CAMBRIDGE STUDIES IN AMERICAN LITERATURE AND CULTURE

Self and sensibility in contemporary American poetry

Cambridge Studies in American Literature and Culture

Editor: Albert Gelpi, Stanford University

Advisory Board:

Nina Baym, *University of Illinois, Champaign-Urbana*
Sacvan Bercovitch, *Columbia University*
Richard Bridgman, *University of California, Berkeley*
David Levin, *University of Virginia*
Kenneth Lynn, *Johns Hopkins University*
Joel Porte, *Harvard University*
Mike Weaver, *Oxford University*

Books in the series:

Robert Zaller: *The Cliffs of Solitude*
Peter Conn: *The Divided Mind*
Patricia Caldwell: *The Puritan Conversion Narrative*
Stephen Fredman: *Poet's Prose*
John P. McWilliams: *Hawthorne, Melville, and the American character*

Self and sensibility in contemporary American poetry

CHARLES ALTIERI
University of Washington

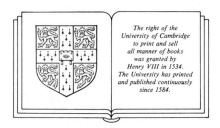

*The right of the
University of Cambridge
to print and sell
all manner of books
was granted by
Henry VIII in 1534.
The University has printed
and published continuously
since 1584.*

CAMBRIDGE UNIVERSITY PRESS

Cambridge

London   New York   New Rochelle

Melbourne   Sydney

Published by the Press Syndicate of the University of Cambridge
The Pitt Building, Trumpington Street, Cambridge CB2 1RP
32 East 57th Street, New York, NY 10022, USA
296 Beaconsfield Parade, Middle Park, Melbourne 3206, Australia

© Cambridge University Press 1984

First published 1984

Printed in the United States of America

Library of Congress Cataloging in Publication Data
Altieri, Charles, 1942–
Self and sensibility in contemporary American poetry.
(Cambridge studies in American literature and culture)
Includes index.
1. American poetry – 20th century – History and
criticism. 2. Self in literature. 3. Creeley,
Robert, 1926–   – Criticism and interpretation.
4. Ashbery, John – Criticism and interpretation.
5. Rich, Adrienne Cecile – Criticism and interpretation.
I. Title. II. Series
PS325.A38   1984   811'.54'09353   83-7855
ISBN 0 521 25396 9 hard covers

Contents

v

Preface

The older a literary critic gets, the shorter his prefaces become. It takes only getting older to see why. One's dependencies become so diverse, so intricate and recurrent, they either cannot be stated or appear mocked in the stating. Some cannot be stated because a testimonial to all those students and colleagues whose thinking has affected the critic's sense of his subject would be as long as the book. Others politeness prevents. In my case getting older has entailed recognizing how much I feed on anger, and how much I have had as a critic of contemporary poetry to feast upon – from an academy that does not care about the subject and from subjects who think they do not care about the academy.

It is easier and ultimately more gratifying to name those to whom one cannot express sufficient gratitude. Because I do not type, I have been inordinately dependent on the secretarial staffs at the Center for Advanced Study in the Behavorial Sciences, New College of the University of South Florida, and at the University of Washington, especially to Cheryl Mathisen, who has the dubious honor of expecting my dependencies to continue. My infirmities at least give me a unique position from which to appreciate their professional dedication and more than professional compassion and tolerance. Because I cannot write much while teaching, I am also in a position to be especially grateful to the National Endowment for the Humanities, the Guggenheim Foundation, and the Center for Advanced Studies for a year of those purest academic indulgences – writing and talking to stimulating peers. Finally, because my pleasure in writing exceeds my talents, I want to thank those editors who helped me work parts of what became this manuscript into shape and who have given permission for me to exhibit here the results of what they initiated. My overall argument expands two essays published by Thomas Gardner in *Contemporary Literature*. Doug Bolling of *Par Rapport* helped with some materials that enter the first chapter, Cheryl Glickfield of *Chicago Review* with the objectivists, Bill Spanos of *boundary 2* with the Creeley material, and Joe Riddel, guest-editing an issue of *Genre,* with Ashbery. Riddel had the especially difficult task of cleaning up what I wrote when I was trying to break my dependency on smoking. Al Gelpi had the kindness to believe that this synthesis of materials could be a coherent book and the tough intelligence to help bring the product this far toward that goal.

I save for last those dependencies that make dependency one of the deepest pleasures I know. Parts of this book, as well as periodic renewals of my faith in academic life, stem directly from conversations with Carl Dennis, Bill Matthews, Dick Blessing, Charles Molesworth, and Marjorie Perloff. For severely testing my faith in broader segments of life, and ultimately for transforming the tests into an education in the love that wills dependents and dependency, I dedicate this book to my wife, Joanne, and my children, Philip and Laura.

1

Self and sensibility in contemporary poetry

I

> I want a hero: an uncommon want,
> When every year and month sends forth a new one,
> Till, after cloying the gazetteer with cant,
> The age discovers he is not the true one.
> Of such as these I should not care to vaunt . . .

Of such as these I cannot choose but vaunt. Lacking Byron's wit, one in our time has only the ploy of taking up provisional stances toward what years and months send forth. I want a hero because I want to introduce dramatically some of the problems and powers I consider characteristic of contemporary American poetry. There is of course no such entity as contemporary poetry. But if we hone our razor sharp enough, there is no such entity as a poet or a hero. At best we have bundles of poems that are bundles of words. So much for analytic logic as a tool for establishing foundations. What we can take as a significant entity is relative to functions. All functions, though, are not equal. If we want to understand a general situation that contemporary poets might share, we need to construct a hero, however provisional a one, as our emblem for cultural pressures manifesting themselves in individual choices.

Byron's concern that fame gives too many of us our fifteen minutes in the limelight is in some respects inappropriate for contemporary poets. Part of our wanting a hero involves wanting someone who can get the lights to focus on poetry at all. Nonetheless, we have some fairly clear indexes (in addition to obscurity) of what would constitute a representative contemporary poet. Take David Young, for example. He began serious writing around 1960, won a Yale Younger Poets' prize, developed his current style in the aftermath of a failed cultural revolution, publishes regularly in prestigious places, and edits an influential journal of poetry and poetics. It seems plausible, then, to take his writings on poetics as one way to understand the dominant intellectual climate in which the reading and writing of American poetry is fostered. There are better and different poetic and critical voices, but I shall argue that we fully appreciate claims for their stature only if we begin with a stance more representative of what we might call "the poetry world." If we want to understand or situate the power and the pathos of our best writers, we must begin with the problems and pressures they try to overcome.

Young's poetics depends on two fundamental themes – the importance of "sincere" poetic emotion and the writer's capacity to project his or her mastery of craft. The ability to use language "in exciting and brilliant combinations" is the first, most striking sign of significant poetic work. Mastery over language then becomes Young's means of reappropriating New Critical ideals: By carefully wrought "texture, movement, and diction," a good poet "renders" rather than "describes" an experience. By acknowledging that they are made out of words, not ideas, the best lyrics avoid the "fatal discursiveness" of "verse essayists" like Wakoski and Ammons and show language's "power to express what we had thought inexpressible." As his basic example for rendering the inexpressible, Young chooses William Stafford's "Ceremony," a poem from the 1960s that clearly indicates the lineage for all too much contemporary poetry:

> On the third finger of my left hand
> Under the bank of the Ninneicah
> a muskrat whirled and bit to the bone.
> The mangled hand made the water red.
>
> That was something the ocean would remember:
> I saw me in the current, flowing through the land,
> rolling, touching roots, the world incarnadined,
> and the river richer by a kind of marriage.
>
> While in the woods an owl started quavering

with drops like tears I raised my arm.
Under the bank a muskrat was trembling
with meaning my hand would wear forever.

In that river my blood flowed on.

Against this "humility," Young sets the "essential egomania" of James
Dickey's "The Poisoned Man." From the contrast there springs a virtual
catalogue of standard contemporary poetic values. "Ceremony" has "an
authentic grounding in experience and consciousness" and "an authenticity of voice . . . believable and natural"; it manifests a quality of not
being "manufactured" or "pretentious" but of at its best moments having
"surprised" the poet; and it builds to "a final image that glimpses that
loss of self associated with visionary experience and with most great poetry."[1]

It is difficult not to use a term like "ideology" to describe this reasoning. An extremely confident, commonsense voice treats values as obvious and morally significant that are in fact rife with internal contradictions undercutting the very attitudes he tries to authorize. Young envisions
an ideal state where mimetic criteria of naturalness and an ethical standard of humility can be integrated with moments of visionary self-
transcendence sustained by careful attention to craftsmanly control. Yet
the naturalness is difficult to reconcile with the desire for visionary self-
transcendence, and the insistence on rhetorical control hard to link with
anything more than a stage humility. Young wants his naturalness, and
he wants it purified of all traces of contingency, just as he wants a rhetoric that does not belie the antirhetorical stance it stages. In these desires
Young is an excellent mimic of Stafford's poem, but not a very acute
critic of it. Naturalness in Stafford is so elaborately controlled, one won-
ders how any feelings not certified as "poetic" can flow on or how any
humble self can swim in such a river. The poem itself utterly lacks fluidity because we are never allowed to forget how each detail must perform the symbolic chore of preparing for the "surprising" visionary con-
summation. Stafford apparently wants to put the violence of *Macbeth* in
a comprehensive context, but here the stage properties in fact reduce that
natural context to sheer cultural artifice.

If we judge such contradictory stances, we reason not the need, nor
the emotional pattern in which the needs find expression. But if we avoid
the necessary critical distance – toward contradiction per se and toward
the possible forces producing precisely these confusions between sincerity and self-consciousness – we may collapse reason into an expression
of need. Criticism offers obvious examples of both poles: the unsympa-
thetic critique of recent literature as without qualities or without firm
intellectual standards[2] and the gushing (or politically deferential) sym-

pathy with poems like Stafford's. But the most striking consequences appear in the work of Helen Vendler, the most sensitive and most capacious critic of contemporary poetry.[3] Vendler's great strength is her ability to capture the basic distinguishing qualities of individual poets so that we can see how the writer responds to the demands of making mature adjustments to modern life. But the sympathy lacks firm intellectual or cultural contexts, and thus constitutes a partial trap. Maturity becomes her version of what I shall call a lucidity term. It provides an existential norm allowing her to judge the experiences poets present. How, though, can one define maturity or imagine seriously defending or attacking it? The concept is on the one hand too flexible to be a firm measure of context and on the other too narrow to produce ways of valuing experimental styles. Thus there are occasions when in order to preserve sympathy Vendler must distort the writer, for example, by treating Ashbery as a Keatsian romantic without analyzing the thematic import of his style.

More important, with her standard there can be no serious speculative challenges to an "adult, tragic sensibility" and no inquiry into epistemological and social principles. Ultimately her poets become confined within dramas of coming to terms with a necessary domesticity. Such dramas, social versions of Young's humility, leave the imagination little to do but to console us for our losses and align us in elegant ways with the psychic economies championed by ego-psychology. Her conservatism makes few demands on the critical intelligence of her poet or on her power as a critic to challenge and provoke that intelligence. By concentrating on poets she can praise on her terms, and by immersing herself in each individual poetic sensibility, Vendler cannot develop a framework for describing the pressures that impose such terms or for measuring a poet's achievement in expressing or perhaps overcoming those pressures. I need hardly add that we may pay the price of such critical stances in seeing our poetry become considered (even by writers) as monkish and marginal an art as manuscript illumination.

II

Providing an alternative critical model, however, is much harder than pointing out the need for one. My efforts to produce one will require a good deal of patience and willing suspension of concrete detail on the part of the reader. Instead of emphasizing individual poets, I shall try to outline a set of problems and cultural pressures that constitute a common situation. In this context the measure of the poet is how thoroughly and how complexly he or she negotiates what all must face. In other words, I intend to concentrate on what is involved in calling Young a "representative poet." Clearly his is not the only style for contemporary poetry, nor do his arguments reflect an explicit consensus among poets. Nonetheless, Young does represent the values of a group I shall try to describe as the dominant mode in contemporary poetry, that is, the mode that is most influential in the domains of literary education and prestigious publications. His concern for modest, highly crafted narrative structures producing moments of sudden illumination and his desire to correlate sincerity with rhetorical self-consciousness reflect two basic values shaping most contemporary poetry. In fact, the agreement is so striking that one is tempted to take these values as also characterizing a large segment of the society poets can be expected to express.

However, because these values are so central it is a mistake to deal only with what might be called the direct or mimetic features of Young's representativeness. Once poetic values become dominant they tend to organize discourse in such a way that even those with very different commitments find themselves compelled to shape their work so that it addresses these central issues. Poets, after all, are extremely sensitive to values implicit in a culture, and they are extremely eager to define their specific place within or against prevailing tastes. We can take Young, then, as articulating some basic parameters for a site where the conflicts shaping the future of poetry will probably have to take place as poets engage the styles and values he champions. Some poets make the conflict an explicit basis for self-definition, whereas others reveal only implicit traces of the struggle to resist or correct the emphasis of the dominant mode. In either case, if critics can adequately map the site, they can both suggest a dramatic context for poetic choices and establish comparative standards for assessing the work resulting from those choices. Then, because we share the same social world as the poets, we have a cogent basis for describing how they in effect speak to and for us.

Literary history is such that even this brief introduction requires several qualifications and clarifications. I do not mean to say that Young is in fact a spokesman for a group or that contemporary poetry comprises one seamless network. Rather, I hope to show that there is a useful level of abstraction on which we can see both what Young shares with a dominant mode and how those shared values force others to articulate competing positions. On this level, moreover, we discover some ways in which it becomes profitable to treat many of the major directions in American poetry as sharing a single cultural enterprise. There are obviously many other ways to map the scene, but mine I hope will help us appreciate both the pathos and the power of a considerable number of the best poets who came to poetic maturity in the seventies. If this map is to prove perspicuous I must not confine myself to conscious authorial intentions. Poems and arguments express cultural tensions in a variety of emotional configurations, ranging from deliberate self-expression to the unconscious betrayal of symptoms. When we try to define cultural contexts, we must consider what poets mean, what they can see that others may not have intended, and what they reveal as possible unconscious pressures on their work. Once we admit these types of data, we also need criteria for assessing them somewhat different from those we would use if we were concerned only with the intended meaning of a specific poem. I suggest a criterion of retrospective intentionality: We speak validly about cultural contexts when a competent community can agree that the author might be persuaded after the fact to accept a given account of his selections as he was writing. Such a criticism will not produce certainty. But if we agree to it as our ground rule, we have a norm for forming disagreements and suggesting lines of further argument or research that might make agreement possible.

Retrospective intentionality has the further use of emphasizing the complex interplay of first- and third-person positions that go into reading works as participants in a social drama. We need to see as writers see in writing, and we need to see as writers might see themselves through the lens of complex comparative and historical accounts. In an earlier book, on the poetry of the 1960s, I concentrated on recovering first-person experience. I attempted to trace the careers of individual authors as they encountered problems and worked out tentative resolutions. This model of reading seemed to me necessary for that poetry because the poets worked primarily in abstract, speculative terms testing possible stances that might illuminate and sanction a general philosophical attitude toward experience. As we shall see, the situation of poetry is now quite different. Most poets are not as concerned with a series of interrelated explorations of abstract ideas as they are with bringing single poems to complex rhetorical resolutions. Their context, then, is less the ramifications of a concept or the relation of a concept to the individual life than the history of style and the rhetorical choices it makes available. This means that critics will find it most useful not to trace the dialectics of a career but to elaborate the pressures on the rhetoric poets use to control particular experiences. Within a first-person perspective, control of rhetoric is a matter of intentions. But we shall find that the social constitution of rhetorical strategies requires us to see poets (and poets to see themselves) from the outside as defined by the imaginary constructs available to them and at times blinding them to emotional investments in what they think they control.

In *Enlarging the Temple* I tried to imagine writers as they imagined themselves. Here I shall seek ways of imagining the writers seeing themselves from a distance, as if they were simply agents working within a definable set of relations to other writers and to society at large. From this perspective the expression of individual sensibility is not an end to be realized but a sign to be interpreted and assessed in terms of the place it creates for itself amid competing styles and common needs. In this critical context, choices become dramatic for other than psychological reasons, poems have clear exploratory purposes, and poets become actors within a culture. We allow ourselves a language for treating a variety of poets as responding to the same historical conditions even if they do not provide explicit discussions of contemporary society. Within this language we can address the strange duality inherent in a contemporary literature – that it can move us as much by its pathos, for what it shows but cannot master of our cultural situation, as by its power to determine aesthetically and interpretively what otherwise would determine its expressive structures. Finally, by constructing a common network for choices and common demands for self-reflective judgments, I think we make it possible to establish shareable criteria for determining who might be our strongest poets. I shall grant that mantle to John Ashbery and Adrienne Rich, but as we consider the terms of their success we will recognize some fundamental unresolved issues that may dictate a basic agenda for the poets in the eighties. This lack of resolution is compounded by an irony that plagues criticism. Poets usually stay several steps ahead of their critics. As we produce contexts for judging them we begin to see that the best among them have already made similar or better judgments of where poetry must go. So our judgments are likely to prove most useful not as assessments but as introductions to the imperatives producing constant change in the poetry world.

III

I fantasize results while I still need to justify my assertion that we can approach poets as participating in a single cultural enterprise. As I suggested in speaking about representativeness, it is not easy to determine the level of abstraction that makes a term like "single" neither a tautology nor an evasion of crucial differences. The term is warranted only if a critic can describe a culture writers might share and elaborate an approach to stylistic choices that connects them to that culture. There is no way to speak about art as art without honoring distinctive qualities of individual works and individual sensibilities. However, I think it is possible to concentrate on features of individual achievements that invite comparison among works and that connect specific emotional economies to general cultural and intellectual traits. My emphasis will be on how the poem structures the course of a feeling, understands its artistic coherence as testimony to specific mental and aesthetic powers, interprets its resolution as a model for aligning the sensibility to sources of value, and finally makes its claim on the attention of the audience an emblem of how an author can represent choices as worthwhile, as worthy of attention and respect from a community. I cannot say that poets intend such generalized features, but I hope to show that it makes good sense to ask how the release of the imaginary that is poetry becomes an index of the fundamental terms for self-regard that poets adapt from their society and cultural heritage.

As the context of such readings I shall attempt to sketch two basic sets of historical pressures on the images poets construct. One set of pressures is literary: a need for poets to engage the shattered heritage of an overoptimistic and overheated romanticism that nonetheless committed poets to qualities of personal speech incompatible with the formal, contemplative styles of the 1950s. The other is social and existential, for as romanticism fails it leaves poets the enormous problem of facing in themselves and their world the questions "what to make of a diminished thing" and what to make of one's resistance to that reduction. As poets develop myths of poverty or mature disillusion, they must worry whether their fictions in fact serve to exaggerate the poet's self-importance and minimize the true nature of what we have lost or are losing. They must wonder how to create poems that are not exercises in the self-evasion Young exemplifies.

Constructing a dominant contemporary mode helps give us concrete access to the nature and effects of both kinds of pressures. When I speak of a dominant mode I refer to a critic's ideal type, nowhere fully evident but established and reinforced by overlapping strands in a variety of influential poems and poetic statements. More concretely, in positing such a type we try to capture what holds Young and Stafford together. I define a mode as a stylistic type, more abstract and flexible than a genre, which carries a distinctive ethos or set of values in part characterizing the writer when he or she adopts one of the styles it controls. Satire is a good example of a mode that characterizes authors in a way relatively independent of specific historical contexts. The variety of Byronic styles in nineteenth-century poetry constitute another mode closely tied to social history for its associations. A mode becomes dominant when the ethos it idealizes develops institutional power – both as a model for the ways in which agents represent themselves and, more important, as the basic example of what matters in reading and in attributing significance to what one reads.

As Young shows, a model of reading can appear ideologically neutral in proposing general values for interpreting texts from a variety of styles and periods. But if we examine it carefully we see that what appears general is in fact quite particular and quite at odds with what those styles had authorized for previous generations. We see here one aspect of a feature in a dominant mode that has wide ramifications: It shapes a good deal more than it positively describes. As a mode achieves hegemony, even its opponents or those seeking only to stand outside it find themselves forced to take up positions that are strongly influenced by what they reject. The dominant mode creates a situation in which all acts of self-definition take place largely on its turf. These processes of acceptance and rejection operate on several levels, so it is not implausible to see poets explicitly rejecting basic aspects of the mode in the name of principles in fact fostered by the same system of values – just as Eliot was perhaps never so romantic as in his rejecting romanticism because he sought a deeper and broader notion of self-consciousness. Ultimately a dominant mode is an abstract version of Harold Bloom's father figure. But when we treat the source of pressure on poets as cultural rather than familial, we allow ourselves to engage and take seriously a broad set of conscious projects for testing and transforming inherited materials. Moreover, this cultural stage allows poets and audiences to share the same oppressor, so we can take as potentially representative both the problems and the possibilities poets produce in their struggles.

I am all too aware that particular claims about a mode's being dominant are always contestable and often difficult to adjudicate. How one shapes a dominant mode will control all the subsequent stories one can tell. In my case the shape will emphasize philosophical rather than aesthetic matters. Nonetheless, to restate Newman, no one is likely to risk death for an iamb or an alliteration or even a finely wrought overall form, but people will do so for ideas that can be sustained by compelling images. So I feel that my biases may at least lead to one version of contemporary poetry that clarifies and deepens our understanding of some poets and also offers other critics a framework they can oppose by producing competing accounts. My confidence, however, is no excuse for not being as careful as I can in developing my account of dominance. The obvious models for such an account are either quantitative or qualitative, but neither will quite do for staging the drama of attractions, repulsions, and transformations that is contemporary poetry. If one proceeds only quantitatively, one might be able to tell what kinds of poems are most often published, but there is no way to make transitions from frequency to power. Without some qualitative measure we cannot distinguish between styles that are simply popular and styles that influence those poets who require or deserve critical attention. But purely qualitative judgments of dominance simply use dominance as a synonym for excellence. They return us to the ideal of paying close attention to individual poets without worrying about shared contexts and problems.

If we want to understand a writer's choices, or even many of our reasons for valuing the work as a form of relevant contemporary news, we need to blend the two kinds of criteria. Qualitative ones help us see what the best writers make available; quantitative ones show what some segment of the culture seems to desire from what is available. The former indicate models that should influence, the latter the general conditions of what has in effect wielded power. Both conditions can be substantially satisfied if we use as our bases for establishing the dominant mode the assumptions of those poets and critics who govern the distribution of prestigious awards or publishing contracts and (not coincidentally) shape the principles commonly taught aspiring writers.[4] If we can locate such common assumptions, we will have found just the right tension between ideal images of poetry that hold the allegiance of writers and actual stylistic practices that border on cliché. From these poles we generate the process of change, resistance to change, and illusion of change that is literary history.

Jonathan Holden offers a very useful strategy for discovering basic assumptions of a dominant mode that no empirical survey is likely to elicit. We can locate influential shared assumptions by specifying those reactions most commonly evoked when we ask a poetry workshop to suggest revisions for a poem written in the past. A typical contemporary litany is easy to reproduce: Craft must be made unobtrusive so that the work appears spoken in a natural voice; there must be a sense of urgency and immediacy to this "affected naturalness" so as to make it appear that one is reexperiencing the original event; there must be a "studied artlessness" that gives a sense of spontaneous personal sincerity; and there must be a strong movement toward emphatic closure, a movement carried on primarily by the poet's manipulation of narrative structure.[5] Such a list of traits is not (and Holden does not intend it to be) a substitute for a synthetic account of the ideological and affective complex this mode helps produce and reinforce. Providing that account, without the political baggage and confident explanation that normally accompany claims about ideology, will be the task of my second chapter.

For now I will offer only a provisional summary. In Stafford's poem we find several features that will prove paradigmatic. The work places a reticent, plain-speaking, and self-reflective speaker within a narratively presented scene evoking a sense of loss. Then the poet tries to resolve the loss in a moment of emotional poignance or wry acceptance that renders the entire lyric event an evocative metaphor for some general sense of mystery about the human condition.[6] The two most popular variants consist of making the scene a more intense moment of psychological conflict (as in heirs of confessional styles) and extending the evocative metaphor by a more discursive and tonally complex reflective summary (as in Richard Hugo, David Wagoner, and the heirs of Elizabeth Bishop). In all these models, the poems must clearly illustrate the controlling hand of the craftsman, but the craft must remain subtle and unobtrusive. So the formal burden lies primarily on elaborate vowel and consonantal music. The central aim of the art is not to interpret experience but to extend language to its limits in order to establish poignant awareness of what lies beyond words. There is virtually never any sustained act of formal, dialectical thinking or any elaborate, artificial construction that cannot be imagined as taking place in, or at least extending from, settings in naturalistically conceived scenes. As shorthand I will call this the scenic style, and in my second chapter I will try to make clear the sources that created it, some of the ideological effects it has on the poets' images of the self or their terms for emotional authenticity, and some of the problem areas it creates for its practitioners as well as those who struggle to revise or escape it.

IV

Establishing a dominant mode is only a starting point. Once we have a plausible one, the crucial critical act is to locate the internal faults or points of slippage where problems arise that require poets to try out new possibilities or old traditions. Here drama begins, and criticism obtains modest but defensible dialectical terms by which to deal with the pressures of contradictions or needs unsatisfied by the very sources that produce them. Finally, here we begin to see how problems specific to poetry echo or at least afford analogies to aspects of American cultural life. It may even be the case that because we are likely to know our own culture better than any other, we have in the study of contemporary poetry a paradigm for testing the ways stylistic features imply or are implicated in these larger cultural theaters.

I think I must begin my analysis of specific tensions by briefly outlining what I take to be the central conflict shaping both the literary and the existential pressures I spoke of earlier. Our lyric poetry remains within the romantic tradition, and that tradition can best be understood as a reaction against Enlightenment strategies for idealizing its secularizing activities. Enlightenment thinkers wanted to preserve as many of the values sanctioned by religion as they could. This desire led them to create dual roles for their primary weapon – the ideal of reason. Reason could be wielded as an essentially critical instrument, seeking out and destroying structures of belief based on metaphor and superstitions only because reason also possessed positive values based in fact on the very Renaissance metaphoric system it was bent on destroying. Reason could overthrow illusion because it seemed to be the feature of man closest to the structure of the cosmos, if not to God. Hence in self-knowledge humans also freed themselves to grasp the order of things, already latent in the powers of mind. There were doubtless other sources of authority for the ideal of reason; it was, after all, sustained by advances in science. But in its early phases the passion for science itself derived from Christian ontology, and that ontology created a background providing intensity and dramatic flair for the light-bringing process. The ideals of Baconian empiricism do not engage enough emotional life to establish this theater on their own; nor do they afford the dramatic principles required for appreciating what takes the stage.

For most writers, these dramatic principles take the form of a conflict between what I shall call ideals of lucidity and ideals of lyricism. The tension between these ideals makes for the longest-running play in our cultural history. Situations and characters change, but the dual roles Enlightenment reason must play through all these guises – demystifying ideals and idealizing a model for a sense of values that resists all demystification – keep the central conflict as obvious as it is oppressive.[7] I take lucidity and lyricism as attributes of reflective stances that emerge in relation to three dichotomies basic to modern thought. The easiest dichotomy to describe is the standard one between fact and value: In the process of replacing a symbolic religious tradition it seemed imperative to cleanse facts of all latent or intrinsic meanings not determinable by laws of nature or pseudolaws of social science. From the point of view of self-consciously lucid stances, the values could only be explained as personal preferences, and thus continuous with an empiricist sense of individuals. All claims about them as objective or transcendental were the kind of lyrical illusions that led Nietzsche to treat artists as deserving the thinker's reproof – "Could you not watch with me one hour?" To watch with the thinker would require adopting the thinker's language, one based on a second, related dichotomy between descriptive and emotive language. Finally, these changes in cultural values become instances of a third dichotomy between a sense of history as essentially a chain of different, incompatible social situations and a classical ideal that one could find models of behavior and sources of imaginative energy in the past that afford a potential best self for one's action in the present.

Lucidity and lyricism mattered because they enabled thinkers to characterize themselves as taking strong stands within the basic contradictions of their age. Here, for example, is Baudelaire in "Muse Venale" complexly setting a stage lucidity against a pathetic public lyricism:

> il te faut, pour gagner ton pain de chaque soir,
> comme un enfant de choeur, jouer de l'encensoir,
> chanter des te deum auxquels on ne crois guère.

I choose Baudelaire because by the time of romanticism the relevant roles had grown quite complex. The choice of lucidity carried its own lyrical *frisson* because it allowed writers to identify themselves at once with and against an essentially demonic force. As the Enlightenment devoured its own progeny, the spirit of lucidity could become a model of authenticity whereby the beleaguered lyrical consciousness embraced its own enemy. Shakespeare's villains became Byronic heroes. Writers who wanted to preserve the standard lyrical ideals, however, did not have it so easy. To defend lyricism is to stand against the march of history, so the defender must either adopt the role of eccentric or indulge in complex redefinitions of the nature of the lyrical. The obvious strategy would be simply to align lyricism with a faith that literature or literary attitudes can somehow sanction what the spirit of secular lucidity denies. This is largely what Northrop Frye does in distinguishing myths of concern from myths of freedom, or what Hazard Adams does in his division between allegorical and antiallegorical stances. But if we only maintain these dichotomies, we ignore the competitive and dialectical efforts of writers both to overcome the authority lucidity models assert and to claim a higher lucidity for their ways of seeing. Given the power Enlightenment values hold over most intellectual disciplines, those desiring alternatives cannot simply reassert old positions. They must invent new ones or new reasons for restoring old ones. This is why those who resist pure lucidity stances claim some deeper, nondiscursive truth for their own values. And this is why such thinkers invite conflicting judgments – for example, that they are blindly indulging in superstitions or that they have in fact located areas of experience for which established descriptive language lacks sufficient terms and relational principles.

Therefore I shall take "lyricism" as a term applicable to all attempts to use what literature can exemplify as a model for affirming in ostensibly secular forms predicates about the mind, person, and society that were the basic images of dignity and value in religious or "organic" cultures. The pressure of lucidity drives writers to react by developing psychic economies that can restore a world compatible with our imaginative forms of ideal personal qualities. And, indeed, in projecting these economies the lyric serves as the richest form. Here the world's adequacy to the demands of the self is most immediately and intensely tested, without the full-scale displacement of the imaginary or the subordination of mental to social forms that are typical of the novel.

We have, then, a history of attempts to defend the lyrical as in fact the true form of lucidity (for example, in Coleridge's and Richards's appeal to a logic of poetry or in Fichte's making idealism a "poetic philosophy"). But this union becomes increasingly problematic because we find it growing more difficult to countenance metaphysical speculation or appeals to psychologically "deep" versions of subjective life. Once Enlightenment oppositions permeate our discourse about values, lyricism may be condemned to continual self-doubt. The models of what constitutes knowledge, or even what constitutes legitimate terms for discussing values, grow increasingly skeptical of what cannot be empirically demonstrated. Thus there is a constant temptation for poets to respond by rejecting impersonal thought and turning to the pure form of their myth, to the idea that it is only in terms of the intensity of first-person experience that an authority for values can be established or defended. Yet once this move is made, there is no way even to talk about what the imagination discovers without bringing more doubts than clarity to what we would assert.[8]

In modernist writing lyricism and lucidity played out their drama in essentially public arguments about cultural and religious matters. The modernist adventure, its dream of making differences that would make a difference, depended on the hope that artists could establish philosophical and cultural stances that would satisfy both demands. Art would become analytic as a means of attaining new states of lyric sensibility. Then poetry would not only be as well-written as prose, it would also recover for the imagination the power to carry on the forms of thinking co-opted by the mind's more prosaic forces. These formulations now appear one among the many illusions we inherit as literary history. In reaction, contemporary poets try more limited, personal ways of resolving or minimizing the conflict. By insisting on specific scenes and by placing authority within the qualities of personal experience, they risk very little, probably too little, that invites the demystifying spirit. Instead of challenging other models of lucidity, the scenic mode works subtly at its edges, hoping to elicit glimpses of a life that makes isolated individuality bearable.

Without hopes for changing society, poets nonetheless try to move and console those who must suffer its contradictions. So the contemporaries tend to develop plain lyric stances capable of satisfying society's empirical standards for explanation and representativeness. This process allows them to treat their lyrical features as continuous with practical experience – six perceptions in search of a transcendental vision. When the moments of vision are asserted, the empirical context helps naturalize them. The poet need not argue for any special properties of the mind or nature that might authorize visionary insights, because these sudden moments of illumination can appear self-authorizing so long as they occur within anecdotal presentations devoted to a form of dramatic coherence we find in our standard descriptions of action.

It is poets' desire to resolve tensions between lucidity and lyricism within the empirical personal voice that leads to the particular slippages and problems I shall concentrate on as central to the dominant mode and to the need for exploring alternative styles and ideals of imaginative activity. Three particular problems invite analysis, each a function of the ways the scenic mode envisions personal identity. The first of these is also present in traditional literary works but is rarely so closely involved with the sources of the power the poem tries to present. As we saw in Young, the desire for sincerity or naturalness, for poetry as communication, seems continually in tension with the highly artificial means required to produce the desired effects at a level of intensity adequate for lyric poetry. The effort to create the image contradicts the image, and we find it hard not to become suspicious about the values claimed for the ethos of naturalness. If we prove so easy to move, or if we are so willing to ignore the artificial means required to produce the desired effects at a level of intensity adequate for lyric poetry, it becomes difficult to trust any of the emotions produced by claims for direct expression. Yet the obvious alternative, the extreme forms of reflexivity exemplified by the post-modern novel, seems a dead end for the lyric. Unless one finds new models of emotion, there is no way to concentrate extended analyses of what I call "rhetoricity" into the compressed forms of attention the lyric demands.[9]

From this contrast we arrive at a second closely related problem in generating believable and satisfying lyrical emotions. Because lyrics seem so closely under authorial control and that control easily becomes suspect, poets must worry about closing poems without falling into the trap of presenting a smug, self-satisfied lyrical persona constantly transported into visionary states by the poet's apt metaphors or turns of events. The scenic style encourages achieving closure by a leap from the narrative to the visionary levels, as if sensitive experience reached its climax in moments of resonant silence. This leap, however, expresses serious difficulties in the style's overall emotional economy. We see that the manipulation of detail belies the purported concreteness of description. Moreover, the desire for vision equates intense lyric emotion with the somewhat passive role of making sudden discoveries within contingent aspects of events. There is thus no deliberate composing a self with the power to make and sustain generalizations. Finally, the pursuit of resonant silence may not allow the poet to say enough, may not purchase enough in vision to pay for what it costs poetry in eloquence, especially when a cult of silence makes it easy to luxuriate in vague emotions. At the least, the dream of controlled transcendental glimpses narrows what poetic language can do, and at the worst such emotions allow no way for poets to deal conceptually or even imagistically with the grounds and implications of the very sources of eloquence that make them poets.

These tensions between sincerity and rhetoric manifest their most general consequences in the ways poets must grapple with reconciling first- and third-person attitudes toward the lyric self. Since romanticism, at least, the lyric "I" – in poetry and in the cultural imagery poetry has engendered – provides our deepest model of a fully personal inwardness. The mystery, depth, immediacy, and essential privacy of our experiencing lyric emotions seems public testimony both to the uniqueness of private experience and to its ultimate communicability. If we can identify with what we read, we should be able to share similar experiences with those who participate in the same culture. Yet that very possibility of communication entails dependencies on a public order that seem powerful invitations to the ironic or deconstructive angel. If everything can be named in a public language, where does the "I" depart from the "he" or the "she," or where can we begin to present ourselves as unique by virtue of qualities of our subjective experience? Yet if we allow that angel to be our only voice, we may buy our irony too cheaply and ignore the possibly genuine mysteries inherent in our experience of first-person states.

The poet's problem is to maintain this balance, to acknowledge the dependencies of the "I" on a public order and rhetorical strategies while still testing what can be distinctive about the qualities created in specific reflexive uses of that order and those strategies. Such balancing can involve complex redefinitions of how we understand the personal and impersonal, or the psychological and the rhetorical, as well as the possible interrelations among these poles. The danger in contemporary poetry, and in contemporary culture, is that we see the ironic, depersonalizing forces so clearly that we flee into forms of extreme privacy that we hope are as inviolate as they are inarticulate. But even this privacy then seems all too public a symptom of a collective need for some richer notion of the personal.

All three problems appear most clearly in the scenic style's treatments of poetic personas. In order to create the effect of sincerity, the poet cannot establish much distance between the authorial presence and the dramatic voice. There is little irony and even less drama of the self engaged in projecting and testing masks or "heroic" possibilities. Too much sincerity makes such projection a terribly vulnerable act. Instead, we get a severely restrained directness, a personal presence pared of all distinguishing qualities that would prevent an audience from taking the speaker as continuous with the poet's "self" and from identifying fully with the emotions expressed. Such easy identifications ironically result in collapsing speaking and responding into a narrow state of self. The poems concentrate emotions instead of encouraging a lyric dialogue among competing voices in the self or among ideas the self tries out as interpretations of its experiences.

All this becomes especially problematic because the poems' claims for the unity and singleness of feeling are belied by our awareness of how much the rhetoric serves to depersonalize the emotion. Stafford's ending is all too clear an example of an apparent direct simplicity that, under

scrutiny, opens onto parts of the self rather desperately and falsely produces what he claims to discover. Once we recognize the divisions such
moves attempt to conceal, it is not difficult to be tempted by the poststructuralist faith in a diffuse, multiple self. But this faith, too, may be
oversimplified because it uses another all-encompassing scheme. For poetry we need simply to recognize the phenomenological pressure such
complexity and complicity create. Doing so gives us access to the power
of pathos in poets like Stafford, and it helps us appreciate the efforts of
other poets to capture the interplay between a desire to be personal and
a desire to acknowledge the multiple rhetorics through which a person
may be glimpsed. We produce a context for understanding the poets'
needs to open their poems to a play of tensions between the self represented and the variety of motives that go into the process of producing
and using representations. The representing self must share stage time
with the dramatized actor playing his or her roles within a single constructed scene.

V

The richer our sense of the problems in the dominant mode is,
the fuller is our grasp of the motives for difference in a wide range of
contemporary poets. I shall develop three general categories that I think
outline most of the fundamental choices available to those reacting against
scenic values. By emphasizing abstract classes, I can shift attention from
the internal tensions one finds in specific poetic careers to conflicts inherent in the stylistic strategies available to a variety of writers. Then concrete choices can be understood as options defined by and caught up in a
literary culture. We surrender some of the variety we could obtain from
a survey of poets, but if we gain a complex sense of common problems
we may ultimately do more to enhance our appreciation of the distinguishing qualities within that variety.

My first category is the most general. Poets reacting against the problems I described as basic to the scenic style are likely to attempt transforming the mode from within. Although they do not deny prevailing
ideals of personal sincerity and the impact of resonant silence, poets like
Carl Dennis and Robert Hass try to acknowledge the pressures and opportunities for imaginative play afforded by self-consciousness about the
motives in rhetoric. Their poems usually replace natural scenes by somewhat lightly held elaborate conceits that invite us to consider the control
of poetic rhetoric as a crucial dramatic feature of the personal states expressed. The second poetic reaction I study is far more radical. Instead
of transforming a dominant style from within, it insists on analyzing the
historical misconceptions that lead us to desire a poetry so tied to the

sincere emotive self and so confined to dramatic, experiential shapes for producing emotions whose authority resides in their intensity as privileged moments of awareness. These criticisms derive from two basic poetic doctrines. At one pole we find Robert Pinsky defending in modified form the ideals of classical discursiveness fostered by Yvor Winters. At the other pole we encounter the heirs of objectivism who see romanticism itself as already too discursive, too willing to treat poetic emotions as functions of opinions and assertions rather than as states of meditative rest established by the mind's power to construct objective forms.

The poems that derive from such efforts to redefine lyricism strike me as interesting achievements and significant indications of experiments poets must explore. Yet I am more concerned with the way these attacks produce as many difficulties as they find in what they oppose, because these difficulties indicate the depth and persistence of the general problems I have been discussing. Pinsky's efforts at discursiveness do not, in my opinion, establish a new authority for the poetic imagination, but leave him even more dependent on romantic strategies for ennobling the personal voice than are those he attacks. Similarly, objectivism succeeds all too well in objectifying emotion, but it does not allow enough personal voice in a time when the more we pursue self the less we understand personhood, and it cannot integrate its demands for formal and meditative closure with complex enactments of the processes of poetic thinking.

For these processes of thinking we must turn to my third category, once again consisting of two quite different traditions. Here we find poets who make the conditions of speaking their central thematic concern. Scenic presentation must be dismantled in order to maintain a sharp opposition between the specular self generated by a poetry of completed thoughts and the multiple selves allowed expression by a conjectural poetic faithful to the act of thinking. Robert Creeley's recent work provides a good introduction to this mode because it turns against his earlier objectivist commitments in the hope of capturing the multileveled spaces and shifting focuses of attention characterizing the mind in action. However, the traces of objectivism that remain create serious problems for this new style because a desire for spare resistance to metaphor becomes terribly constricting when one wants poetry to express the life of the mind. What Creely cannot do, John Ashbery can – superbly. Creeley helps clarify why I consider the mode Ashbery exemplifies to be the most interesting and most promising of contemporary styles.

Ashbery sets his own quasi-discursive reflections in sharp, often witty, and penetrating contrast to features of himself (or the self) expressed as self-staging lyric desires. The aim is thus to have poetry free what lies "underneath the talk . . . / The moving and not wanting to be moved, the loose / Meaning, untidy and simple like a threshing floor."[10] In seeking these loose meanings and attendant emotions too fluid and diffuse for the narrative structures of the scenic mode, both Ashbery and Creeley distribute the theatrical subject of traditional lyric emotions into a series of "positions," of rhetorically based stances the poet then observes and plays on in reflective self-consciousness. This duality focuses attention on the complex play of motives producing the slippages and self-evasions that one glimpses when one tries to stand outside the desires that writing sets to work or to play. Similarly, both poets treat the rhetorical struggle for closure primarily as a point of departure rather than a form of resolution, and this treatment entails re-imagining the nature of the self and hierarchies of feeling associated with it. Once again the experimental tradition has a rationale. If writers suspect that traditional forms of coherence ignore the most important aspects of experience, they obviously must invent new literary styles. Within these styles the self can be understood as a force whose various desires and "sites" create a mobile field of lyric attachments, and suspension of conventional forms of organization becomes a way of gaining access to motives and feelings that may underlie and evade our all-too-theatrical modes of lyricism. Both poets seek to develop new lyrical possibilities by giving the ludicity of self-consciousness and the duplicity of rhetoric their full play.

In many respects Ashbery is for me the major poet of our minor age. He most fully articulates its basic problems and transforms their terms into new possibilities of knowing and feeling ourselves in our world. Nonetheless, it would be silly of me to treat his as the paradigmatic way to grapple with the problems I have been discussing. His contemplative stances are too narrow; his emotions too delicate, passive, and self-reflexive; and his poetic structures too repetitious to warrant exclusive allegiances.

More important, if the values I use are to be useful to criticism, they must be capacious enough to help us appreciate a variety of contemporary projects. This task obviously applies to all my readings, but I address it directly in an extended discussion of Adrienne Rich. She is perhaps as strong a poet as Ashbery is, yet she is the contemporary poet most radically opposed to all Ashbery stands for. If the general contexts I construct are appropriate, our discussion should make the poets delineate one another's strengths, while indicating how the two approaches challenge poets of the eighties to modify their scenic heritage. Rich's basic strength is not in the complexity of her self-consciousness but in its rigorous intensity and her determined effort to test beliefs by their practical, ethical consequences. Self-consciousness to her is less a matter of attention than a means for making a self. The test for self-definition is the qualities of poetic speech one can produce as one's vehicle for expression and as one's bond to an audience. Where Ashbery insists on diffusion as an alternative to the specular self, Rich insists on a deeper, more self-reflexive concentration on the needs and power of will. Her stylistic experiment is to make poetic language a clear mode of discourse, so that it transcends aesthetic standards and invites judgment in terms of the sense of community it fosters and the powers of action it affords that community. In her most recent work she realizes that she best achieves those goals if she dramatizes the power of coming to terms with the emotional consequences of her political ideals. Poems cohere in a volume, and the self coheres to the extent that it acknowledges the necessity of conflict and the difficulty of reconciling competing demands on its private and public aspects. Self-consciousness must recognize the claims of irony and self-disgust if it is to forge a plausible, activist alternative.

It is by no means clear to me that even these two poets suffice to give poetry a vital place in contemporary intellectual life. In fact, it is by no means clear to me that I can successfully resist the claims of irony and self-disgust in relation to the criteria I employ for judging poetry. So I at least honor my commitment to self-consciousness in a brief conclusion where I speculate on the limitations of my position and some of the practical consequences for poetry in the eighties should my position be right or, perhaps better, persuasive.

VI

There is one feature of my effort to construct critical principles that requires further elaboration here. I think any assessment of contemporary poetry must take into account the power of writers to address problems basic to their social situation. For we read contemporary literature as commentary on, and often as a plausible alternative to, a specific cultural plight. Yet I know of no model for linking literary work to social context that resists the Scylla and Charybdis of reductionism in practice and blind self-staging for practitioners who claim to possess the fundamental truths about literary values. My compromise is to avoid all explanatory hypotheses. Instead I shall be content with an essentially phenomenological treatment of a limited set of psychological problems informing characteristic attitudes and anxieties of the cultural groups poets primarily write for. Then readers can fill out for themselves the possible application of my claims while they reflect on the poetry. Relying heavily on these readerly powers, I shall here attempt only to clarify some very abstract relations between contemporary poetry and problems of identity and rhetoric underlying a good deal of the anxieties in the lives of upper-middle-class intellectuals who respond to tensions between lucidity and lyricism.[11] In this undertaking I shall not worry about how literature might be a picture of actual social causes or a powerful critical instrument with distinct social uses. I wish I could provide these accounts, but my own projections seem to me even more hollow than those I read. I must be content with drawing analogies to a limited social group. At least this stance allows me to serve what I take to be the primary social role of poetry: that it offer concrete experience of possible and plausible worlds that foster individual powers of self-reflection without tying the individual to one of the explanatory schemes competing to dominate the political marketplace.

By keeping my account abstract, I hope to suggest applications beyond the social group I try to describe, and I hope to align poetry with a variety of specific issues that might fall under the general categories I explore. Initially I shall simply try to expand the three problems I have just been describing in relation only to poetry. Then I shall try to suggest a general contemporary condition informing all the problems and requiring radical imaginative speculations. The tone and style of this discussion will be much more dense and concise than the remainder of the book. If readers grow impatient or skeptical, I ask them to give my next chapter a hearing before deciding that this is another book they do not need to read. Perhaps I should have made the ensuing discussion an appendix, but that would defer the sense of cultural analogies that I think enhances our reading of contemporary poetry.

If we concentrate on common contemporary forms of representing ourselves to ourselves, we find the clearest analogies to the poetry emerging with respect to the issue of sincere expression. Most of us have little but sincerity and intimacy to believe in as ultimate values, yet all our means to such goals seem contaminated by the overdetermined qualities of our public language. There are virtually no terms we might apply to the self or to intimate experience that do not also carry elaborate fantasies shaped by advertising or the repetitive banter of journalism and television drama. We everywhere encounter parodies of our deepest desires, until desire becomes difficult to distinguish from a despair that the desire is not ours but that of some public demon who possesses us.

From this general condition I draw two further correlations. Poetry is not the only form of activity torn between two basic attitudes toward the self: a desire to produce emotional and intellectual structures that define a coherent self and a desire to revel in the freedom of stationing one's attention within the play of energies generated and distorted by our need for closure. These problems of closure then reappear on an even more general level. For although most of our most sophisticated thought concentrates on exposing the limitations in analytic reason, we find no very satisfying alternatives. If we now think values precede and shape our determination of facts, or at least of their relevance, this conclusion leaves us no decent account of values, only a desperate sense of our need for one. We have license to resort to existential notions of freedom, but we distrust any sense of self that could authenticate the choice, and we suspect that gaining such freedom only ensures that we can be what Creeley called happy solipsists. On the other hand, we are besieged by therapies promising to cure us of both isolation and our desire for analytically derived standards, but the resulting processes seem to use the dream of cure largely as a means for avoiding internal inconsistencies and external criticism.

We most clearly see abstract analogues between the scenic mode and the essentially narcissistic upper-middle-class intellectuals if we attend to popular modes of self-presentation. Dramatic structures in the scenic mode beautifully reflect the dualities of the "laid-back" style. We have seen that the poets choose dramatic structures where nonconfessional, nontheatrical, personal voices record a moment of "poetic excitement" or "heightened sensitivity" grounded in and explained by the specific event. Yet in order to make the personal experience testify to possibilities for lyric values that are in fact in the world, the personal voice must combine self-assertion with an effort to erase the qualities of will that mark it as individual. Self-abnegation seems the safest vehicle for authenticating the deeply personal. A self whose heightened sensitivity allows it to dissolve into the feelings created by its perceptions and reflections testifies to the immanent, transpersonal force of the experience. Now, however, the desire for individuality and the desire to achieve public meaning encounter a contradiction that it is all too tempting to try to suppress. The self projected as the vehicle for lyric experience seeks a public identity, yet it trusts no public symbolic form as a vehicle for its distinctive qualities, especially for the actual personal qualities that have been incorporated into the poetic event. Our lyric poetry exemplifies the desire to claim that an experience is significant in the precise way "I" engage in it – important both because it constitutes a claim to the esteem of others and because, in its intensity, it becomes potentially representative and hence a bond between the self and others. But the very terms for esteem and representativeness seem at once necessary and impossible; the conditions that make both the experience and the self special consist precisely in their resistance to all public measures.[12]

The "sincere" self, then, is one poets are tempted to posit as always beyond language. Heightened sensitivity is a path to secular transcendence. But secular transcendence has no ritual, no public confirmation of the patterns that warrant the pursuit. And for most contemporary poets, claims about form cannot replace ritual, since they only return one to the inflation of modernist metaphysics. So, like the child spoiled by his parents' indulgences but unable to attract their attention, the sin-

cere self has no theater on which to stage itself except the theater it constructs. But such construction is pure rhetoric, the traditional opposite
of sincerity, because the individual acts of self-staging shape what is made
to appear as natural. As we shall see, poets can treat rhetoric as the area
where sincerity manifests itself; that is, they artfully reconstruct in order
to make for others the truth of what they felt. But this claim may only
push the problem of regression back one level. There is still a claim to
transparency dependent on forms of action that belie and betray the agent's
desire to possess what he or she also wants to keep mysterious.

If the projected intimacy can conceal such dilemmas, it is likely to have
strong immediate claims on our feelings. We can identify with lyric emotion without the disturbance of reflecting on what makes such identifications so attractive. But these emotions remain vulnerable on two fronts:
they encourage a desire to be even more radically "authentic" and self-
disclosing or self-present; or, on the contrary, they tempt us to search
further back beyond the manifest state for those needs and masks in the
emotion which make the expression a possible form of self-evasion. As
we engage these problems, we can produce either enhanced sublimity
or the threat of speechless paralysis. Neither condition can quite be
subsumed within the traditional humanistic dualities of union with an
exalted nature or entrapment within an endlessly regressive self-
consciousness. For in contemporary poetry a specific relation to nature
is usually not at issue. The drama is less epistemological then psychological. What matters is not unity with nature but what that unity is a figure
for – that is, harmony between the selves we represent as significant to
ourselves and others and the forces we dimly recognize (or fear) as shaping and distorting the desired representation.[13]

At this level of the problem, modernist impersonality is no longer a
possible cure for what romanticism creates. However much we deny the
idea of a unified, substantial self, we cannot easily deny traces of our
personal styles that resist objective language. To the suspicious contemporary mind, the efforts at imposing impersonal controls on an emotion
are likely to appear signs of personal anxieties. We are tempted to treat
the stance of objective observation as in fact one of the self's most "interested" or subjective ways of producing or maintaining private desires.
Coleridge's "imagination" seems less relevant to our age than Lacan's
"imaginary," because the act of creative synthesis of self and world is
precisely what we must question. The "I" confronts or reveals its own
duplicity in a hall of inevitably self-distorting and self-ennobling mirrors. Charles Olson foresaw the problem: We would become paralyzed
by the interference of the lyrical ego. But Olson's work seems to most
poets proof that the effort to escape only deepens the disease because it
gives one's ego a free reign to claim that it can reinvent the world on its

own terms, under the guise of an objectivism closely linked to a poetics of the local. Olson's objectivism now appears to be primarily a strategy for indulging in attributions to the self as object of all that Olson had the good sense to suppress in the position of subject. So whatever the abstract poetic doctrine, it seems that few poets can escape the dilemma of having to make of an ineluctably parodic lyrical ego the basic instrument for resisting the deadening impersonality of a consumer society.

Personal expression is a notoriously slippery and duplicitous notion – the more seductive because it seems so innocuous and healthy a value. The problems derive from the kind of tensions we located in discussing representativeness: the desire to meet some public measure of significance and the impulse to have a deep, uninterpretable source of energy ensuring that the self is not simply an actor on a public stage. There must be something driving the self to offer revelations and something that resists the revelations, some source of activity that is only suggested in the contents of one's acts or discourses.[14] Selves must be deciphered within the world and against it, just as poets need public expectations or traditions and need to contrast their individual achievement to this context. In psychological terms, these tensions create endless vacillations within the self between the power of the first-person stance and the pathos in the fact that first persons become third persons, creative acts the instances of some general category. As readers of these vacillations, we encounter the inherent duplicity between subjective and objective genitives. An expression of the self can be one that is intended, the self's act, or one that is symptomatic, the act of a self not in control of what it manifests. Finally, all these confusions of subject and object, deep self and intelligible actor, add up to two incompatible but necessary ideas of the person, one stressing its incoherence as a set of desires and embedded ideological structures, the other inescapably caught up in the fact that such differences – of force and of content – seem to have a coherence or compatibility among levels that we find in no other being – indeed, in no other place except the manifestation of the first person.

When we cannot decide whether signs are intended or symptomatic, we find it very difficult to decide what is the specific text for a critic to read. Conversely, we become suspicious of the moves critics make to break this impasse. When critics promise a cure for some interpretive disease, we wonder if they are not in fact taking a normal condition as the disease so that they can claim to have a crucial cultural role to play and the authority to maintain the role. Conceptual strategies projected as cures for conceptual diseases become suspect as perhaps casting what is normal in the form of a disease so that the critic can hve a role to play and authority to wield.[15] This suspicion dominates the work of thinkers as diverse as Wittgenstein and André Glucksman – and for good cause, since it extends the tension between sincerity and rhetoricity to the question how we produce coherent interpretations of experience. The lyric's struggle with the nature and status of closure, then, captures some of the richest and deepest senses in which various forms of coherence become problematic. Closure is normally envisioned as a resolution of duplicity, either by Russell's gesture of eliminating the properties of the speaker that loop back to complicate or cancel the semantic message (as in the Grecian liar paradox) or by transcending the oppositions in some third integrative term. The third term can take many forms, from Hegelian logic to the modernist romantic image to the New Critical myth of sacramental metaphor.

The best practitioners of the dominant mode in contemporary poetry have seen the failure of all those options. Yet they are even more desperate for closure because the state of self organizing the emotions is so fragile and passive – a lyric dandelion. However, the only forms of closure left are a resolution in some small visionary sense of a silence beyond language or a highly artificial discursive conceit whose logic controls all the particulars. Each mode of closure, moreover, is haunted by what it cannot be: Too large a claim for silence returns us to *symbolisme* and the romantic image; too comprehensive or serious a use of discursive metaphor entraps us in an anachronistic bardic role of imposing vague profundities on the narrow basis of scenically grounded lyric emotions. Most important, the very desperation for closure, under such clear historical constraints, calls the gesture itself into question. Our analytic efforts at imposing conclusions become roles in the drama of personal needs, so that the psychology generating them becomes more significant (more fascinating?) than their philosophical import. For the act of producing such desperate closure once again makes inescapable the presence of a will or levels of motivation not consciously contained by the rhetoric. The rhetoric cancels its own power by not taking responsibility for its capacity to make elements appear coherent and resolved. Then it seems that what is most "real," most in control of the text or the agent, is most outside the intentional act. We feel we need new critical lenses in order to adjust for the distortion of meaning produced ironically by the agent's apparent resolution of conflicts and contingencies.

There are two morals here. First, the hermeneutics of suspicion is not merely an academic or psychoanalytic enterprise. It is demanded by the gulf between representation and acts of representing everywhere evident in psychic life. The more a represented scene seems to resolve all the explicit emotional tensions, the more we suspect that it has ignored the full play of forces that go into making the resolution. When we think we control our "sincere" expressions, we are prone to ignore what speaks through us. But what happens when we recognize this dilemma? Here we begin to see how attention to the personal dimension of lyricism and lucidity begins to open up new philosophical possibilities. Roland Barthes once said that our languages desperately need a mood of speaking lightly – especially, I might add, about ideas like "desperation." Similarly, Yeats characterized myths as fictions to which we give about 70 percent assent. It seems to me that the major dimension of poetic and cultural life that makes most high modernism seem somewhat anachronistic (and that perhaps justifies the use of concepts like "post-modern") is our capacity to adjust to incompatible systems without feeling paralyzed by their inconsistency or lack of unity.

In a critical age we cannot do without discursiveness. Indeed, the contemporary poetry most aware of the issues we are discussing tends to meet demands for lucidity by incorporating a good deal of discursiveness within the poetic experience. Such poetry recognizes a need to deal with qualities inherent in our practices as explaining and interpreting animals. Yet this very use of discursiveness tends to set the critical spirit against itself and to replay the major irony of post-Enlightenment culture – our inescapable critical need to question all the forms of discursiveness we produce as our instruments for explanations. Now, to deepen the irony, we must find in apparently outmoded poetic traditions the terms for developing new attitudes faithful to, or even instructive for, our living within these conditions. The New Critics emphasized how poetry works as a nondiscursive alternative to the simplicities of argument. Now our most interesting poets, especially David Antin and John Ashbery, can reverse those priorities: Nondiscursiveness sits within the very heart of argument because poetic conventions can be manipulated to focus attention on the overdetermination latent in all our discursive practice and habits of thought. We can even learn to take lyric pleasure in this excess of signification and the strange interpretive romances it can attract us to. Attention to overdetermination produces speculative instruments guiding us in turning thought's desire for closure against itself, so that we can make a lyricism out of lucidity. By what I call a poetics of conjecture many contemporary writers attempt to redraw our conceptual or poetic maps. They approach on the level of thought the same desire or need to maintain incompatibilities we find in our sense(s) of self.

Consider the following allegory, loosely based on Ashbery's *Three Poems*. "I am a 'solipsist,' and I want to present that condition in a literary text," thinks the writer. But solipsism is logically incompatible with "literature" because literature offers a condition and probably an attitude as representative or exemplary. One cannot be a representative solipsist. Yet how do we know anything about solipsism if there are not representative solipsists? We are in a dilemma that may be only a disease caused by our forms for philosophical discussion. Nonetheless, as Wittgenstein showed, naming diseases does not cure them; in fact, it tends to deepen further our distrust of names. The disease at least seems concrete. And indeed, in this concreteness the disease can be a creative source leading the writer to extend contradictions so that they appear constitutive of some features of spiritual life. Contemporary poetry, we are constantly told, takes loss as its central starting point. But loss is the supreme and sublime instance of a concept whose very use partially belies it while opening new ways in which traces of what is claimed to be absent become an effective presence, in our thinking and in the forces disclosed by our thinking.

Each of the problems I have discussed generates particular concrete pressures and fascinations. These are the stuff of poetic drama. But as we attend to specific contemporary lyric actions, I think we shall begin to see how all of them are episodes within a larger cultural shift in our very idea of what constitutes an appropriate or resonant stage for reflective thought. It is difficult on this level of generalization not to turn drama into melodrama. But without it, I think we will not be able to understand two central factors of the contemporary scene: how speculative criticism now attracts much of the audience and the energy the last decade devoted to poetry and how some poets do in fact continue to serve as antennae of the race as they face this general condition in their own way.

The most obvious way to state the distinctive condition of thought that takes itself as self-consciously contemporary is to speak of reason as systematically revealing its own unreason. This appears as the final lucidity, a light that swallows itself on the perverse model of the black hole. Ours is an age in which glimpses of the dark side of Enlightenment ideals invite the exploration of new generalizing attitudes that may take us beyond the basic opposition of an ideal of "truth" set against an endless irony despairing of truth. Heidegger and Wittgenstein began the process by setting themselves the task of thinking simultaneously with and against the philosophical traditions of the West. All thinking, for them, requires brackets, and generalization becomes valid primarily through the representative presence of a single consciousness trying to free itself from or see around the very discursive practices to which it is condemned. Now their actions become codified as our dogmas.

Derrida and Foucault lead to André Glucksman's generalizations. Glucksman insists that Hegel's model for philosophy expresses a paradigmatic example of the psychological and political forces that the ideal of reason produces. Hegel's orientation reveals a powerful connection between an image of mental action as negation and an ideal of total rationality with the authority to arbitrate among facts in the world. Born of total negativity, the reason has no dependencies. Its own internal structure, dialectically traced out, is its only arbiter, and that freedom appears to give it the right to project a model for all orders. The self-born can be the self-knowing and can thus impose its principles on people or facts mired in their own contingency. But if reason is in any sense contingent, that is, if it has interests and stems from a position, it is only one of many competing frameworks for order – a rather bad one, in fact, because it lacks the dramatistic terms needed to handle the play of mo-tives involved in the process of positioning.

Within Anglo-American thought the same tendencies are given less apocalyptic form in the tradition that runs from Austin to Richard Rorty.[16] Here the attack is on what Rorty calls "foundationalism," whether it be based on an image of a rational order or on an empiricist faith that we have available firm discovery procedures for resolving "meaningful" dis-putes. For Rorty, purposes and communities determine inquiry: There remain conditions of objectivity relative to practices. For Glucksman, on the other hand, reason can never grasp or justify the specific desires that produce our political actions. But however one defines the nature of pur-pose and its relation to discursive criteria – a task that I suspect is the major philosophical one of our decade – we can abstract from these dif-ferent views an account of the tensions involved that will, I think, help us place the various strategies poets use as they develop ideas of the per-son and modes of relatedness appropriate to the time.

As I intimated in describing Glucksman, we can state the sense of rea-son's unreason as an awareness that within all our efforts at description there is a condition of positionality that at once threatens and overdeter-mines descriptions. My account echoes Sartre and dozens of sloppy lit-erary allusions to Heisenberg. That is no accident, because those thinkers identified the presence of the problem in specific areas and began to de-velop analyses of being positioned that do not reduce to nineteenth-century perspectivism. Like Sartre's freedom, position is not equivalent to a per-sonal stance the agent controls by reason and judgment. Rather, the idea of position derives simply from recognizing that descriptions are over-determined, but that as we seek the source of overdetermination we en-ter an endless regress of competing codes, desires, and levels of reflection and concern. A position is a place from which someone speaks, but the place itself is positioned by the cultural practices and the personal history and needs of the speaker. This means, ultimately, that all authority is at best provisional: No one discourse can claim to speak for or over another since there are enormous difficulties in translating between positions or deciding how they might be commensurable.

There are many levels of experience where the relevant positions over-lap. But as we get more general, as we try to decide, for example, whether philosophy governs sociological terms or a sociology of knowledge governs philosophy, we begin to see the ramifications and suspicions such competition breeds. We need discourses, but we cannot trust them, a condition leading Ihab Hassan to coin the marvelous term "indetermanency" as a description of post-modernism.[17] We are never without values and criteria – hence immanence – and we are never sure of their relevance – hence our sense of indeterminacy.

VII

If I were to write a theoretical statement on the subjects we have been discussing, I would quarrel with most of the assumptions I take here as basic features of contemporary consciousness. I think we can avoid many of these dilemmas, at least on the level of philosophical argument. But the fact remains that our poets, and probably our basic emotional investments, have not avoided them. So at the least they constitute a necessary framework for understanding our literary tastes and for perhaps thinking our way through to alternative standards. The Enlightenment has given all to reason and has come to this. But we may be able to take up the kinds of stances and assumptions proposed by thinkers like Richard Rorty, or even Derrida, as the beginnings of a new faith. The future, however, is not my topic here; nor is conceptual argument my method. Rather, I employ some of the conceptual matter from arguments as a stage capable of framing and forming poets' imaginative efforts to describe their world and to invent ways of living in it without succumbing to a narrow sense of lucidity. As an example of these efforts, even the scenic mode, the villain of their work, must be acknowledged to have a good deal to offer in the emotional energies it organizes and the tensions between description and construction it exemplifies. By relying on sincerity and directness, the dominant contemporary mode tries to confine the positions of the ego to predicates we comfortably use for discussing motives in conventional dramatic frameworks. These allow the experience of lyric sensitivity to appear representative without engaging the duplicities inherent in more abstract thought. Ultimately, poets hope the manifest sincerity will produce sufficient power to erase all the dilemmas of regressiveness.

If taking someone's word leads to communion and extends our sense of our own power, we may be foolish to question it further. However, I am convinced that if we stop here we purchase our lyricism too cheaply. The better we understand the pressures these scenic strategies try to resist, the more we see how the more radical stances become necessary.

There are duplicities within these efforts at self-authorization that eventually mock the poetic enterprise unless they are confronted. Some means of confrontation can remain quite conservative. Robert Hass, for example, transforms the scenic mode so that it can carry a sense of complex personal voice that makes the ironic stance pale by comparison. But the ultimate reward for taking seriously the themes I have been developing is the access they give to contemporary forms of inclusiveness that recapture for different situations the imperial imagination central to our greatest poetry. Here Ashbery reigns supreme because he dramatizes a power to position oneself so that one can think the very condition of being positioned – an activity Wittgenstein illustrates beautifully in his attempts to imagine how people with different faiths assume general attitudes toward thought.[18] In what Beckett calls "the old disposition," which continued through most high modernism, the "noblest" lyric poetry sought to identify its own lyric activity as a step toward momentary ecstatic union with some transpersonal principle of creative energy. Logos became a *natura naturans* or active form or unconscious speaking through and as poetry at its most intense. And the intensity in turn justified the poet's claims to possess authority in that voice: What emerged could serve at once to measure the present and to project an ideal future for those who could be moved (in every sense) by what they heard. For contemporaries there is too much motion to hope to hear or respond to any single still point.

But the dream of figuring forth a sense of source, of what we understand ourselves as standing on in our motion and emotion, remains alive. If we are dismantling reason's stage, some poets at least are trying to read through our constant sense of duplicity a wholly other dream of ultimate grounds. Rilke began it by making divine the lack or absence Mallarmé saw at the heart of language, its silence. Now, though, the romantic dream requires a very nonromantic mode of approach. Our center is at best a centering that takes form when the mind occupies a site at the margin of any single drama. There several paths of thought cross, each overdetermining and undercutting its neighbor, but in the process revealing traces of what moves and holds our motions.

Here in the interplay of emotion and of vacancy, here where all our crossings among poets lead, one finds two distinctive and exciting imaginative stances. At one pole there is John Ashbery's meditation on all that flows from and within that absent center which drives us to a language aware of its strange, self-reflexive forms of liminality, and at the other pole we find in Adrienne Rich a radically opposed insistence on taking responsibility for all creation as embodying and ultimately depending on Woman's imaginative will. Even these poets rarely produce a contemplative site adequate to all the duplicities our language and our world continually impose upon us. Yet were the enterprise of tracking those duplicities not an intriguing end in itself, the project we begin here may justify itself simply by preparing us to see how much we need such moments and how they may in fact continue to make available what must suffice.

2

The dominant poetic mode of the late seventies

I

The concept of ideology is probably too dependent on ideologies to be of much critical use. But if we take a step back from current controversies and simply bracket any impulse to make our claims about ideology support large social visions, we can use a loose sense of ideology in order to situate most serious contemporary poetry. In making this claim I assume that any writer likely to last has the ambition to express and to transcend his or her literary culture. So by identifying the common terms of that culture we in effect establish one basic struggle taking place in the works. Second, I assume that in responding to cultural pressures the poets encounter forces stemming from complex affiliations they have with social classes, canons, and sets of poetic and social principles, all likely to overlap and be in tension with one another. Each area of inquiry is complex in itself, and things are not made simpler by the series of regressive dependencies among beliefs that any analysis is likely to turn up.

Such problems require a high degree of generality in my initial description of a dominant mode.[1] I propose to achieve this generality by adapting from standard accounts of ideology two basic principles. When we speak of ideological aspects of some phenomenon, we normally refer to some component of false consciousness and some dimension of emotional investment on the part of the ideologue. However, it has become all too evident that insofar as we equate false consciousness with being mistaken or partial in one's view of social realities we introduce an endless chain of charges, countercharges, confessions, and assertions of justified irrationalism. I prefer to interpret the dimension of false consciousness as an aspect of quality rather than truth: In other words, in this study "ideology" refers to what happens to any discourse, however true or valid, when it must be framed to organize practical behavior or produce justifications for a group larger, more diverse, and less possessed of the relevant skills than the group of those who could work out the intellectual position with the fullest rigor and deepest complexity. Then, if ideas become so organized, it is easy to explain how emotions get involved. The process of simplification invites the adapting of ideas to images and pieties deeply embedded in our forms of self-regard and ideals of behavior.

If one can isolate a dominant mode, one has a clear social group within which to search for ideological commitments. From among the many different communities concerned with poetry as a high art in the United States, I shall seek this mode by isolating the assumptions characterizing the taste of what can with the most justice be called a poetry establishment. There is no single, sinister cabal, but there are clear signs of shared taste and vehicles like fellowship boards that make it possible for the taste to take on institutionalized power. Richard Hugo once said during a reading that when he and David Wagoner were graduate students in the backwater of Seattle, Washington, they would occasionally speculate on what their fate would be in the hands of the eastern literary establishment. Since then, Hugo added, seeing that he was editing a Yale series and Wagoner was editing Princeton's poetry collection, they had *become* the eastern establishment. Even if this is fortunately not the whole truth, one can grasp the presence of shared assumptions simply by looking at the kinds of poetry not published by those presses or by the larger poetry journals.

This does not mean that there is one rigidly enforced style. But it does suggest that we can hope to produce a level of abstraction at which we can define common principles of judgment responsible for such distinctions. We are not likely to find strong, crisp poetic doctrines governing taste. Instead, we normally encounter somewhat vague, very general principles loosely melded from basic styles and specific doctrines held by major writers of the previous generation. A poetic ideology is usually a somewhat muddy blend of literary and existential values that are adaptable to generalized public forums like the review or the classroom. Such values take shapes that allow persons to make judgments while covertly reinforcing their own commitments. Thus there is a literary version of the conservation principle established by W. V. Quine: When we develop descriptive terms or evaluative principles we try to adapt to change and contradiction with the minimum loss of those fundamental elements which provide self-esteem or give direction to cultural practices. We bend at the edges while trying to preserve a center intact. The deeper the emotional investments in the particular sphere of experience, the greater the stake in the conservation principle – even when, as in poetry, there is a competing demand for originality and distinctive personal styles.

Examples work better than abstract definitions when our concern is for the ways in which beliefs get codified and issue in judgments. So in this chapter I shall return to Young's discussion of Stafford and compare his values to those of Stanley Plumly, another poet who has published influential essays on poetics. Each poet has a somewhat different sense of audience, Young's more pedagogical, Plumly's more a community of writers; but these differences serve largely to lead us to the abstract space where we can recognize the beliefs they share and the contradictions they suffer. In order to articulate what is common about their ideas, I shall place their values within a brief sketch of the changing pressures on poets in the past three decades. Then, as a measure of the consequences of such beliefs, I shall devote the rest of this chapter to analyzing two poems that can serve as paradigms for the aesthetics of the dominant mode. I hope to show how Plumly and Charles Wright each manifest considerable talent but nonetheless encounter serious poetic problems deriving in large part from their assumptions about the art. The poems turn out to be as moving for what they fail to achieve as for what they control, thus leaving us an image of traps it will be difficult for even the most brilliant and self-aware contemporary poet to avoid.

II

The Stafford poem Young praises is not a bad one. It is, though, a bad example for his case because its naturalness is so literary and its literariness ultimately so evasive and self-protective. Within his contemplative sincerity Stafford seems to feel no responsibility to reflect upon the rhetorical figures producing the poem's moment of vision. The conjunction of bone, blood, river, muskrat, and hand composes a resonant sense of elemental realities, which in turn supports the poem's final invocation of the concept of meaning for an event whose resonance must lie outside language. But this careful use of the inexpressibility trope is never acknowledged as a trope. The audience is left with two reactions

– a sense of being moved and a suspicion that roughly the same emotions could be produced endlessly by simple variations on the formula.

I am obviously exaggerating, but I wish I felt a larger gulf than I do between my parody and my reactions to the poem. Stafford's treatment of emotions makes him all too susceptible to the ironic reversals worked by deconstructive thought, and that vulnerability helps explain why poetry has such a marginal status in our society. It simply fails to satisfy our standards for self-awareness about the means we use to gain our ends. The poems reflect our emotional duplicity without our practical intelligence. As an illustration of their failure of intelligence, consider by contrast what Roland Barthes makes of the inexpressibility trope. He asks us to be wary of the surface appeal, to look beyond the claims of visionary presence to the implicit needs that are in effect revealed by the signs of rhetorical effort. Why should we be so anxious to have meanings that hands wear forever in mystic marriage with muskrats? Are we perhaps simply trying to evade the banality of the quotidian, the inevitable sense of sameness and repetition that accretes around what is in fact there to be expressed? If, for example, someone were sick in the hospital, it would be an insult to send a note that said simply "Condolences." But do I in fact feel significantly more complex or inexpressible emotions? Is not my message very plain, and is not that the reason I cannot just state my "meaning"? It is only in order to make a typical situation seem special and in order to distinguish my response that I in effect unexpress the expressible and write an elaborate "sincere" note. We convince our audience and ourselves of sincerity and depth of feeling by inventing variations on what in its simplicity and commonness might be the accurate statement.[2]

I do not wish to endorse Barthes's implication that all romantic mystery is so easily demystified. That endorsement might be bad metaphysics and certainly would make for a very limited poetics. We clearly need a stance like Barthes's, if only to keep poets from embarrassing us with bald contradictions about the emotional experiences art creates. But in so collapsing lyricism into lucidity terms, Barthes is too willing to replace depth by mere cleverness. Young and Stafford are engaged in negotiating a difficult passage between two destructive forces; on one side lies the interminable self-consciousness that cripples so much of contemporary writing and on the other the false sublimity and vacuous prophecy of what passed as speculative poetic thought a decade ago. Yet neither failing can destroy the power of lyric feeling or our cultural needs for it. So they must seek lyric states whose authority lies simply in the quality of emotions captured by verbal nuances as the poet narrates the psyche's adventures amid dramatic scenes.

Young's is probably the most common, but by no means the most sophisticated, formulation of the values shaping the dominant mode. For more complex examinations of sincerity sustained by the craft of scenic construction we can turn to Stanley Plumly's intriguing two-part essay "Chapter and Verse." Plumly faces the contradictions in Young recasting the nature of sincerity in poetry – from the scene represented to the poet's control as a rhetorician. Sincerity is a quality of self-conscious authorial performance, not of dramatic illusion. And this approach in turn allows Plumly to offer a sharp distinction between the work of his own generation and that of its more vocal predecessors. Where sixties' poets like Robert Bly, Denise Levertov, and Charles Olson shared a desire to make poetry capture "experience in capital letters," those who developed styles in the seventies could insist on poetry as primarily a mode of discourse.[3] Poetry remains a form of experience, but not an illusionistic one based on elaborate adventures of immediate discovery. Rather, the experience is of the ways in which a given rhetoric controls our relation to events we encounter through our identification with the reflective authorial voice.

Implicit in Plumly is a sense that the previous age demanded poets willing to overextend themselves by dreaming that society's values could be revalued through exemplary acts of altered or redeemed consciousness. Poetry sought to be "experience in capital letters," then, because poets felt that intense poetic experience might serve as witness and proof of the power of mind to recover numinous values trampled underfoot by the assumptions of liberal industrial society. Now that the desire to transform society, or even to transform long-standing aspects of American personality, has come to seem to many at best escapist and at worst another of the illusions Americans create to avoid the contradictions in their lives, poets have sought quieter, more distinctly personal and relativistic ways of adjusting to what seem inescapable conditions. Thus Plumly defines the basic motive of younger writers as a quest for carving out distinctive personal qualities within an accepted space of public discourse. Instead of seeking to make the poem a testament to new ontological or psychological frameworks, younger poets impose on themselves the more limited, although also perhaps more poetically taxing, criterion of "the relative believability or authenticity of the poem's voice, its rhetoric."[4] The task is not to transform the social but to make voice an index of how we can register the complexity of the given and thus develop our personal powers for responding to experience. Since the 1960s, "tone seems to have displaced the image as a 'technique of discovery.'"[5] What the image had offered as a means for getting beneath surfaces, tone affords as a means for dwelling sympathetically and intelligently within inescapable public and personal facts and conditions. What now seems an irresponsible commitment to public responsibility in poets like Bly, Levertov, and Ginsberg authorizes by contrast the refusal of poets in the seventies to claim responsibility for anything except the quality of their interpersonal relations.

Ours is an age that must come to terms with failed expectations and, worse, the guilt of recognizing why we held such ambitious dreams. So it is not simply the case that we reject ideas that poetry can help transform the self or the world because these ideals are anachronistic delusions. It was we, not others, who held these illusions. Those of us who indulged in the dreams of the sixties, but now take what we can from a society we still do not believe in, cannot assume so objective a stance. It is hard not to see these old hopes and roles as either pathetic blindness to social facts or disgustingly self-evasive efforts at self-promotion. What took the guise of idealism nags us now as a reminder of how cheap and easy it is to proclaim our differences from the domestic, political, and literary authorities that formed us. The very terms that allowed us to dream of power and possibility now in large part indicate how we so easily mask private needs by our public assertions. Under such suspicions, there is not much space for the self-projection that makes compelling lyric stances. For many of us the only available forms of nobility are either the supple and clever deconstruction of our past assertions or the cultivation of temperaments so delicate, nostalgic, and resigned to the art of survival that they can thrive on emotions too fine to be contaminated by the demise of one fiction about values after another.

This simple social context is one framework that makes us see why Plumly is so concerned with the rhetoric of poetry as its principal "technique of discovery." It matters less to have new vehicles of knowledge than to be able to dramatize the powers that remain for us in our constricted world. Plumly distinguishes two kinds of rhetoric, each a way of making control the primary factor and of treating poetic emotion as deriving from a timeless, asocial source of lyric speech. At one pole, that of the "prose lyric," we find poets concentrating on the power of voice to create complex tonal balances for simple, virtually transparent actions. At the other pole is the poetry of image that seeks the deep, timeless emotions that accompany the act of transforming contingent features of experience into the stillness of the emblem. Each mode, in turn, obviously echoes a dominant style of the sixties: "Tone" derives from the adaptions of Williams's techniques of contiguity in poets like Lowell, whereas "image" clearly continues the sixties' fascination with the surreal. Yet in both cases, a rhetoric that was considered the means to elaborating some idea of "deep" content now becomes the dominant source of emotions simply by virtue of qualities in the authorial act.

III

Wallace Stevens is perhaps our most suggestive theorist of literary history because he elaborates what I take to be the central metaphor required for such analyses – the metaphor of pressure. "Pressure" is a term that pertains to both external and internal forces, so it allows critics to approximate the struggles writers have as they develop themes and explore stylistic strategies. Poets are subject to pressures from their culture, from personal situations, from styles they inherit, and from the demands inherent in the content with which they choose to work. But at the same time, Stevens reminds us, external pressures elicit imaginative energies asserting a counterpressure that can produce a distinctive imaginative stance toward the materials.[6] The case is simplest in individual lines, where the poet's manipulation of conventions can give us a fresh sense of his or her particular grasp on a perception. The same processes of transformation may be located in complete poems (as in Yeats's use of the sonnet in "Leda and the Swan") and in the general shape a poet gives a volume or a career. The more deeply we understand the relationship between external pressure and internal counterpressure, the more fully we can both measure the distinctive achievement of the poet and recognize the possible uses an audience can make of that poet's stance in order to resist those external pressures. For Stevens, it is because poets exemplify such powers that we can imagine their measure to be their capacity to involve the lives of other people in their work.

I define the force of a poem as its capacity to produce this involvement. The pressure metaphor, then, enables us to give a partial explanation of this sense of force: There are very real literary and historical factors oppressing the imagination and requiring mental exertions closely tied to our experience of physical labor. Literary pressures appear through those ancestors or styles most consistently combated and revised in a poet's work, and historical pressures are revealed in the themes, styles, and situations the poet emphasizes as the chosen means for at once expressing and mastering them. The means for this mastery are correspondingly doubled. There is first of all simply the counterpressure the poet puts on linguistic and structural elements in order to assert free intelligence with respect to inheritance.

But for craft to become also a historical force, the poet must adapt these aesthetic means to constructing what Olson called "stances towards reality."[7] Counterpressure on the line, diction, or structure becomes also a cognitive pressure testing the validity of psychic powers and potentially public values that we want to explore through new imaginative attitudes. The historical pressures on Wordsworth's art, for example, were constituted primarily by Milton's sublimity and the excessive attention to the act of writing without a corresponding sense of new ideas in Gray and Collins. The social pressures Wordsworth articulated in the very process of resisting them can loosely be called the empirical, utilitarian, and mechanistic features of the Industrial Revolution. Then, in seeking a language free from the excesses of Gray and Collins, yet capable of competing with Milton while attending to common nature and anti-heroic circumstances, Wordsworth managed to make the dramatic stage for his new diction a model for possible ways the imagination might make and perceive relationships. Wordsworth's development from "An Evening Walk" to "Tintern Abbey" consists not simply in replacing associative and chronological structures with synthetic, dialectical ones, but also in using the symbolic logic of imaginative memory to project organicist values, dynamic powers of the mind formed by Wordsworthian habits of attention, and images of a possible society that might prove an alternative to the values shaping the course of the Industrial Revolution.

When we turn to the sixties, it is fairly easy to see how what Plumly takes now as a pretentious claim to "experience in capital letters" seemed then one of the few valid ways to resist the aesthetic and cultural pressures imposed upon writers by their immediate heritage. In the fifties the display of artistic intelligence had come to seem either a decadent aestheticism, putting very little pressure on actual realities, or a surrender to a narrow Christian humanism represented by second-generation New Critics. Juxtapositional styles and complex levels of internal relationships had been developed by modernists precisely to locate new sources of mental energy in an age dominated by simple poetic descriptions on the one hand and political bombast on the other. These styles had grown enervated, and lyric richness had become the end rather than the means the poets had expected it to be. It seemed that poetry could be saved from decadence only by shifting the basic use of poetic intelligence from concerns for aesthetic complexity to concerns for emotional intensity and speculative scope, even if the price had to be the rejection of traditional expectations about craft and about coherent symbolic patterning as a structural principle.

Accompanying and in part informing these changing views on poetry was a radically new sense of how poetry might resist the dominant cultural pressures. From high modernism through the fifties, the major antagonist of the arts was conceived to be a cultural barbarism in middle-class life that might be mollified or escaped by cultivating the aesthetic imagination and the energies available from the traditions that exemplify it. For younger poets in the sixties, the antagonistic pressure of barbarism remained, but high culture began to appear as part of the problem rather than a basis for resistance. The Arnoldian dream of replacing religion by culture had failed, as had most versions of faith in the form-creating imagination as man's partial access to the creative Logos. Thus younger poets felt the need for versions of religious experience not already compromised by Western history. Yet because complicated forms of reasoning and intricate self-reflection seemed preempted by these failed stances toward reality, the poets had little but the intensity of extreme emotional states, the sharpness of perception, and the sublimity of momentary religious visions as their means for giving authority to their new perspectives.

Lowell's confessional style marks for me the crucial turning point because it makes the self, shorn of intellectual and cultural traditions, the necessary source of authentic lyric feeling. Yet the self can be manifested only in continual conflict, psychological and aesthetic, with forms of understanding that might interpret the intensity as a means to some sense of transpersonal powers. Lowell's confessional style tries to deny artifice by forcing the poem to stay within the forms of coherent subjective experience. Instead of argument, structure must rely on arrangements of synecdochic details from the "pure prose" surfaces of common life. This move secures what might be called existential authenticity, but it encounters the problem of energizing or valuing those details while resisting the lyric energy of the gracefully twisting, pattern-making mind. The plainness of surface becomes a challenge to generate a sense of depth, while distrust of intellect leaves little but private emotion and the space of a nameless anxiety with which to fill the gap. Moreover, the insistence on prosaic surface reinforces a profound sense of cultural alienation; if one sees only naked physical particulars, perhaps invested with private meanings (which the poet makes resonant), the traces of cultural symbols appear only in alienated and alienating form. The emotion is all in negation – impotence raised to the level of lyric song – so that drama in a world without significant action depends on the ego's melodramatic capacity to suffer. The mind's power to produce formal balance must be replaced by the sublimity of the emotive self as it rages within the confines of metonymic particulars: "In this urn the animal night sweats of the spirit burn."[8]

Lowell made magnificent poetry of his plight. But he could not be imitated – even by his own later self – partially because the authenticity of suffering does not brook constant repetition and partially because the logic of Lowell's emotional rhetoric was all too clear. Once one reduces the imagination to a surface of contingent details, the "I" is likely to discover itself without grounds: "I myself am hell; / nobody's here."[9] To place there somebody or something more powerful or less pathetic than the anxious "I" became the quest of most self-consciously post-modern

poetry in the sixties – from Olson's myths, to O'Hara's glittering surfaces, to Ginsberg's blend of hipster and guru in search of alternate realities. All in effect labored to escape what Robert Bly saw was a confusion
in confessional poetry between "poetic excitement" and the "nervous
excitement" of lyricized anxiety: "For the confessional poet anything less
than an abortion or a cancer operation really doesn't justify the machinery. A poem becomes a tank that can't maneuver on soft ground without
destroying it."[10]

Bly's criterion of "poetic excitement," however, would prove equally
problematic. Like Lowell, he judged that the lyric state depends on transforming a prose world sheerly by the movement of specific perceptual
energy the poem can sustain. For Bly the sources of that energy were
located in forces deeper than the ego, to be disclosed at the poem's conclusion by a sudden leap inward to surreal emotive states. But the terms
for achieving lyrical intensity were equally melodramatic, at least in most
of the work Lensing and Moran would call poetry of the "emotive imagination." Thus Paul Breslin could say of this dominant mode of the
late sixties and early seventies that its pursuit of the deep image escaped
the Freudian ego of confessional poetry only to rely on an equally problematic and theatrical Jungian self.[11] In the pursuit of "poetic excitement"
it is difficult not to rely on self-consciously poetic subject matters and
effects, and it becomes all too easy to confuse poetic thinking with bardic
prophecy. Moreover, everything that might distinguish between thinking and fantasy or that might produce cultural resonance for metonymic
objects was contaminated by what seemed Western culture's complicity
in the Vietnam War. Poets had to make large pronouncements because
their task was to provide cultural alternatives, and there was no way to
distinguish between rhetorical intensity and plausible visions of an alternate society. Thus what began as an attack on the confessional pursuit of
raw experience earned fifteen years later the same criticism from Plumly.
Now, in fact, the condition Plumly identified might be characterized as
a poetry left only with a rhetoric of experience. For we see all too clearly
how the self in these deep-image poems often confined its intelligence
and feeling to what Robert Pinsky called "a more imagistic than thou
attitude."[12] The depth of the deep image seemed to depend on a simple
twist of the same rhetorical cloth from which epiphanies were mass-
produced.

My complaints have been stated too boldly and generally, but their
relevance is not difficult to demonstrate. Bly's work, in fact, illustrates
why the lyricism–lucidity conflict would require Plumly's critique of the
dominant mode in the late sixties and early seventies. "Surprised by Evening" is not one of Bly's best poems (which tend to be his prose descrip-

tions), but it clearly demonstrates the effects of a psychic economy shored up by an emotive imagination without the backing of contexts that sustain a reflective, controlling tonal intelligence:

> There is unknown dust that is near us,
> Waves breaking on shore just over the hill,
> Trees full of birds that we have never seen,
> Nets drawn down with dark fish.
>
> The evening arrives; we look up and it is there,
> It has come through the nets of stars,
> Through the tissues of the grass,
> Walking quietly over the asylums of water.
>
> The day shall never end, we think:
> We have hair that seems born for the daylight;
> But, at last, the quiet waters of the night will rise
> And our skin shall see far off, as it does under water.[13]

Bly wants here to exemplify a mode of imaginative attention in which the mind becomes aware of a sense of mystery in natural experience. The poem produces a "slip inward" to an order of psychic reality where analogies allow the mind to discover grounds of being it shares with natural processes beneath the ego and the discursive intelligence. Thus one becomes aware of a numinous source of value and psychic integrity. In order to develop this state aesthetically, Bly puts heavy pressure on the poem's timing and on the power of the images to escape limited rational concerns, so that initial fascination can be transformed into sudden secure discovery of what skin, water, night, and imagination share. But even on this level his success is questionable, since the images recall the preciosity of the *symboliste* Yeats and the "at last" lacks any powerful dramatic motive. More important, by ignoring other pressures the poem should respond to, Bly invites us to see his work as more determined by cultural pressures than determining an adequate response. The poem puts all its intelligence in the service of denying the reflective, analytic mind and equates a state of vision with essentially passive absorption into the quiet waters – fit materials, perhaps, for what Plumly would decry as Bly's monotone voice.

Moreover, the lines are flat; the language is not completely under control (e.g., the several meanings of "asylums" do not all get resolved in the poem); the phrasing, syntax, and stanza units are remarkably repetitious and the easily evocative "of" phrases downright embarrassing. In order to create a sense of mystery, Bly keeps the poem's surface as loose and contiguous as those of Lowell and Snodgrass. Yet his poem lacks the dramatic pressure they derive from emphasizing the psyche's state of need.

Its diffuse emotion is not tempered by sharp recognitions or verbal wit; what is left is only the passive associations of fancy masking as active imagination.

Finally, the poem cannot take responsibility for what craft and intelligence it possesses. Bly is very skillful at embedding analogies and personifications in order to establish a context for the final explosive images. The apparently contiguous details are as self-consciously "poetic" as in Stafford's poem. Yet Bly wants his rhetoric to count also as immediate concrete perception. Thus it is difficult for him to acknowledge the rhetoric without projecting an ironic context undermining the truth claim in the analogies. All romantic poetry, as de Man and Paz point out, dances delicately between analogy and irony, but few poets go as far as Bly in insisting on the unconscious forces revealed in these analogies. So long as one makes analogy dependent on a dramatic perspective (where analogy is acknowledged as part of the stance) or uses it as the basis for reflections on the symbol-making mind, one can transcend the irony inherent in using elaborate structures to justify claims that one has discovered values within the immediate experience of nature.[14] In the work of Bly, however, the represented claims for immediacy are belied by the very act of writing that stages them. The clanking of Bly's verbal machinery, then, ironically calls our attention to a will to poetry that the poem's interpretive structures cannot accommodate. The will to the poem is sadly incompatible with the cognitive claims projected, so an impossible burden is put on artificial texture to support the poem's assertions. The ultimate irony in Bly is that his need to sustain religious claims solely in terms of the lyric mystery projected by evocative images puts cognitive pressure on precisely those features of his literary culture that are already under a great deal of stress and thus readily demystified. This is why he must shrink from acknowledging his own rhetorical acts; otherwise he would have to deal with the charge of manipulating the easiest and thus most easily suspect terms on which one can hope to achieve lyric assent to more than lyric propositions.

This withdrawal from a demonic lucidity in order to make essentially lyric emotions serve cognitive needs highlights two basic problems in our literary culture, both directly addressed by younger poets who call attention to their own constructive activity and make tone a demystified source of lyric emotion. The first concerns our fundamental assumptions about the nature and value of intense emotional experience. If we insist on intense emotions, we are likely to lead psychic lives that function in terms of binary oppositions: Either we welcome all experiences as valuable because they fit standard lyric categories of love or pain or religious exaltation, or we posit ourselves as dead, flat, nauseated beings resenting the empty artificiality of cultural forms and the deadness of nature. When experiences do not fit our emotional grammar, we turn either on our-selves or on the world as inadequate. Literary sensibilities tend to blow up the descriptive gap between feelings and the lyric predicates we assign to them into a metaphysical gap between self-consciousness and objec-tive realities or the lives of other subjects. Alternatively, we may impose on experience an unacknowledged theatrical rhetoric that satisfies our emotional needs but invites ironic dissolution and disillusion. We need only remember the weight Bly puts on his analogies and the need his poems exhibit to maintain the illusion of a single, coherent, dramatic movement toward a climax. We inherit a situation, then, in which the attempts by younger poets to put skeptical pressure on these assump-tions about emotion will be characterized by the need to alter conven-tional expectations about metaphors as vehicles of knowledge and about coherent, illusionistic dramatic structures.

The second problem concerns the effects on lyric voice when a poem is asked to carry the burden of restoring to a culture large religious vi-sion, however secularized or psychologized. It may be that the very depth of our need makes it impossible for any single mode of mental or imag-inative activity to do the job by itself. In seeking to do too much, in seeking to make dramatic situations essentially representative moments exemplifying the working of larger metaphysical properties, poems may end up doing too little. This condition is manifest at each of the polar extremes explored by poets of the emotive imagination.

Galway Kinnell's *Book of Nightmares* has often been attacked for its strained rhetoric, but the important question is why a poet of such talent should get trapped in problems very similar to Bly's. The answer lies, I think, in the task Kinnell sets himself: In order to sustain and to resolve the level of intense, theatricalized suffering of the poem's often brilliant nightmare visions, Kinnell must be able to elaborate a metaphysical scheme equal to his demonic moments and capacious enough to justify a fully bardic stance. But Kinnell's ideas are very thin, and so he is forced to rely on the verbal gestures of intense emotion grafted onto conventional romantic postures. Here is the dramatic climax in the central fourth sec-tion of the eighth poem:

> and the bodies of our hearts
> opened
> under the knowledge
> of tree, on the grass of the knowledge
> of graves, and among the flowers of the flowers.
>
> And the brain kept blossoming
> all through the body, until the bones themselves could think,
> and the genitals sent out wave after wave of holy desire . . .

and I understood
the unicorn's phallus could have risen, after all,
directly out of thought itself.[15]

This section continually affirms the onset of knowledge, but after such knowledge, what but bathos can follow? What do trees know or bones think, and, above all, what more than a small lyric can be resolved by such a limited moment of final understanding? Knowledge and holy desire belong here to the realm of unicorns because only an abstract mythic frame will not immediately reveal the ultimate triviality of this resolution. As he reaches for a high style, Kinnell's general Rilkean stance collapses into a Blakean version of "Dover Beach," and the very attempt to transcend the personal by ontological reflection leads only to restating the basic problem as a solution; we are back with the dream of intense personal relations and isolated pastoral moments as the only alternative to the lucidity of nightmare vision. If one persists in seeking resolutions, nightmares demand not a momentary intuition but a sustained imaginative framework akin to a religion. Instead Kinnell's poem offers mostly exercises in lyric sensibility masquerading as thought. The skeptic might glory here in exposing such poetry as a pathetic and portentous attempt to take God's place, with an imaginary phallus our only weapon.

If the bardic voice fails because its reach exceeds its grasp and produces mock heavens, the other characteristic stance of the emotive imagination – the deflection of religious needs into understated recognitions in a kind of plain style – fares no better. This plain style so slackens the cognitive pressures on the poem's details and ways of developing relationships that it renders consciousness as too passive and narrow to enact or act upon any moments of insight the poem might bring. Lyric intensity here takes a form radically different from that of the best romantic poems because it is won only at the extinction of personal energies. James Wright's work is an important test case here because he and William Stafford remain influential on Plumly and his peers. Charles Molesworth, in a superb essay, states succinctly the source of Wright's problems. Wright's central myth, he tells us, is "that the poet must lose himself in things, for only there will he find his tongue." One can celebrate a unity of the self, then, "only when the self turns over its powers to its own emotions . . . , when . . . the soul is willing to dissolve the ground of its own being."[16]

In articulating these dissolutions, Wright works both with and against Bly's exaggerated lyricism: His best poems either develop covert analogies into lovely moments of lyric surprise ("A Blessing") or move toward self-deprecating modesty and sudden shifts to public wit or private self-consciousness ("In Reference to a Rumor . . . " and "Lying in a

Hammock . . . "). Yet both modes easily lapse into unreflective, almost automatic gestures as they reach for general import. The self-deprecating poems tend to become merely exercises in the topos of modesty because the poems lack sustained irony and turn so much on surprise that the final gesture seems theatrical and pompous – an assertion of self masking as humility. This unconscious theatricality, not qualified by the poem's reflection on the act of writing, is even more pronounced when Wright makes the shift to surreal images carry emotional and cognitive pressure. Imagine how easily the following concluding images might become aspects of complex and ironic states of desire and reflection on desire in an Ashbery poem: "I float among / Lonely animals, longing / For the red spider who is God"; "Their sons grow suicidally beautiful / . . . and gallop terribly against each other's bodies"; "When I stand upright in the wind, / My bones turn to dark emeralds." [17] From the perspective younger poets share with Ashbery (though few would salivate with his perverse irony at the second of my quotations), these images are too theatrical to serve as claims to sudden visionary awareness but must be seen instead as indexes of a desire itself demanding careful, self-conscious reflections.

Wright's dilemma is a moving one, although its full pathos is never confronted in his poetry. He needs to dissolve the skeptical, rational intellect, and to make poetry of this process he needs striking imaginative constructs of sufficient emotional and intellectual weight to make moments of vision do the work of the intellect. Some of the European and Latin-American surreal poets can do this, but for Wright the unconscious is won only at the cost of greatly reducing our sense of the powers of poetic language and, indeed, of all human powers. In responding to a poem like "To Flood Stage Again," the mind does nothing but register contingent particulars with no life of their own or ability to demand capable response from the poet. All the lyric effects depend on a shift of levels, from perception to a final evocative moment of self-consciousness: "I open my eyes and gaze down / At the dark water." [18] What surprise the ending might have is to a large extent vitiated by its formulaic nature: At least seven poems in *Shall We Gather at the River* begin with the "I" located in a specific landscape and then, maintaining the illusion of an experience unfolding in the present tense, elaborate loosely related particulars and associations (with a few "darks" sprinkled in for mystery) until all the details become coherent preparations for a sudden leap in attention that warrants shifting the stance of the "I" from observer to lyrical participant in deep forces. [19]

Moreover, most of these final gestures involve no complexity of tone and lead to no attempt to reflect upon the moment of vision. This putative absoluteness of insight, which precludes further reflection, creates something close to what Hegel called the "bad infinite," a form of mystery depending more on vagueness and surprise than on any sense that the mind has located structures that genuinely exceed its own powers of comprehension. Such final and banal assertions of mystery tempt one to suggest that Wright's wish that his words be grass, like Bly's that "the talkative be silent, / and the dumb shall speak,"[20] is all too close to realization. The aim may be to bring despair to a point of religious transcendence, but the result is a capitulation to society's view of poems as mere emotive cries seeking desperately to escape realities and ironies that only a lucid and demystifying consciousness can face.

IV

These extremes toward which the emotive imagination tends make it clear why a poem like Stafford's "Ceremony" can continue to exercise considerable power. Stafford's poem has neither the excessive reach of Kinnell nor the formulaic passivity of Wright. The speaker engaged in concrete actions, and the somewhat stagy use of detail creates a complex particular relation to a scene so that it is the entire event, not only some final moment of delivery, which takes on metaphoric weight and extension. Such poetry becomes increasingly influential in proportion to the ways the extremes it denies come to appear melodramatic or conventional. Thus poets coming to maturity in the seventies took as their models the least pretentious poets of the sixties, those who most emphasized craft and gave qualities of unaffected naturalness to their scenes and concluding images. Young poets would learn from Wright and Stafford to make believably resonant deep images, from Richard Hugo to stress musical vitality and "hardheaded" tonal complexity, and from poets like Donald Justice and David Wagoner to elaborate scenes into delicate, somewhat distanced thematic reflections.

Such training produces the two forms of rhetoric Plumly describes, those of tone and of the image. As Plumly is all too aware, there are many variations on the basic model, but in order to understand poetry today we must see how the fundamental structures emerged as a response to historical and cultural pressures. Younger poets must avoid the embarrassing excesses of their predecessors, but their project is strongly affected by the enormous constraints that the emotional ideals of that poetry continue to exercise. As Plumly brilliantly demonstrates, the new poetry brings more personal intensity and a more complex tonal control than was common in the poetry of the emotive imagination. Moreover, in the pursuit of naturalness, the younger poets generate dramas that can rely less on the image because the representativeness of the poem is less what the poem "discovers" in nature than how its "I" implicates a universal "I" facing general human dilemmas. Yet the emotional range of their dramas remains quite narrow, because the "I" remains largely a passive recipient of experience and the poet still pursues a state of resonant silence prepared by a single dramatic sequence. The ground for the resonance is different – the reflective psyche replaces analogical nature – but this difference does not change the model of how poems move us and present structures for emphasizing the places where value and lyric emotion may be located in experience. All the power resides in the way the scene elicits sensibility, whereas in Yeats or Stevens or Pound the crucial task is to build from the scene an act of mind that draws out speculative possibilities. These modern poets test cultural as well as personal resources for extending the materials into a more capacious meditative space with consequences for the way in which one takes responsibility for one's actions.

Plumly's "December, 1945" offers a striking example of the contemporary effort to transform the romanticism of deep-image poetics while retaining its basic structure for creating "poetic excitement":

> How the dry day goes, lapidary,
> wind against the grain –
>
> the gray grass, the kindling
> of the whole stark tree,
>
> the brick-and-straw burning of the sun,
> field, fallow, flame:
>
> my grandfather's foundry,
> long into dark, cast iron, cast clay,
>
> cast weed – stoke and bank, baked bread,
> loaves the size of furnace doors,
>
> lifted, left to cool all night, to make
> of each day the requisite stones of hunger.[21]

The poem's frame is pure Bly and Wright: We move from a setting that could be Minnesota wheatfields to a final surprising image that shifts inward to make all the external details become momentary elements in the spirit's life. The means of the motion here are quite different – not the prosaic flow of Bly's sensations but a version of Pound's monosyllabic crispness of sound forming intricate patterns and sustaining an elaborate syntax that testifies to the powers of art as composition of the mind. Yet all that self-consciousness is put in the service of a sense of emotional depths that is essentially a cautious, aestheticized version of Bly. Plumly makes psychology carry the burden of metaphysics – Jung easily Freudened – and employs a highly crafted tactile sense of the qualities of articulate silence to compose the space of mystery Bly projects by ponderous adjectival phrases (not unlike "stones of hunger"). The content preserves the same broad contrasts we might expect from Bly: nature's dry, bright flame set against the dark, cool textures associated with the dead foundry and with the war evoked by the title.

Plumly's strength and contemporaneity reside in his way of extending the symbolic range of the cold stone. Nature's otherness becomes a tactile equivalent of psychological states where we confront ambivalent memories of our dependence upon the authority figures who nourished and oppressed us. Plumly uses Bly's techniques of surprise to reinforce precisely this difference. As the dark elemental quality of the stone is suddenly transformed into a sense of hunger, the space of mystery shifts from some *Gott-natur* to the silence carried in the interstices of personal memory. Memory keeps mystery secular while providing a context in which tactile scenic particulars take on emotional significance. The tactile image enables us literally "to identify with the source of emotion" (as Plumly puts it)[22] in its evocative reticence. This reticence, in turn, balances memory between abstraction and physical incarnation. And the delicate complexity of memory's ways of retaining presence dignifies the self-conscious craft because it puts a heavy burden on the control of voice, so that its quiet attention to details becomes testimony to the speaker's capacity to maintain a balanced attitude. Cultural changes demand the reticence; Plumly makes of that necessity a subdued heroic way of surviving the residues of our historical losses.

V

Plumly insists that the rhetoric of the contemporary emblem poem is radically different from this tonal control because it attempts to absorb the action into "an emotion perfected rather than performed" and extends voice into a silence that leads to a sense of sources for that voice beyond the "I."[23] Yet his own poem clearly employs an emblematic movement in order to give memory both power and pathos. Conversely, a pure practitioner of the image, like Charles Wright, appears to rely on structural principles and states of feeling quite similar to Plumly's. I think we witness a condition in which the poets need to assert differences in order to convince themselves that what they share with their immediate predecessors does not cripple them. Yet although the poetry is virtually of another magnitude than that of Bly or the bardic Kinnell, it is hard not to begin to wonder whether it is worth perfecting ever-finer instruments to explore mines that are largely played out. The work begins to appear as a form of evading other possibilities and of reinforcing models of sensibility with little place in our intellectual or practical lives.

In order to test my claim we must be clear on what the emblem-making instruments can do. The sixth section of "Skins" is vintage Wright:

> Under the rock, in the sand and the gravel run;
> In muck bank and weed, at the heart of the river's edge:
> Instar; and again, instar,
> The wing cases visible. Then
> Emergence: leaf drift and detritus; skin split,
> The image forced from the self.
> And rests, wings drying, eyes compressed,
> Legs compressed,
> Beneath the dun and the watershine –
> Incipient spinner, set for the take-off . . .
> And does, in clear tear: imago rising out of herself
> For the last time, slate-winged and many-eyed.
> And joins, and drops to her destiny,
> Flesh to the surface, wings flush on the slate film.[24]

The master trope here is analogy, exactly as it is in Bly and Plumly. The structure, too, depends on a typical progression toward a surprising yet resonant image, here picking up and fulfilling the notes of imminent doom that begin with "forced," "constricted," and the latent pun on "tear." The poem then brings all the notes of fatality to resolution in the particular figure of the mayfly flush on the water become "slate film."

Yet Wright offers several distinctive variations on the established mode. Most emphatic is his way of reversing the direction of analogy. The poem carries all the metaphoric weight of resurrection motifs, but the thematic burden is not on transformation but on repetition, not on leaps to inward freedom but on allying ourselves with outward necessity. The mayfly speaks for us by entrapping us in its destiny, not by freeing us to make metaphors that sustain our dreams of transcendence. Freedom there is, even a romantic sense of unity with nature, but here under the insistence that what persons have to celebrate is less their grandeur than their smallness, less their freedom than their elegant participation in a universal cycle. Metaphor itself becomes a figure not for escaping nature but for reinforcing its ultimate power.

Because analogy and participation play such central roles, Wright makes control of the reader's position carry the burden that control of authorial tone carries in Plumly's poem. The poem begins by having the reader's eye come in from a distance, picking up only the wing cases that signify a drama not yet registered. "Then / emergence" creates a lovely shift from emptiness to life and from pure physical description to an abstraction that carries both a sense of natural movement and the beginnings of the rebirth analogies. Now Wright can balance our attention between release and constriction until the moment of flight, which allows eye and mind to expand once again.

But this expansion does not quite restore the freedom of the eye one had at the poem's beginning. For as we stand back to take in the entire flight and its meaning as destiny, we too are tied, "flesh to the surface," and unable to see the river for the slate film that signifies our own entrapment. "Entrapment," however, is too strong a word, too romantic and not sufficiently attuned to the way Wright, even more than Plumly, relies on the ornate artifice within the naturalistic setting. As the poem entraps our natural vision in an expansive scene marked by the endless repetition of destiny, its verse becomes a highly alliterative synthesis of Pound and Hopkins. The poem's flesh joins to another surface, that of pure art which can embrace destiny because such submission is the price it pays for the forms of freedom achieved by beauty and rich poetic reverberations. Artifice here serves functions directly opposed to those achieved by the romantic image: It insists on the mind's freedom, but the alliterative patterns suggest that the work of freedom is to bring us to embrace our condition as flesh. Words become flesh not to transform it so much as to give it weight, to caress what must die and in dying bring beauty flush to material surfaces. Like Plumly, Wright seeks fulfillment in what is perhaps the last metaphysic left to Western culture, a sense of silence becoming tactile substance. But poets must wonder if all this beauty might reduce us to registering delicate surfaces, so that it becomes an extremely precious substitute for our public destinies. Whether tone or image is made primary, contemporary naturalness seems ineluctably tied to an elegance of pastoral that must produce a constant theme of loss as its only sustenance within contemporary life. Wright's beautiful poetry of acceptance makes it difficult to accept his form of beauty.

3

The pressure to transform

I

If we are to extend our discussion to other poets, it is crucial that we understand both the appeal and the traps in the work of Plumly and Wright. Their modesty, for example, ought not to be underestimated. As relatively young writers they accept the need to master craft before taking on ambitious speculative projects. And they make craft an index of an intelligence and civility often sorely lacking in American poetry. More important, their refusing the imperious ego in favor of subtle and resonant feelings for the basic rhythms of life and growth enables them to preserve qualities of life that may be closer to extinction than many of the animals we are trying to save. Yet their emphasizing elaborate craft subsumed within quiet, relatively simple contemplative states may be at once too much and too little an antidote to mainstream contemporary life. The refinement concentrates power, but it also absorbs them almost entirely into the scene, leaving little room for reflecting on the evasions, duplicities, or even positive consequences inherent in their stance. Control of craft is ultimately not control of the self; it is only channeling the self into a theater that may not be appropriate for its needs or sufficiently critical of its deeds. If we concentrate on craft we are tempted to confine critical consciousness to areas of aesthetic judgment – a site where we will not find most of the poetic materials that make it worth making judgments about craft.[1]

Let us return for a moment to "December, 1945," this time trying to view it from the point of view of a poet wondering about the values of writing in this style. The virtues would be at least as evident as I made them in my comments. But it would be difficult not to see how the poem reduces the history it calls up to private family analogies, concentrates hunger in evocative tactile sensations at the margins of a reverberating silence, and ennobles the self simply by virtue of its complex nostalgia. The concentration on memory makes possible a rich play of tones in a quiet meditation, but it also enforces on the poet a passivity that appears to encourage a self-indulgent, emotional bath in that nostalgia.

By so narrowing the powers of mind, poets purchase an emotional theater incapable of staging any capacity to generalize with respect to the present or of engaging the concerns about power, motive, social contradictions, and delusive rhetorics that appear to be basic interests of our literate community. Too wise to hope for more than momentary glimpses of deeper realities, too skeptical and cautious of false poses to attempt connecting such moments to coherent argumentative contexts, and too despairing of possible changes in a democratic society that brought Ronald Reagan to power, poets like Plumly can articulate only a spirit aware of its own fleeting recognitions and domestic ambivalences. The speaking voice offers a delicate recording instrument, but only by becoming, on the dramatic level of the poem, a precious and passive witness dominated by the scene. Both content and style are deliberately timeless, as if lyricizing a psychological nostalgia in order to evade the more public loss our culture has experienced with respect to the sixties' hopes for change. And in becoming ahistorical, the poets let history return in the form of symptom. The slow, self-congratulatory isolation in their scenic development parallels a cultural order devoted to luxuriating in adventures of a private sensibility not responsible to discursive thought. In defense of spirit, these poets nonetheless vindicate what philistine critics have always claimed: When *Mourning and Melancholia* constitutes our bible, poetry runs the danger of becoming a psychological hot tub. At our most self-critical we must fear we are returning to a kind of poem Pound called in *Gaudier-Brezeska* "an asylum for the emotions," where artistic skill becomes a means for warding off intellectual scrutiny.

In this chapter I want to spell out one set of options available to the imaginary poet with this reaction to Plumly. There are many versions of this poet, but they remain discreetly silent, under the apparent idea that poets can utter general complaints but should not be harsh on those who are roughly peers in status. So we must indulge in critical speculations.

By observing some poets whose work clearly reveals a careful and complete engagement in trying to preserve many of the values of the dominant mode while resisting its dangers or excesses, I hope to make explicit the terms on which that mode may be transformed from within. The poets we shall consider here share the need to restrain bardic ambitions while anchoring poetry in naturalistic and psychological contexts where the emotions are precise and demystified because of the sense of personal sincerity sustaining them. Yet they also recognize the trap of so literary a sincerity, since it easily reduces the lyrical self to a narrow seriousness carried by the single-minded intensity of the authorial voice. Stafford's humility and Wright's balance are almost doggedly, inhumanly consistent in their capacity to register sensitivity. Similarly, the crafted naturalness appears at times almost frozen. So if the restrained, artful mode is necessary, poets must develop speaking selves with powers to play against literary sensitivity. This process will entail finding ways to exert a counterpressure on experience less centered upon the passive meditations of memory or reflections on natural scenes.

More important, a new seriousness will depend on being able to hold seriousness as a rhetoric allowing the poet strategies for looking around the lenses one uses to concentrate emotion. This play with "absorption" can take many forms, all I think based on making part of the poem a meditation on its own force as a creative act. Plumly and Wright are certainly aware of their rhetoric, but the rhetoric never becomes self-reflexive in any explicit way, or even in a way that changes the register of the lyric emotion. Thus Wright makes the physicality of composed sound a means for deepening his sense of a fulfilled submission to flesh. But rhetoric is treated entirely as the function by which art supplements scenic effects. The poet does not call much attention to the power such acts could wield as exemplars defining and testing general attitudes the self might assume. The scenic rhetoric does not establish a poetic mode that can fully acknowledge the complexity of the self trapped between lyric self-indulgence and a critical narcissism paralyzed by the play of light on the broken mirror of the reflective mind.

II

Charles Simic's "Forks" makes a good example of how recognizing such limits becomes the basis for new poetic strategies:

> This strange thing must have crept
> Right out of hell.
> It resembles a bird's foot
> Worn around the cannibal's neck.

As you hold it in your hand,
As you stab with it into a piece of meat,
It is possible to imagine the rest of the bird:
Its head which like your fist
Is large, bald, beakless and blind.[2]

The deliberately unpoetic subject sets the tonal key for the poem. Here the rhetorical virtues of invention and judgment are as much ends as means, because through them Simic's stance becomes part of the poetic metaphor. The poem makes it appear as if the more ridiculous or unpoetic the subject is, the greater will be the freedom from conventional lyric stances and the possibility of exploring modes of playfully holding ideas so that poetry can deal with large themes without bardic voices or strident and portentous insistence on its symbols and metaphors.

If a central characteristic of recent intellectual life is the need to operate with loosely held, often internally contradictory intellectual structures, each more or less adequate to specific situations, the imagination must learn to articulate its own privisional status, without even the help of a supreme fiction. Seriousness becomes inextricable from casual thinking and fortuitous angles of vision. Sketches or notebooks were a formal gesture toward this kind of awareness in the sixties, but the poems often belied the implications of their frameworks. In Simic, on the other hand, the manipulation of this casualness establishes formal energies with the power to balance the familiar and the unfamiliar, the casual and the lyrical. Thus, in the sequence of which "Forks" is a part, Simic so overdetermines common objects that all specific dramatic urgency is suppressed, emphasizing instead mind's capacity to play within its constrained roles. Flush to the surface, it is not fixed in its fate. The poet's tone need not be tied to a single event but can in itself dramatize the mind dancing between invention and judgment.

The most pronounced feature of "Forks" is its flattening the surreal into a self-consciously manipulated rhetorical mode, a strategy also prevalent in contemporary painting. Automatic writing gives way to a poetry as carefully controlled as Wright's, but with the "poetic excitement" all in the perspective. Distance replaces Wright's and Plumly's identification with their subjects, but distance leads back a sense of destiny and materiality like Wright's, now, though, adapted to a generalized image of human actions. The fork as a cultural object returns us ironically to a recognition of how much of our being as natural creatures our civilized structures can express. The pure wit of the visual comparison to the cannibal's necklace creates a pressure that modulates into a more serious suggestion that our unconscious expressions of appetite render us, if only in this respect, as simple, as blind, and as terrifying as a mindless bird.

But the distance and playfulness deny the easy negative associations of this equation and preserve at once pity for and some freedom from the state rendered. Dramatic image and authorial act play off one another as man's roles of victim and eater do in the poem's analogies.

Moreover, by accepting a distanced perspective and the accompanying recognition of poetic space as metaphoric discourse, Simic can risk returning to obvious poetic devices inappropriate for poets seeking pure encounters with experience. The final alliterations, for example, hark back in a lighter, more self-conscious way to Tennyson's "On the bald street breaks the blank day," with Simic's reference to blindness nicely linked to the general sense of animal nature by the rigorous necessity of the alliterative chain. But the necessity is so clearly a constructed one that in recognizing the blind limits of the body the poem affirms the freedom of mind. By ignoring demands for immediate ethical relevance and intense dramatic experience, Simic defines a possible form of psychic survival, precisely in accepting the distance between mind and empirical behavior and between poem and a world it can nonetheless never escape.

It is not difficult to see what Simic shares with Plumly. Both equate rhetoric with a sense of the qualities of authorial self in relation to an imagined setting, and both seek an ultimately imagistic form of closure and emotional impact not explicitly connected to the major concerns of their cultural heritage. The difference lies primarily in Simic's separating the rhetoric from the scenic level, so that it does not reinforce a dramatized person but elaborates the implications of an authorial stance exploring new modes of feeling. If Plumly's rhetoric is so tied to scenic effects that it deprives poetry of powers of self-consciousness and attitude construction, then Simic exemplifies strategies for opening a more self-reflexive space, playing in and against the scene.

We shall soon encounter far more radical uses of this space than Simic's, but for this chapter I want to concentrate on three styles for extending the play and place of poetic rhetoric that all grow out of the emotive imagination and often coexist with forms of writing that closely parallel Plumly's and Wright's. Thus I can speak with some historical accuracy of efforts at transformation within common assumptions as they begin to fray at the edges. The three transformational strategies can coexist, even within the same poem, but I will isolate them for emphasis and choose as examples poets whose best work usually relies on the specific style.[3] I imagine the three strategies on a continuum defined by the nature of the self-conscious qualities of rhetoric the poem foregrounds.

At one pole we find an essentially impersonal but still naturalistic treatment of scenes that adapts the dominant mode's imagistic strategies to more general, reflective purposes. These poems are not illusionistic – even the speaking voice is clearly a self-conscious poet's working with language as a medium of communication. Thus there is no process of sudden discovery, no moment of heightened sensitivity in a state that transcends language. Rather, the poem celebrates its capacity to use the rhetorician's virtues of invention, judgment, and tact as instruments for locating within the familiar the outlines of some general idea or sense of the human condition. Perception itself, then, is not an end but the means to constructing attitudes and ideas the poet can treat as consistent with other forms of wisdom.

My second style adapts similar strategies to a more personalized stance. Indeed, here the dominant feature of the poetry is the powers of an implicit author as they can be organized and sustained by a poetic rhetoric in relation to a typical situation. The basic qualities of this style are most pronounced when we contrast it to modernist uses of persona. These contemporary poets try to collapse the distance between the agent projected and the voice projecting. Even if the poem involves a distinct persona separate from the poet, the poems treat the persona as a way of extending the authorial consciousness. All personal stances become means for turning self-consciousness about rhetoric into permission for allowing parts of the self to come to expression and to be tested imaginatively for the powers of survival or celebration they provide. In constructing persons in poetry, the writer in this style marks out a space of freedom from the demands for consistency and habitual self-gratifications that characterize the empirical self – while still relying on a form of sincerity, because the pressure of empirical need remains foregrounded. Poetry becomes a drama of possible identifications and the motives informing them.

My third example of transformations places the freedom of invention and person in a more radically experimental context. It makes self-consciousness about rhetoric into a speculative instrument by elaborating extended conceits while not providing links that will produce any obvious coherence. Here invention begins to chase its own tail as the poem requires us to pursue forms of relatedness that are obscured by the ideals of coherence typically found in scenic lyrics or in metaphoric chains strongly controlled by single thematic orientations. The new poetry is all in the drama of increasing the level of fancy while inviting us to speculate on a mysterious source that might organize these fractured parts of the world.

In all three styles, the most important factor is a renewed sense that language need not seek its fulfillment and full resonance by erasing itself into a tactile silence. Despite the gravitational pull of an evanescent and shimmering sublime where only the lyric imagination can live, the poets will, can, and perhaps must show the power and discipline to celebrate the modes of attention by which language carries us beyond perception, beyond even the evocative image.

III

That such a desire for reveling in the power of language need be neither set against nor reduced to the evocativeness of the image is clear in the ways Stephen Dunn uses the elaborate conceit. Poems like "Day and Night Handball" in fact preserve the evocative from the precious by dramatizing poetry's power to recover the familiar:

> I think of corner shots, the ball
> hitting and dying like a butterfly
> on windshield, shots so fine
> and perverse they begin to live
>
> alongside weekends of sex
> in your memory . . .
> . . . .
> I think of a hand slicing the face
> of a ball, so much english
> that it comes back drunk
>
> to your opponent who doesn't have
> enough hands to hit it,
> who hits it anyway, who makes you think
> of "God!" and "Goddamn!", the pleasure
>
> of falling to your knees
> for what is superb, better than you.
> But it's position I think of most,
> the easy slam and victory
>
> because you have a sense of yourself
> and the court, the sense that old men
> gone in the knees have,
> one step in place of five,
>
> finesse in place of power,
> and all the time
> the four walls around you
> creating the hardship, the infinite variety.[4]

This has all the dramatic naturalness of the scenic mode, but little of its serious urgency and no tactile closing image. Dunn also shares with the poetry of the sixties a sense of radical immanence. Yet the ground of immanence here is not nature but culture, and the realism in no way seeks to disclose an act climaxing in heightened perception. For Dunn the enabling act is "I think," an act that fulfills itself not in silence but in the precision of articulate generalizations, of what was ne'er so well expressed. Thus all the description is suspended as an extended metaphor. Wright's sensuality remains – the metaphor depends on making one feel pure absorption in the act – but it too takes purely civilized form as an enhancement of a mind willing to achieve seriousness by playing self-consciously with the stuff of sense and sensation. The poem itself is the ultimate game, the "I think" under conditions that test all the mind's powers. Thus the constant enjambment plays a vital role, maintaining the flow of the game while keeping a rhythmic control that will not allow the poem to be carried away by its metaphor-making powers. This control, echoed in the discipline of addressing purely public domestic contexts, indicates how the lyric energy need not derive from "experience in capital letters." A poetics of discovery gives way to a poetics based largely on social measures of discourse, that is, on the wit and invention that produce conceits and on the acts of judgment that call attention to the cognitive values of the metaphors and of the tones manipulating them.

For Dunn the poet is a person speaking to other people, and his performance depends on exhibiting traditional qualities of public speech – pith, wit, freshness, and wisdom. The poem discusses important issues, but it addresses them by appealing to an ordinary standard of sensibility rather than by setting up the poet as prophet or exemplary figure whose rhythms of perception we must imitate, however provisionally. Here, having judgment involves trusting in the reader's ability to appreciate civilized finesse. In this social context, tone and judgment become the exemplary states of mind that, in a romantic tradition, take the form of stances of attention and involvement in dramatic encounters with raw experience. Compare, for example, Dunn's images of the poet and of the relationship among desire, ironic limits, and pleasure in those limits as source of imaginative pressure with two famous images of poetry dominant in the sixties: Levertov's image of the poem as the effort to make every step an arrival and Lowell's comparison of the poet with a skier traversing a dangerous slope. To Dunn, Levertov relies upon an indefensible monistic vision and undervalues the discipline and sense of limited, artificial structures that in fact awaken the mind to the vital sense of presence. Lowell's remark, on the other hand, becomes an ironic reminder of how even at his best Lowell had a melodramatic sensibility prone to treat basic pleasures in pompously heroic or tragic terms.

The poetics Dunn exemplifies shifts the sources of cognitive pressure on a poem from the desire to capture large, resonant truth in intense experience to a sense of poetic emotion as inherently diffuse, quiet, and reflective. Poetic emotion depends on an interplay between poem and world, balancing the poet's capacity for invention against the capacity for dramatizing acts of judgment and controlling the inventions. But as powerful as Dunn's work is, his form of control, his absolute mastery perhaps, exacts a substantial price. No poem is without a sense of personality, but Dunn's poems come close because genius dominates genesis, and wisdom passion, so that the universality is abstract enough not to need any pressure of dramatic context on the authorial voice. Dunn frees invention and judgment, but the total equivalence between the poem's theme and the self-reflexive stance of the poet makes the four walls appear too confined a poetic stage. Personality is all too well disciplined, without sufficient acknowledgment of the forces impinging on it.

IV

Louise Gluck's "First Goodbye" makes a strong contrast. It exemplifies a second strategy for transformations, open to several significant variants. Dunn's distance and impersonal conceits cannot in her eyes produce sufficiently intense lyric emotions. One cannot escape the dramatic personal voice if one wants powerful poetry. But one can make the plight and power of that voice something that extends far beyond the scenic. For the drama Gluck relies on a specific lyric persona, but she then makes the idea of a persona a central factor in the poem. The relationship between poet and persona embodies the tension between rational and imaginary versions of the self that complicates our motives. The creative act of the poet is not primarily a generalized model of interpretive intelligence. Rather, what must be generalized is the power of will and fantasy that writing enables:

> You can join the others now,
> body that wouldn't let my body rest,
> go back to the world, to avenues, the ordered
> depths of the parks, like great terminals
> that do not darken: a stranger's waiting for you
> in a hundred rooms. Go back to them,
> to increment and limitation: near the centered rose,
> you watch her peel an orange
> so the dyed rind falls in petals on her plate. This
> is mastery, whose active
> mode is dissection: the enforced light
> shines on the blade. Sooner or later
> you'll begin to dream of me. I don't envy you
> those dreams. I can imagine how my face looks,
> burning like that, afflicted with desire – lowered
> face of your invention – how the mouth betrays

the isolated greed of the lover
as it magnifies and then destroys:
I don't envy you that visitation.
And the women lying there – who wouldn't pity them,
the way they turn to you, the way
they struggle to be visible. They make
a place for you in bed, a white excavation.
Then the sacrament, your bodies pieced together,
churning, churning, till the heat leaves them entirely –
Sooner or later you will call my name –
cry of loss, mistaken
cry of recognition – meaning
someone who exists in memory: no voice
carries to that kingdom.[5]

Surprise here is not essentially a means to lyric effects. Surprise is virtually a taunt, signifying the speaker's power to exorcise her pain by imposing on her lover a set of images she controls and a desire for symbolic meanings she can withhold. An opening "go from me" to other women quickly changes into an increasingly vicious manipulation of the scene so that he must see in his desires essentially figures of death or absence and must feel the other side of sexual mastery. Thus it is precisely when she controls by dissection what he must see that she can tauntingly make the theme of mastery explicit. Mastery becomes freedom over metaphor, so that by the poem's conclusion poet's metaphors and demon lover's powers become inextricable, and the sacrament's physical sexuality appears as only an outward sign of some unfathomable epistemological drama. The space she creates intensifies what the voice displays – a frightening coldness after sexual ecstasy. This is the sphere where names matter and where the capacity to stage one's passion retrospectively as coldness becomes mastery. He must call her name because she yields him no power to name what he seduces. So she forces him to recognize "that kingdom," where the imaginary displaces the satisfactions of desire, and the only sexual cries are voices that cannot master their own absolute loss.

V

Carl Dennis is usually concerned with a very different kind of power. Distance for him is a means not to dominate but to deflect. Instead of using self-consciousness about artifice to intensify a single drama, Dennis develops a range of passions available for contemplating the self after the event. He often stages himself as resembling the male lover in

"First Goodbye," but always as a test of where he can stand toward himself to find a way of picking up the pieces without any melodramatic laments. Here, as in some of Dunn's poems or David Wagoner's, the extension of the scenic mode constructed by the allegorizing force of the conceit becomes itself a vehicle for self-reflexively establishing personal attitudes by which fancy successfully cheats and thus survives oppressive realities. Conceit in Dennis usually takes the form of the slyly ironic Jewish fable. The allusion to dramatic situations preserves enough concreteness to allow the experiences alluded to their affective bite, while the distance between the maker and his scene opens a large and varied field for tonal effects and contrasting angles of vision. Such effects place lyric emotion within the context of a complex interpretive personality. Notice what becomes of Young's cult of humility (and of Gluck's cold rage) in a poem like "Clara Hopes for a Lie":

> At the corner, when we met by accident,
> You were true to your word and turned away,
> Crossing the street in the rain,
> Practicing the miser's virtue, honesty,
> The cheapest substitute for a gift.
>
> There are other moods to swear by . . .
>
> Why can't you be like my cold tight-fisted minister
> Who stands in the pulpit Sundays
> Exhorting love? Would the world be improved
> If the sermon dwindled to confession
> And the minister settled for honesty,
> True to himself, a man he's never admired?
>
> Why can't you ponder the country
> You've never laid eyes on
> As you walk home in the rain,
> Undistracted by the poor, bare fields
> We will always have with us?[6]

The poetry is all in the blend of pathos and distance controlled by the authorial voice balancing the roles of playful philosopher and thinly disguised sufferer of Clara's plight. We are not asked to identify with some carefully rendered moment, but to reflect upon the general human needs we can sneak up on from the poet's angle on Clara's angle. At the same time, the need itself appears in all its inescapable commonness – Yeats's mask theory adapted for ordinary life.

This poem, however, does not carry through the intelligence established by the constructed situation. The allusive wit of the last stanza does not prevent it from relying on standard poetic emotions of desolation. Dennis, I think, is not confident enough of the lyric power of his elusive sensibility, so he reaches for the surprising, scenic, tactile image as a basis for emotional resonance. Ironically, the conventional quality of the image virtually absorbs and cancels the semantic emphasis on the poignant necessity of such fictions.

Compare this poem to the conclusion of "The Veteran," where Dennis uses conventional lyricism for subtle tonal and reflective purposes:

> Once it was hard to believe
> That the birds I watched for hours,
> Darting and perching, had no opinion
> About me, and would have none.
> Now I'm tranquil even if my city,
> Known far longer, doesn't look my way.
>
> If my strengths and weaknesses aren't needed here,
> I can imagine a city where they are.
>
> I was knocking at my own door yesterday;
> I was looking in the window, wondering
> Who could live in this small room,
> So plain and empty. Today I stand inside
> And look out, mindful of the trees,
> The birds, the planet.
>
> If I can't tell what will happen
> It's because I'm free. The birds
> Will sing their song for ever.
> They'll always be birds. They can't stop.
> I could forget myself in a minute
> Even now if I stopped dreaming.[7]

Dramatically, the last line is all surprise and shift inward. We expect some more "substantial" term than "dreaming" for the self-consciousness contrasted to the bird's unconscious song. Dennis, however, makes the surprise a means of opening self-reflexive levels for the poem. The last image reminds us that our need for self-regard often makes us construct imaginary selves and audiences. Fantasy blends with the simplicity of statement to earn Dennis the right to handle us, and himself, gently. There is no way to stand outside and judge without feeling the invitation to "stand inside and look out." This, Dennis might say, is the principle of poetic justice and the nature of artistic making. To provide a context for this looking at once within and without is why the birds come.

The final contrast could be pure Sartre in its absolute opposition between the blind self-sufficiency of nature and the anxiety of the freedom inherent in the first-person perspective. But pure Sartre is too self-theatricalizing, or not subtle enough in its philosophical arrogance. Freedom in Dennis' poem is poised between two conditions. There is, first, a wish for a total denial of our need for affirmation, in order to allow a self-forgetfulness without even the temptation of song. Balancing this is the complex evocativeness of the final line. We are inescapable dualists – for Lacanian, not Cartesian, reasons. For the idea of necessity without song is an imaginative counterfactual confirming our inevitable involvement in the unreal. We dream, and we dream of not dreaming; therefore we are condemned to subjectively constructing versions of the world where the self might matter and the dream have substance. The very force that keeps us from self-forgetfulness – this dreaming – is our song. Silence is only its pale substitute, a rhetorical fiction to keep us attempting lyric expression.

VI

Dennis and Gluck emphasize attitudes, not scenes; the imaginary becomes a means of extending personality. Robert Hass extends that means into the more difficult task of constructing a full sense of an authorial person. Plumly has written superbly on him because Hass is our best example of rhetoric employed as sincerity. But it will not do to treat rhetoric in his work as primarily the means for creating complex apprehensions. Hass is at least as interested in the powers that work through the process of apprehending as he is in the specific understanding of an experience he achieves. This is why his best poems are so fluid. Poetic style is inseparable from personal style, and the complexity of person depends on not allowing any single attitude to congeal into lyric self-congratulation. The person takes form in and as the voice capable of integrating a variety of lyric moments. An easy way to say this is to assert that Hass makes books, not poems, because he wants his range of creative acts to make poetry coextensive with ordinary life. But Hass's real distinction lies in making individual lyrics carry a sense of a full personality that transcends its moments of heightened sensitivity. This ambition carries substantial risks. The poet at times seems to cultivate sanity as if it were a hothouse plant, grown in books and domestic settings but preserved from any full encounter with rage or ecstasy. When passion is dared, one often feels as if the danger existed in order to prove Hass can keep his composed maturity intact, within immaculately articulate aural and syntactic arrangements. Yet at his best he approximates the capacious flexibility of Wordsworthian domesticity. Vision can expand into wisdom, and his somewhat stagy "intelligence of hunger" becomes a genuine hunger of intelligence to absorb scenic materials within a sense of a balanced human voice capable of speaking to other persons.

The basis for Hass's transformations and the sense of person they create is a technique borrowed for the lyric from larger units of poetic composition. In compressed form, the poet foregrounds not a single dramatic process but an emblematic rhythm for relating and integrating various aspects of the self. The poet's mind moves from the hunger of loss, to the erotic moments memory of loss makes possible, to larger contexts and attitudes that enable him to blend lyric ecstasy with discursive generalizations and a rigorous sense of the limits of imagination. As the best single example of his sensibility at work, I have chosen "Meditation at Lagunitas":

> All the new thinking is about loss.
> In this it resembles all the old thinking.
> The idea, for example, that each particular erases
> the luminous clarity of a general idea. That the clown-
> faced woodpecker probing the dead sculpted trunk
> of that black birch is, by his presence,
> some tragic falling off from a first world
> of undivided light. Or the other notion that,
> because there is in this world no one thing
> to which the bramble of blackberry corresponds,
> a word is elegy to what it signifies.
> We talked about it late last night and in the voice
> of my friend, there was a thin wire of grief, a tone
> almost querulous. After a while I understood that,
> talking this way, everything dissolves: justice,
> pine, hair, woman, you and I. There was a woman
> I made love to and I remembered how, holding
> her small shoulders in my hands sometimes,
> I felt a violent wonder at her presence
> like a thirst for salt, for my childhood river
> with its island willows, silly music from the pleasure boat,
> muddy places where we caught the little orange-silver fish
> called pumpkinseed. It hardly had to do with her.
> Longing, we say, because desire is full
> of endless distances. I must have been the same to her.
> But I remember so much, the way her hands dismantled bread,
> the thing her father said that hurt her, what
> she dreamed. There are moments when the body is as
>   numinous
> as words, days that are the good flesh continuing.

> Such tenderness, those afternoons and evenings,
> saying blackberry, blackberry, blackberry.[8]

The poem contains one basic lyric scene, the memory of the woman. But Hass is careful to control his own penchant for delicacy by placing this memory (and memories it releases of other scenes) within a larger dialectic of loss and recognition, or distance and presence, on both philosophical and dramatic levels. Movement then works structurally and thematically to balance various aspects of loss and to place the reflections within the conversational context of shared needs. This movement pulls against the naming power of language, toward the evocative tactile silences of poets like Plumly and Wright. But it simultaneously makes the referential properties of language crucial to one's sense of personal powers to connect memories to the present. At one pole the contrast between "everything dissolves" and "remembered how, holding / her small shoulders" makes memory virtually a physical force and enables the image of her to extend into the childhood river, archetype for all erotic presence. But to rest within such sensations would be to enter a pure lyricism whose converse side is the anxieties of loss. By placing memory within reflective and social contexts, and by delaying over memories so that their relations become a force for resolving the uneasiness of the present, Hass also dramatizes powers of understanding and compassion fostered on loss. He places his final celebration of presence so fully within a complex syntax of personal apprehensions that the tactile evocations of the repeated "blackberries" are probably their least important properties. What stands out is the capacity for self-reflective appreciation of the speech act in its ramifying contexts. In the encounter with loss and the mind's power to dwell on what the encounter releases, presence becomes not a matter of touch but a profound sense of how consciousness feeds on limits and makes of them the consolations of a flexible human speech, in our time by virtue of its freedom to spread focused attention over time.

Hass's volume *Praise* extends this sense of person and interprets it in a way directly relevant to my concerns about the relation between stylistic and cultural transformations. The volume begins with an epigraph that recalls Stevens's firecat in Oklahoma:

> We asked the captain what course
> of action he proposed to take toward
> a beast so large, terrifying, and
> unpredictable. He hesitated to
> answer, and then said judiciously:
> "I think I shall praise it."[9]

Virtually every element reverses a feature of the dominant mode of the sixties, yet the alternative need not rely on perceptual and tactile images.

Hass's setting is social, not the record of an isolated individual, and the source of wisdom is a cultural figure, to be trusted because of experience at a regular enterprise. The demonic force is not named; an allegorical figure will do because Hass wants to address the intellect and not tie the pressure on imagination to any specific description that may dissolve into mere ideology. Then all the enjambment stages a crucial difference in attitude: The poem seeks not a moment of heightened sensitivity but the signs and effects of careful, hesitant reflection. Reflection produces a lively link between qualification and a sense of quality. The poem is about necessity (like Wright's), about our having to face the point where history and nature leave us. Yet within necessity, we can hesitate (the colloquial use of "I think"), creating a space where the powers of thinking become (as in Dunn) inseparable from a quiet, refined power to hold off existential anxiety and accommodate ourselves to what makes demands on us.

The remainder of the volume examines the constraints or limits on the imagination we must face if we are to give a responsible praise. Our recognition of limits becomes our permission to continue lyric song. The final poem is addressed to Hass's daughter, but since in it we all approach the condition of children it could almost serve as a prolegomena to any future poetry:

> That is what I have
> to give you, child, stories,
> songs, loquat seeds,
>
> curiously shaped; they
> are the frailest stay against
> our fears. Death
>
> in the sweetness, in the bitter
> and the sour, death
> in the salt, your tears,
>
> this summer ripe and overripe
> It is a taste in the mouth,
> child. We are the song
>
> death takes its own time
> singing. It calls us
> as I call you child
>
> to calm myself. It is every
> thing touched casually,
> lovers, the images
>
> of saviors, books, the coin

I carried in my pocket
till it shone, it is

all things lustered
by the steady thoughtlessness
of human use.[10]

On the one hand Dennis's song is put in the ontological shadow of death. We hear echoes of Bly's and Rilke's meditations on a silence that holds us as we ripen toward it. But while death sings us, our song is given other directions: The poet's counterpressure depends on his finding a form of believable direct address to save him from the isolated natural scene. And the continuing vitality of lyric poetry depends on shifting its ground from nature to culture. Then we need no myths of the prophetic bard, no preciosity, and no absorption in solipsistic memory. We need only the attention to those miracles that sustain us even though we have never learned properly how to praise them. Our need to praise is the motive for continually transforming established lyric modes.

VII

Simic, Dunn, Gluck, and Hass each seek a form of mastery. As they deflect the scenic mode, they also create models of personality (or impersonality) capable of composing scenes for rhetorical purposes or using rhetoric to dramatize personal powers. They want the dramatic force of character in confessional poetry without the egocentric theatrics. And they often achieve a muted version of it. But the achievement can easily appear a serious limitation on their work. For when poetry requires psychological versions of Dunn's handball court, the process of exclusion tempts other writers to explore the other side of the walls, what perhaps can never enter any game with rules or even be subsumed under the self-conscious presentation of personality.

The attempt to link personas with the poetic voice is easy to see as a simple domestication of the romantic imagination. That recognition, in turn, produces a strong counterpressure to resume within nonbardic stances the romantic fascination with processes of mental life that cannot be represented at all. There must be strong passions that drive us to highly controlled conceits. This line of questioning will eventually require a complete poetics based on sharp oppositions between a poetics of completed thoughts and one devoted to the uncertainties and duplicities of thinking. But among poets shaped largely by the dominant modes of the early and late seventies, the efforts to engage this condition are more rhetorical than epistemological. They concentrate on articulating poetic attitudes where radical invention is continually aware of its own provisional status. The poet's task is to capture what underlies and belies the artfulness of the conceit by taking its rhetoric one step further: The fancy of the conceit must so stress invention that it calls into question any conventional logic for establishing coherence among mind-forged materials. With strategies like catalogues that suggest a rationale but yield only possibilities of coherence, themselves at once overdetermined and underdetermined, or implicit narratives and arguments that do not readily suggest a governing intentional motive, these poems make lyricism of all that resists lyric conventions. There, in our suspicious age and in our frustration with Dunn's four walls or Hass's mastery over his beast, we may have to locate the actual site of our most compelling emotions. Our lyric lives may depend on forces that continually resist the very desires for discursive order that they produce. Plot, theme, and character need not be the basic organizational elements of a work; rather, they appear as symptomatic materials manipulated by forces we recognize only as traces of some undefinable source.

From this perspective, the desires we live by are essentially illogical, atemporal, and so resistant to cultural forms that they can only be misrepresented by any discourse seeking to describe or make lucid their concealed features. If truth must be seen as Heidegger's *alethea,* the disclosure of what had been concealed, there can be no truth about the psyche. Try to speak of personal desires, and you find a large component of the impersonal and the theatrical; try to judge behavior, and you find that judgment itself depends on motives and principles themselves demanding judgment; try to represent desire, and you find the terms themselves presenting desires and altering their object. Under these conditions, it seems better to let one's desires for significance and truth remain implicit: Let invention play among the mind's resources, and let the self disperse among its many selves in the hope that nonempirical, relational patterns may reveal new and deeper pressures that affect our actual stances toward reality. As John Ashbery puts it, "Underneath the talk lies / The moving and not wanting to be moved, the loose / Meaning, untidy and simple like a threshing floor."[11] In other words, the romantic distinction between ordinary logic and poetic logic may be inescapable for the kinds of cognitive pressure poems can put on experience. But we must be careful not to interpret this distinction as a simple contrast between external and internal or symbolic modes of relationship. Ordinary language may be too committed to depth and coherence rather than too committed to superficial and contingent connections. Ordinary language may not be attentive enough to the loose and apparently arbitrary folds in the surface of events where fantasy and psychic demand continually merge and diverge from one another, just as the self blends with and collapses into a congeries of selves.

Albert Goldbarth's "Song in One Serving" is a good example of poetry attempting to adapt the scenic lyric to these self-reflexive concerns.
Goldbarth combines a powerful sense of lyric control with a prolific fancy
that continually plays against the organizing conceit. Its central poetic act
is negotiating the hazards in the rhetoric that generates lyric feeling:

> This is the song in which a raccoon turns over
> at the side of the page, a tire tread indelibly
> catching rain on his belly, and I laugh. In this piece
> ankle-bones mean to snap down a chain-gang's length
> like a string of firecrackers, and some are meant to let
> a chill wind in at their breakage, and some designed to
>   confound
> all epoxies. Here, a Pakistani student receives an F
> in Comp 101, though the sweat on his forehead phosphors,
> though the sweat on his forehead manifests itself
> with the corporeality of phlegm, and he must be deported;
> see him? driving wet-eyed through the downpour,
> listen closely to the sound of a small brown paper bag
> of bones beneath the wheels: the raccoon. In this tune
> nothing's dry, and even the rigid MP rubbered up
> against the damp is thinking more of his frilly wife found
> in the sergeant's arms than of guarding the base, you can tell
> by one yellow drop of adrenalin too much as it trickles
> out the eye and makes a cross with his knife-edge line
> of mouth, or by my guffaws. Agnes, what you saved
> from me at the party after our high school prom is pronged
> this morning by a surgeon's spear; too bad. Go home,
> need desperately to have your husband say he loves you
> anyway, and find a note: he's just found out
> about the sergeant, he's leaving you. And Sarge?
> is gone to war; this afternoon, inside a song like this,
> he ships out for Karachi, Pakistan having bombed
> two-thirds of our Eastern coast; the general wipes
> thick sweat from his forehead and thinks, before his camel
> explodes, how demolition reverses his failing grade
> more surely than just repeating the course. Bridges
> fall, mutts pee on wooden legs, bullet-holes appear
> in the nipples of half the nation's convents; great!
> This is a poem in which I exorcise all my superfluous
> hate. Let it dish up gall in another plate.[12]

The opening lines initiate a process of self-reference in search of self
and of a logic that will make the lyric energies all cohere as one serving

whose unity establishes resonance for the excessively flat narrating voice. This process leads us to take the central conceit as posing a basic, implicit question: How can the entire work be a "song," given the ambiguity of its deictic reference to "here" and the absence of any clear mimetic object enabling us to attribute motives to the content of the writing? Goldbarth in effect mocks the illusion of dramatic presence in poems of "Experience" like Wright's by insisting that the relevant present is not a situation outside the poem but the pressures within the poem to make connections not displaced by the imaginative release of writing. The interpretive container in dramatic texts here becomes the contained, the object, whose terms of containment remain implicit. Yet simple metapoetic ironies are all too common. Goldbarth must make the metapoetic stance interesting, and he does so by overdetermining fantasy details so that they pull against the narrow self-sufficiency of the space and time of writing. We are asked to see that the fantasies themselves are at once revelations and concealings of some compulsive source of desire that the willed self-conscious distancing of the poem cannot master.

The opening details, for example, play the song against a set of violent desires or memories that render the laugh somewhat hollow and call attention to the ineffectiveness of gestures of "meaning." Then the references to the Pakistani student and his F set a purely trivial cartoon fancy against the tensions connecting the F to the implicit violence and failure of the opening. Sweat, wet eyes, and especially the "corporeality of phlegm" pick up the rain and introduce a series of references to liquids that come to function as insistent reminders that even fantasy figures derive from and lead back to real constraints in the physical order. Thus deporting the Pakistani becomes something more than a flip mockery of failed American dreams. Metapoetically, the Pakistani must be deported from the text because his failure evokes a corporeality and an anxiety denying the possible self-sufficiency of aesthetic or fantasy space.

Now pattern begins to emerge on many levels. The images dealing with fluidity are perhaps the richest because they establish relations among the frustrated and unstatable desires. Yet the very appeal to pattern serves less to fix meaning than to mark the radical difference from traditional poetics, because the poem cannot reach the forms of closure accessible to Dunn's equally abstract will. Pattern seems obsession in an otherwise random or contingent associative surface; pattern works against authorial freedom to insist that Fancy can in fact cheat very well, deceiving elf that she is. Nothing remains dry in poem or fantasy space because inescapable yet unrepresentable corporeal pressures push against sheer fabrication. Thus the Pakistani modulates into the rigid MP, mock figure of Stevens's mock rational figures. His rigidity, however, only entraps him in fantasies that are trivial, make him ridiculous, and yet form the center of his erotic life. Poem surface and pop fantasy become comments on one another as the representation of desire takes a cheap theatrical form. And now, by repeating the poet's laugh, the poem suggests that it too has an obsessive quality: What is manifest is only a hollow echo of deeper tensions. To acknowledge triviality self-consciously is not to distance oneself from it successfully. Definitive guffaws will not allow us to relinquish our parts in the melodramatic movies we play in our heads. In fact, self-irony itself may already have become another of those roles, whose power depends precisely on the gulf between the form of representation and the unspeakable needs creating it.

The final images of the sergeant's and the general's war effort make explicit the relationship between fantasy and violence and again implicate the poet in his thematic dilemma. "A song like this" now refers both to the poem as artifact and to the kinds of images that justify war in our minds. Violence seems the only possible escape from the failure to reconcile desire and knowledge. Thus the poem turns to its most ironic interplay between linguistic surface and represented desires. Exaggerated rhymes call attention to the ambiguity of "great": The poet's pleasure in his linguistic achievement and distanced irony modulates into a partial involvement in fantasies of destruction. This involvement then motivates a shift to a more formal public rhetoric, though one still undercut by complex self-referencing. Taken as explicit statement, the poem's final lines turn on a complex irony. In exorcising all of this superfluous hate, the poet exorcises only his superfluous hate, leaving unstated and inescapable some central core of frustration and anger. "This poem" will obviously require other supplements as the poet seeks a form of expression that may transcend the superfluous. The poem's attempt to make present a state of mind is inadequate and frustrating.

Thus we must be skeptical toward the poem's final exercise in the romantic subjunctive that asserts a momentary resolution of trouble by readjusting the mind to the world so that the poet may be capable of new forms of perception in the future. Goldbarth invites this skepticism by returning, through the "gall," to the pressure of corporeality carried in the fluidity images. The speaker wants to see the poem as transferring his own anxieties to the reader, but "another plate" is deliciously vague. The other plate may be precisely the level of desire and hatred not representable directly on the surface but continually demanding an expression they will never achieve. The poem condemns the speaker to further poems and more bitter gall, just as the conclusion recalls the epigraph's ironic doubling of the frustrations of understanding: *"Therefore I have cursed what I did not understand, / Therefore I despise myself."* The one thing Goldbarth need not despise himself for is his subtle articulation of the grounds for romantic self-pity in a way that escapes its standard postures. There is in Goldbarth no illusion that poetry can save us from ourselves or our culture, but his inventing fresh ways to put pressure on language in order to capture and to play with our frustrations makes it possible to believe, for a little while at least, that there is in the imagination a power for preserving a sense of the freedom and dignity of the mind that may not be an illusion.

VIII

The poetry we have been considering occupies an imaginative space that I think is characteristic of cultures having outgrown or failed to live up to the promises of a more speculative and experimental time. The space is a realm of middles,[13] where agents speak in the middle register of rhetoric in order to secure values that can be won by turning away from questions of beginnings and endings. Theirs is a poetry that seeks the reasonableness of prose, supplemented by careful craft and delicate emotions that appear to elicit the quiet reflective states. The poets we have been considering fulfill their intentions, so there should be little question about each producing substantial achievements. But if we cannot fault the achievement, we may find the intentions problematic. Taken together, these poems seem somewhat less than a sum of the parts – probably because the sum becomes too easy to calculate. Their lyric emotions are usually motivated by loss or fear of loss, and the structure of relations in the poems mirrors that constricted space. Either attention is focused on the local and domestic or the poem tries to suggest, from the local, general metaphoric glimpses of total life processes. The two blend in lovely lyric moments, and the selves who control the process display highly civilized, sensitive intelligences. But the extended conceit or the well-polished offhand generalization quickly absorbed back into the lyric scene is the most the poetic thinking produces. There is little dialectic between the local and the general – compare Yeats or Stevens – so that the self seems passive and finally somewhat smug in its capacity to produce lyric closure. The dominant impression is of a sense of person constructed around self-confident self-pity and yet still confined to polishing the small change. These poets are fairly young, but at about their age Eliot had produced *The Waste Land;* Stevens, *Harmonium;* and Pound, *A Draft of Thirty Cantos*.

We see, in effect, a redefinition of poetry whose very commitment to the middle range leaves the poets in a position of betweenness vulnerable to attacks from the two basic poles of literary criticism. For the humanist or defender of romantic lyric traditions the poetry is not ambitious enough, not dialectical enough in its attempts to understand and transcend both the modes of understanding and the fragments of personality it offers.

Also, in a more conservative form of the same charge, it seems plausible to claim that the poetry is still not domestic enough, not sufficiently tied to the logics that govern other practices in the world the poems evoke. From this perspective there is still all too much undefended lyricism that only transforms a preciosity about subject matter into the danger of a narcissistic preciosity of lyrical attitudes. Poets find it all too easy to extend what they construct for imaginary personas into terms for defining the self and creating forms of emotional closure that negotiate and control all one's troubles. The troubles themselves come to appear as primarily cause for song, aspects of a rhetoric rather than a true engagement in courses of events not subject to the poetic will.

On the other hand, virtually the same set of conditions can lead those concerned with modernist experiment to insist on exploring much more radical forms of the logic motivating Goldbarth. We need not dialectic but a more suspicious attitude toward all devices that produce satisfying resolutions. Transformations of the scenic mode become last-ditch strategies for preserving a narcissistic lyricism that blinds us to the very needs the poems in fact address. In either case, it seems clear that for many poets the fascination of the personal lyric will not suffice, however moving – or more precisely, because it is so moving – until poets find ways of incorporating within the poems principles for testing, interpreting, and extending the rhetorics of self-presentation and metaphoric closure. Yet the very refusal to lose the world in pursuit of such speculations, and the craft to keep us caring about the world preserved, are no small recompense for the choice to cultivate a space bounded on one side by ordinary life, on the other by poetic assumptions these poets feel worth preserving for what they preserve in a prose world.

4

The paradoxes of contemporary antiromanticism

I

Poets like Hass and Dennis recognize and implicitly defend the compromises they make in their efforts to transform the dominant mode. In their modesty they can clearly define the ground on which they stand. The second group of poets I shall deal with present a more complicated case, for the two styles I shall discuss take as their task a thorough curing of the grounds that produce the dominant mode so that we can begin curing ourselves of the psychological traits which that mode cultivates.[1] But this idea of total cure becomes dangerously seductive. Under it we write, as we often take lovers, with the hope that our good intentions allow us to combine the attraction of old vices with the dream of purifying them into virtues. At times we even succeed, but rarely to the degree that we are not soon back in old habits, all the more seductive because we think we have conquered them. Here I can talk only about poets, although the persistence of problems despite or within the efforts to cure them is one basic source for our general cultural distrust of intellectual "solutions." In this particular case the critical aim is to find imaginative stances not tied to the conflict between rhetoric and sincerity, because they exemplify new ways of understanding language, the role of lyric emotions, and the powers that constitute a person's capacity to posit psychological and social identity. But continually nagging this sense of possibility are constant reminders that even uncompromising efforts at cure may ultimately reveal only how deep and persistent is the disease.

As my example of this need for a cure I shall turn to a third representative text by a poet-critic, this time Jonathan Holden. These discursive texts offer the strongest indications of assumptions that limit poets' imaginative explorations, and thus they justify taking up the issues in an abstract critical language like mine. When poets play critic they may make evident the possible social uses of critics who take them seriously as intellectuals. In Holden's specific case, I want to show how, despite his acute self-consciousness about rhetoric, he remains trapped in the ethos of personal sincerity that, despite his strong case against values like Young's, reverts to evaluative and emotional criteria basic to the scenic style.

These problems in Holden become crucial when we see their consequences for poetic practice. Now instead of Stafford I turn to a younger, even more problematic poet, Mark Strand. Here sincerity and rhetoric enter a strange dance of blind mutual self-congratulation. I do not think Holden would praise the features in Strand's poetry I shall concentrate on. But the important consideration is that one cannot fully criticize him from within Holden's poetics. We can neither analyze the weaknesses nor see their cultural contexts and possible consequences. What Holden cannot do serves in turn to show how important it is that we pay careful attention to the two forms of contemporary poetic theory explicitly devoted to providing analyses of and alternatives for the problems we see in Strand. Both positions can loosely be called classicist, but their values are quite different: At one pole we find a sophisticated neoclassicism best articulated by Robert Pinsky's call for a new discursiveness in poetry, and at the other we find still vital an objectivist tradition based on rejecting all discursiveness and appearances of prosaic relaxation. Both share a commitment to clarifying the ways in which the poems we have considered so far remain trapped within untenable romantic ideals of the mind and of emotional authenticity. And both see the dominant mode as living off the emotional capital of investments that were never very sound, but that at least in their formative stages required a capacious and inquiring spirit now grown enervated.

However, even these promising beginnings lead to serious and instructive difficulties. After spelling out these difficulties, I shall be in a good position to explain why Rich and Ashbery have strong claims to be our most important poets. For in very different ways, both poets directly confront the problem of correlating self-consciousness about rhetoricity with the need to maintain a distinctive and flexible personal presence. Each then provides adequate responses to an overwhelming cultural pressure by imagining roles poetry can play in fostering forms of self-reflection that create new emotional stances and ideas of what a person can be in relation to the language he or she manages to speak.

II

We have seen Jonathan Holden's acute critical mind at work in his treatment of rhetoricity within the scenic mode. Now I want to consider why he cannot do more in using that ability to carve out new areas for poetic inquiry or even to explain the new directions that are emerging. Holden's eye remains keen: He recognizes the importance of conceits as a way of recovering the familiar, he sees the significance of new stances that offer pure hypotheses unwilling to imply assertions, and he offers a fairly rich characterization of Ashbery's aesthetic use of abstraction. Yet notice how little he makes of the idea of "post-modern":

> The true symptoms of the post-modernist poetic . . . originate in a changing rhetorical contract between poet and reader. . . Recoiling from the demands of testimony, yet still committed to poetry that treats of the self, a poet may more find himself drawn to forms that resemble extended hypotheses instead of testimony. . . Clearly the Hugo poem "In Your Young Dream" retains a strong testimonial flavor; but the grammar of hypothesis allows him to mythologize the landscape and the situation . . . the post-modernist mode . . . finds its poem, then, not through the cultivation of discontinuity. Instead, through parody and through the nonassertive epistemology of its propositions, it strives to soften conventional distinctions between fiction and history, and thereby to maximize the poet's freedom playfully to invent.[2]

This is not wrong, but neither is it very strong, especially in context. For this is the concluding passage in Holden's book and the climax of an effort to defend poets like Hugo against Marjorie Perloff's charge that they cook up instant Wordsworth, not suited to the demands of contemporary spiritual appetites. Why, one is tempted to ask, is the fare offered in response critically and poetically so bland?

Perloff's eye is better than some of the specifics of her case. Her alternative to instant Wordsworth is a view of poems as irreducibile because they establish indeterminate but fascinating poetic interrelationships. (In my view irreducibility by indeterminacy is almost as reductive a version of romantic and modern nondiscursive poetic autonomy as is the praise of a softened, personal voice indulging the play of invention.) Holden's response to Perloff offers an essentially "rhetorical" defense of Hugo: that his post-modernism lies in the relationship between poet and world implicit in "borrowing the form from a non-literary source, a dream, rather than relying on standard literary conventions."[3] However, even if we grant that Hugo's version of dreams is not borrowed from an ancient literary convention, we must wonder whether Holden's concerns even allow him to address the core of the case brought by Perloff or to provide much of a defense for Hugo. The problem with his rhetorical defense is that it is precisely the status of rhetoric that is at stake. Perloff's critique concentrates on the lazy rhetorical quality of Hugo's method of sustaining naturalness and honesty by a self-consciously artful placing of details, followed by a celebration of all the parts clicking shut. Perloff sees the well-made poem as repeating the shortcomings of the well-made play, and her criticism applies to hypotheses and rhetorical inventions of all sorts. What, Perloff ultimately asks, is the use your poet can make of rhetoric? Should not the poem question or justify what allows it closure? And how can the poem's energies as energies, not as devices, become exemplary features of aesthetic objects that implicate significant existential concerns?

Here, Holden, for all his intelligence and sensitivity, must be silent because his sense of poetic rhetoric has no place for the idea of texts' interpreting as significant the constructive energies they exemplify, nor does he have any traditional sense that rhetoric controls content as well as a person's relation to his audience. He lacks, in short, precisely the sense of rhetoric's relation to social content that informs the way the classicizing perspectives I shall soon discuss treat the dominant mode. Holden is too much within the assumptions informing the rhetoric to analyze it as anything more than a means, largely because he wants not to let his critique of the poem as testimony shake him from his deeper commitment to a poetry of dramatized personal voices. Some of his reasons should by now be obvious, although their consequences may not be. The idea of self provides an easy ground of emotions and of mystery. If we can no longer find outside ourselves phenomena with numinous qualities – if nature, for example, is simply objective – the self still has, or appears to have, inwardness, mystery, and affective complexity. Moreover, Holden finds himself in the dilemma of having very few options left him. Uncomfortable with testimony, he seems downright scandalized by a view of the poet as engaged in sustained and assertive tests of imaginative thinking and its relation to the will.

The only forms of thinking he entertains are those which revel in their ficticity as pure hypotheses that refuse even to hint at assertion. This means he has no alternative ground of value for the activities of self, now reduced to invention. Only rhetoric sustains the ethos of craft, which seems all the poet can trust. This narrowing of what poetry can be as a speculative instrument has as its corollary what would seem to Perloff (and seems to me) a terribly reactionary, late nineteenth-century definition of the priorities poetry serves. When Holden praises poems, it is almost never for their insight or "news," but for their "poignant" qualities and capacities to be "genuinely moving."[4] The art of poetry he defines as consisting "mainly of the art of infusing feeling into language so that, without the aid of the author's actual voice in performance, language on a silent page can attain the power and immediacy of a singing voice in the ear of the reader."[5] To paraphrase: Poetry is the musical accompaniment of the world as we know it, so that ordinary realities can resonate with a concerned human presence.

The gulf between this and other, more ambitious views of poetry as capable of exercising a constitutive force that offers possible selves rather than expresses given ones is clearest when Holden tries to claim affinities between Plumly on tone and statements like this from Cleanth Brooks: "How can it [the truth of the poem's statement] be validated? When we raise such a question, we are driven to consider the poem as drama. . . We are forced to raise the question whether the statement grows properly out of a context; whether it is "ironical" – or merely callow, glib and sentimental."[6]

For Holden, the two critics share a pressing concern "with judging whether a poem sounds authentic or not" in its relationship to "the crucial role of the rhetorical contract in generating emotion."[7] But small differences reveal large cultural shifts. Where Holden equates authenticity with the authorial presence in the rhetoric, Brooks concentrates on the dramatic elements by which poetic structure renders the intrinsic complexity of experience. What is a means for Brooks is an end for Plumly and Holden – with respect both to what the poem offers and to the way its emotions function. Holden argues that Brooks sees the treatment of a rhetorical contract as producing the poetic emotion. Taken broadly enough this claim can be defended, but it ignores Brooks's crucial concern that what generates emotion is not contract but content, the overall verbal tensions organized by the poem as an objective dramatic event.[8] Brooks in fact suspects rhetoric of tending to destroy objectivity, and hence drama, because it is subordinate to the personal will. This fear explains his resorting to the problematic concept of poetic autonomy. If emotions are left to the rhetorical contract, then they are likely to get subsumed into authors' efforts to persuade others of the truth of the emotions or themselves of their own authenticity. So Brooks gives the poem itself a will by imagining that poetry is a special kind of rhetoric controlled by demands intrinsic to the material.

Because of that power, Brooks can view poems as rhetorics about rhetoric: There are levels on which they are not bound to use rhetoric as the means of communication but can use aesthetic conventions in order to display the nature and limitations of rhetorical constructs. Thus Brooks need not take the person in the poem as primary. Rather, he conceives personal drama in a poem as the result of transpersonal effects that transform life into art and bracket immediate emotional identifications in order to insist upon distinctively reflective emotions. Indeed, it is from a position much closer to Brooks's (although she would deny it) that Perloff criticizes the easy rhetoric in Hugo's poem. Person is an inadequate category for Brooks because he treats poetry not as primarily an art of infusing feeling into language, but as the construction of linguistic objects that examine our terms for feeling and create new possible stances of mind in relation to our existential concerns. One need not accept Brooks's particular version of these claims in order to see by contrast how the stance Holden represents settles for a much-diminished thing: Hypothetical expressions of the tonal self are a fairly impotent source of poetic power.

III

So far we have watched the critical ideals of high romanticism collapse into something close to a repetition of what led to Georgian poetics. Now I want to switch from the effects of personalism on poetic theory and the projects theory authorizes to the actual testimony of what can happen when poets rely on elaborate rhetorical exercises to generate an aura of sincerity. My example may seem an extreme case, the first section of Mark Strand's "Elegy for My Father," but his work in this mode is widely praised by poets and critics of similar persuasion. Nonetheless, if we examine the poem through the eyes of an objectivist or from Pinsky's neoclassical stance, the critical praise is itself an indication of just how representative the poem's vices are.

Most striking to me is the utter passivity, because it makes only the subjective states of the speaker the focus of the poem and produces a narcissism of sensitivity, only reinforced by the strongly foregrounded craft:

Elegy for My Father
(Robert Strand 1908–68)

1   The Empty Body

The hands were yours, the arms were yours,
But you were not there.
The eyes were yours, but they were closed and would not
    open.

The distant sun was there.
The moon poised on the hill's white shoulder was there.
The wind on Bedford Basin was there.
The pale green light of winter was there.
Your mouth was there,
But you were not there.
When somebody spoke, there was no answer.
Clouds came down
And buried the buildings along the water,
And the water was silent.
The gulls stared.
The years, the hours, that would not find you
Turned in the wrists of others.
There was no pain. It had gone.
There were no secrets. There was nothing to say.
The shade scattered its ashes.
The body was yours, but you were not there.
The air shivered against its skin.
The dark leaned into its eyes.
But you were not there.[9]

There is no bardic sublime here, no prophecy and no speculations about cosmic force. The poem in effect cannot get moving in any dramatic way because of the dual pressures of imitated grief and the pull of lyric elegance. There appear only two phenomena: an absent father and in his place an all too carefully composed lyric cry: Was ever father in such manner lamented? We never even get to the scenic. Initial metonymic objects (like those in *In Memoriam*) create a gap that only a series of lyric variations on a theme can fulfill. But this gives us details as abstract as those of the conceits we have examined, here appearing under the guise of what is normally one of our most complex emotional experiences. Yet the lyric freedom displaces any convincing encounter with the father or his memory. Memories tie us to this world. Strand's art appears on the contrary not as a speculative instrument but as pure will to poetry. The details seem chosen primarily to sustain musical and imagistic patterns. Consequently, the father appears as only the vehicle for standard lyric oppositions between presence and absence, oppositions that Strand does not explore so much as exploit. Expressions like "the air shivered" and "the dark leaned" refer less to experience than to the creative writing workshop: Making it new collapses into making verbs active and varying standard affective associations. And when mystery comes so close to mystification, one cannot help interpreting the lack of pressure on the composition as suggesting also a lack of real involvement masking as

sincerity. Composure is all too easy: Compare the different elegaic voices
of Dylan Thomas or Yeats or even Lowell's harsh particulars. Here Strand's
distanced voice makes lyric control seem something close to indifference.
And the aura of mature refusal of romantic sublimities ironically relies
on the easiest of all sublime themes, the theme of loss as a ground for
incantation. The pressure of raw emotion has been so successfully distanced, without the contemplative poise of classic lyric voices like Jon-
son's, that one is tempted to see this poem as ultimately an example of a
refined sensibility concealing and revealing moral bad taste. Passion for
the father simply should not so easily appear a passion for the symbolic
and metaphoric effects the poet can wrest from his father's death.

This kind of criticism bothers me. It makes art too much like life. But
that is what weak art requires: When the conscious act of expression
takes form as essentially a will to poetry, we find ourselves reading against
that will to find the symptomatic conditions it conceals. This particular
set of symptomatic conditions is especially instructive because of the ra-
tios it exemplifies among the will to poetry, passive self-indulgence, and
the pursuit of silence as the self-consciously antibardic poet's way to have
his sublime by elaborating personal poignancy. After five sections, the
work of mourning leaves us this:

6   The New Year

It is winter and the new year.
Nobody knows you.
Away from the stars, from the rain of light,
You lie under the weather of stones.
There is no thread to lead you back.
Your friends doze in the dark
Of pleasure and cannot remember.
Nobody knows you. You are the neighbor of nothing.
It is over. It is winter and the new year.
The meek are hauling their skins into heaven.
The hopeless are suffering the cold with those who have
      nothing to hide.
It is over and nobody knows you.
There is starlight drifting on the black water.
There are stones in the sea no one has seen.
There is a shore and people are waiting.
And nothing comes back.
Because it is over.
Because there is silence instead of a name.
Because it is winter and the new year.[10]

The anaphoric structure is superb: Rhetoric repeats and accepts our submission to necessity. But the bleakness is on the one hand a little too lush in the tragic recognition of necessity and on the other a little too empty in its accepting of the father's reduction to a purely physical universe. I want to trust this willed poverty as a mode of vision, but how can I escape the nagging question that a father so easily reduced to metaphor in the opening is perhaps too easily condemned to the seasons at the close? The poem's very turn to bareness is belied both by its rhetoric and by its crossing between lyrical exultation and obsessive self-absorption. So the poem denies in its act all the dependent sense of otherness it uses as its stage. Effusive, artful grief makes one question both the grief and the uses of art.

IV

The two forms of questioning to which I want to turn now each provide analyses of and antidotes to the form of blindness I attribute to Strand's poem. On the poetic level these questions entail demands for a more complex, disciplined, and aesthetically foregrounded understanding of poetic rhetoric. And on the cultural level they require attempts to come to terms with the limitations in ideas of the person and the emotions that leave us ripe for the seductions of Strand's rhetoric. Yet this very need to encounter directly the cultural sources of poetry's problems will lead less to a sense of liberation than to a sense of how difficult it is to escape both the romanticism forming our emotional attitudes and the empiricist intellectual criteria that drive us to romantic alternatives as our grounds for lyric intensity.

My criticisms of Strand derive primarily from his handling of details. The careful artificiality, highly composed setting, and desire to make all particulars contribute to a single moment of luminous silence all set the poet sharply against a world of practical concerns and common interactions. Here we encounter in extreme form the tendency in scenic poets to imagine the poet as Mill's lonely figure overhearing himself rather than as Wordsworth's man speaking to other men. Absolute scenic lyricism, we might say, isolates absolutely in its quest for moments of pure perception, won from the repetitions of quotidian life. Strand thus helps us see why poets begin exploring possibilities of highly discursive styles that tie the lyrical sensibility to the constraints of continuous thought and the contexts of contemporary cultural life. Even Hass, the most discursive of those we have considered who work in conjunction with scenic values, cannot overcome all of this sort of difficulty in his sensibility. In reading him we find it easy to suspect that his elaborate humanizing of loss may evade confronting the causes of his pain or possible ways of making the sense of loss a principle for actions. Then the efforts to construct a compassionate, reflective voice appear in part as rather desperate attempts to preserve the nobility of a subdued but still romantic ego that must have the world on its terms.

Experimental modernism tried to combat earlier avatars of the "romantic" lyricism by combining an impersonal critical intelligence and collage style with the essentially romantic pursuit of nondiscursive form articulating a distinctive logic of poetry. Now a basic imperative for experiment is to find alternatives to the ideal of poetic logic itself by making discursiveness a central poetic force – whether it be the Wintersian rationalism of Robert Pinsky; the Yeatsian directness of Derek Walcott; the denial of lyric self-congratulation through extended narrative or playful immediacy one finds in Ed Dorn, Norman Dubie, or David Antin; the field for merging free invention, plain talk, and domestic sensibility of James Merrill; or the more contorted "quasi-discursive" movements of John Ashbery, which use self-consciousness to develop a new basis for depersonalized lyricism.

For our purposes the most interesting of these critical stances is Robert Pinsky's. His *The Situation of Poetry* combines a sharp critique of both the cool and the surreal forms of scenic lyricism; an intelligent attempt to root the problems he sees in the enervating of romantic ideals about emotion, the self, and poetry as a medium; and a cogent defense of the values a discursive poetry might make available. Then in his own poetry he shows how a discursive style sustains compassionate, self-reflective intelligence rarely produced within the crafted confines of the scenic lyric. However, his poems also reveal how much more must be done if we are to have major poetry free of the romantic traits whose consequences we have been tracing. In fact, Pinsky may inadvertently show that discursive poetry can be better off radically extending romantic ideas of language and of mind than attempting to suppress what it cannot dispel.

The Situation of Poetry is a profoundly historical book, insisting that the problematic features of contemporary work must be understood against the background of romantic and modern poetry. Judged in this context, contemporary poems all too often reveal "the mastery and elaboration of a way of writing after the motives in life for that way of writing have become obscured . . . leading us to expend force in self-regard at the expense of life, trivializing the ambition of poetry."[11] We are in effect at the end of a radical experiment in envisioning the medium of poetry as allowing artifacts to have "some of the status of an object or phenomenon, rather than a statement." This dream made poets dissatisfied "with the abstract, discursive, and conventional nature of words as a medium for the particular of experience," and thus created two basic problems. First, poets resisting the abstract nature of language are likely to define emotional and epistemological authenticity as making for the self some more direct, more immediate relation to sources of value on the other side of language. Poetry continually seeks to become its other, to gain access to a silent ground that must ultimately prove terrifying and inhuman. Second, once poets no longer trust language to produce emotion by its power of articulating general truths about life, the source for emotions is not the world reflected but the performance of the poet in the act of trying to reflect the world. The problems can become the stuff of great poetry, so long as writers are aware of the tensions they create in relation to ordinary experience and the extraordinary efforts that must be expended to avoid solipsism. In contemporary poetry, however, the sense of problems disappears and the desires stem from largely conventional dogmas. This is perhaps clearest in the ways poets sentimentalize the terrifying, inhuman features of what resists language. And the price is clearest in the ways in which each of the two basic contemporary styles – that of the Dandy and that of the Puritan, the mannered and the laconic voices – collapses the message into the handling of the medium: "The poem is blocked by a sense of struggle, the writer trying desperately to follow his own directive and join art and life more sincerely than the metaphors." Finally, as poetry becomes reified and "gets too far from prose, it may be in danger of choking itself on a thick rich handful of words."[12] Poetic diction ironically becomes the easiest means of making sure that poems do not carry the sentential burden of prose.

If poetry is once again to possess vital energies and compete with other forms of language, it must present a discursive poet "talking, predicating, moving directly through a subject as systematically and unaffectedly as he would walk from one place to another." Notice how different from Holden's, then, is Pinsky's definition of poetry: "The poem is a statement, made in the tone of a human being speaking of and to human beings, with all the excitement of poetry." Pinsky wisely leaves unstated the grounding terms for this poetic excitement that is not based on lyric intensification. He seems to think that one can have poetic excitement without poetic rhetoric so long as the poet fully manifests the virtues of "prose freedom and prose inclusiveness which I have tried to describe with words like 'discourse' and 'discursive.'"[13]

This definition, however, involves Pinsky in paradoxes central to the historical plight of contemporary poetry. The desire to escape romanticism by prose virtues has been in effect the rhetorical enabling act of the romanticism Pinsky suspects. From Wordsworth's "Preface to Lyrical Ballads" to Pound's "A Retrospect" and Eliot's "Metaphysical Poets," the ideal of the prosaic has been used to foster what turn out to be radically poetic forms of thinking and of forming emotional relations. Making poetry carry the burden of prose demands resisting easy emotions and conventional diction, but that resistance may require from romantic poetics the vision of the work as nondiscursive object. If lyrics are to recover the force of prose, poets must experiment with new forms of poetic syntax as possible alternatives to "the generalizing power" of ordinary language, because generalizing, after all, usually appears inseparable from convention. Therefore it does little good to attack poetic diction unless one can define new ways to achieve generalizations while resisting convention. This defining can be done discursively, but not simply by attacking modernist ideas of poetry as a medium. Modernist claims about the medium probably derive from other, more pressing, problems of locating sources of value. Unless one can use discursive means to locate values adequate for a prose world but not evident there, poets will have to pursue radical poetic rhetorics. These rhetorics are, for most major modernist and romantic poets, not escapes from language but desperate attempts to revive its force in situations where the public language and criteria for adequate generalization seem incompatible with the tasks poetry must perform.

This is not the place to debate the nature of modernism. Nonetheless, it is important to see how Pinsky confuses the source of problems with one of the means used in efforts to resolve them. It may be because of this confusion that his own poetry remains trapped in old romantic problems even though it seeks a different approach to the medium. Pinsky's awareness of tradition harms him here because instead of describing and elaborating a way of understanding the generalizing power of language, he relies largely on a negative contrast with poetry that fails to generalize adequately. This reliance leaves his own work asserting a pure language, as opposed to a pure object made of language, while he does not face some of the contaminating properties that have led others to romantic poetics. In attempting to define this ideal of discursiveness, Pinsky reveals inherent tensions within the very notion of a discursive poetry. Discursiveness is difficult to correlate with poetic intensity because the common features of words tend to be so general that they vacillate and block the distinctive moments of vital spiritual life that often transcend all empirical contexts. Pinsky is too bright and too honest not to see the duality, but he is too anxious for a cure to devote full attention to the complexity he sees:

> Definitions of the term "discursive" tend to divide into two apparently contradictory senses. On the one hand, the word described speech or writing which is wandering and disorganized; on the other, it can also mean "explanatory" – pointed, organized around a setting forth of material.

These opposites are reconciled by the radical sense of motion over tension; the word signifies going through or going over this subject. Whether digressively or directly . . . the motion is on the ground and by foot . . . Such a method tends to be inclusive; it tends to be the opposite of intuitive.

It even tends to be earnest; and another way to describe the quality in poetry which I mean to be discursive is to say that it is primarily neither ironic nor ecstatic. It is speech organized by its meaning, avoiding the distances and implications occurring on one side and the ecstatic fusion of speaker, meaning and subject on the other. The idea is to have all the virtues of prose, in addition to those qualities and degrees of precision which can be called poetic.[14]

The most obvious trait here is Pinsky's ambitious seriousness about poetry: The prose lyric governed by rhetoric must become a discursive rhetoric governed by subject matter and thus tied to the public world. But in order to maintain the hope that such seriousness can be effectual, Pinsky must obscure what he initially clarifies. The discussion begins by acknowledging a potentially vacillating, wandering dimension to the discursive. By the second paragraph, where opposites are reconciled, vacillation is reduced to "digressive," and then "digressive" is reduced to being a means for inclusiveness. Finally, inclusiveness (ironically a phrase popularized by Cleanth Brooks as a descriptive term for modern poetry) allows him to collapse "digressive" into "earnest," and all traces of irony, of forces within the discursive that require supplements and self-negation, are erased by the ideal of believable speech. The ideal then produces a definition of the poetic that begs the question how one transcends the virtues of prose. What makes precision more than a prose virtue? Precision about what?

Pinsky's *An Explanation of America* is his attempt to make good on the theory. He produces a discursive poetry organized by the author's quest for poetic precision as he reflects on publicly significant subject matter, with no irritable reaching after feeling or ecstasy. The poem is intended to address large public themes directly, in a way that makes the major emotions and metaphors depend on the generalizing power of language, not on the momentary states of a self-theatricalizing dramatic sensibility. And it insists on recasting the isolated qualities of monologic poetic speech into full public discourse, sustained by cultural understandings that require neither endless ironic self-qualification nor mad empiricist demands for certainty. The poem's basic subject, I think, is an effort to come to terms with the poet's own Americanness, "uneasy in groups and making groups uneasy."[15] Its stage becomes a conflict between the consistent temptation to understand freedom in terms of infinite desire (or the madness of pure metaphor), estrangement, violence, and the isolated lucidity figured in the mountains, on the one hand, and, on the other, a sense of the composition of self and verse one earns by accepting "limits" and defining oneself in terms of virtues and ideals carried within the culture's language. Accepting limits allows one to place American estrangement within the larger contexts of the Odyssey myth and Horatian stoicism, while it also provides as a counterpressure to the appeal of isolated lucidity the structures of generous, hopeful sociality exemplified in Shakespeare's *Winter's Tale*. Within these frames one can treat freedom not as opposed to constraint but as opposed to the slavery within which one cannot give meaning to a life by choosing grounds worth dying for. Such freedom makes citizens possible. And America's mythic value is the pluralism it grants among choices of civic identity.

Pinsky's is a fully conceived American classical republicanism. I cannot give an adequate account of its extraordinary intelligence and of passages where personal speech takes on an intense, high seriousness that is in no way bathos. Compared to Pinsky, James Merrill's cuteness as a means of having and negating discursiveness seems a child's or aesthete's sudden discovery that there are adult issues one should attend to. I must concentrate here on the problems the poem raises – in itself, as a test case for Pinsky's statements about poetics, and above all, as an emblem of how difficult it is to escape the temptation to use the "sincere" poetic subject as one's primary vehicle for developing emotions. Ultimately, I think that Pinsky's attacks on romanticism leave him in another romantic dilemma at least as debilitating as the ones he tries to escape. The problems are probably clearest when we consider Pinsky's desire to supplant illusionistic scenic drama by making subject matter and argument carry the emotional burden. Once he insists on the quality of explicit (non-ironic) discursiveness, he needs a clear way of addressing general public criteria about arguments. Most of our criteria now involve highly specialized measures difficult even to imagine putting in a poem without Merrill's playful distance. And even those which one might call apposite for a polis of generally informed citizens are so diverse and unstable that it is very hard to find common discursive ground. Unwilling either to make ironic poetry of the problem or to become a modern Lucretius or Erasmus Darwin, Pinsky in fact ends up with a Wordsworthian stance very much like Hass's: The measure of the poem is not its argument but the basic human virtues it displays in the stances and rhythms of mind the dramatized poet exemplifies as he or she moves.

The authority Pinsky seeks, then, turns out to be more romantic, less grounded in putatively objective subject matter, than that sought by lyric poets like Bly or Gary Snyder. Without a genuine argumentative discourse to rely upon, Pinsky cannot even defend his sense of the authority of poetic traditions or establish ways to judge the qualities in the poetic acts claiming to represent such traditions. Discursive poetry here exacerbates the distance between poetry and our age's critical models of thought, so Pinsky is left with only poetic sensibility, deprived even of the strategies romanticism developed as sustenance for that sensibility. Discursiveness, for example, precludes the elaboration of dramatic vignettes and the development of juxtaposed layers of experience Williams employs in his vision of America. Modernism became radically nondiscursive less because it was seduced by romanticism than because it was oppressed by its own marginal relation to what had become socially authoritative forms of discourse. Modernist works had to be self-contextualizing, essentially dramatic, constructions, because they had to maintain an adversarial relation to discursive canons. Pinsky seems to want to deny this condition, yet his plain talk appears equally literary, while denying any authority within his strengths. There can be little doubt, I think, that he is best using classical and Shakespearean materials. When he stands naked in a discourse on America, he has considerable lyric strength, but the thought vacillates between a covertly Blyean melodrama of heroic limits in relation to death (Horace as Heidegger, perhaps) and the bathos of warmed-over Yvor Winters:

> The obliterating strangeness and the spaces
> Are as hard to imagine as the love of death . . .
> Which is the love of an entire strangeness,
> The contagious blankness of a quiet plain . . .
> Imagine that the man who writes that poem,
> Stunned by the loneliness of that wide pelt,
> Should prove to himself that he was like a shadow
> Or like an animal living in the dark.[16]

In claiming poetry's power as discourse, Pinsky probably assumes obligations to address issues more specific than these psychologistic twists on an old myth of the American myth. He needs to take seriously the social and scientific issues Merrill wittily gestures at.

Pinsky's problems are clearest in the strategies he uses to frame his reflections within a discourse situation. Modernism tended to ignore questions of audience because it treated poems as the construction of objectified perceptions available to all who would put in the necessary interpretive labor. Pinsky, aware that this myth of objectification evades questions of linguistic generality and social demands, tries instead to recover actual speech through the classical medium of addressing his daughter. But in a long poem and a romantic age, that topos comes under so much strain that Pinsky hedges – he confesses to addressing only the idea of his daughter.[17] The gulf between the idea of an audience and a real audience, however, is precisely the romantic dilemma and one problem with the generality of language. Pinsky leaves himself only a fantasy solution that renders him more vulnerable than the equally awkward forms of direct personal address we find in poets like Merrill, Hugo, Matthews, and Hass. Because his defense of his style depends on the generalizing power of language, Pinsky's problems with convincing speech call his whole enterprise into question and even make one wonder what kind of rationality is possible under such circumstances.

The problems of voice and address are most striking when Pinsky tries to conclude. Deprived of dramatic and narrative coherence, the discursive poem most obviously achieves closure by projecting a sense of having reached agreement on a subject with an audience. Pinsky's solution, his evidence for producing "not a mystic home / But something – if it must be imaginary / chosen from life, and useful,"[18] is to concentrate on his daughter taking a part in *The Winter's Tale,* as if this identification with Shakespeare's romance spirit could resist the figures of estranging landscape and cold lucidity. Yet how romantic is the use of contiguity as a figure for potential transformation, and how broad is the gulf between the private, idealistic terms of the resolution and the actual problems one faces in proposing to explain America. This is romantic ambitiousness, without recourse to irony or to a purely lyric process of producing possible private attitudes capable of sustaining us in the face of society's winter's tale. Thus Pinsky's opposition to poets "who have devised ways of writing which go remarkably far toward embodying, in language, a host of reservations about language, human reason and their holds on life"[19] borders on becoming an unreasonable defense of reason, blind to the unstable ground on which his authority stands. It should not be surprising, then, that other poets will concentrate on precisely those features of discursiveness in motion which Pinsky suppresses – on means of concentrating on the person in the discourse or on the ways discourse questions and doubles itself because of the pressure of nonintentional features, so that it presents a dispersed intentional subject or "authoriality" rather than a self-possessed and coherent subject-making argument.

V

Objectivism gains its power from considerations dramatically opposed to Pinsky's. Instead of insisting on the generalizing capacity of language, it relies on the focusing, concentrative ability of form to transcend subjectivity by giving the mind and feelings life in and as objective force. Yet, as we shall see, it too flounders on the very principles of order it takes as its ground, not because the poets evade the issues of personal presence but because they close off the poetic field so that there is not sufficient imaginative space to handle the complexity of subjective stances and desires. The dream of most objectivist poets is that ideas can be put in things, art things, at least, so that the world satisfies the energies and needs of mind. But the mysteries of subjectivity evade the mastery available within their vision of form.

The objectivist tradition is based on the key term that is also contemporary poetry's dominant value – the idea of sincerity. But objectivist sincerity is a sincerity of the art object as a model for the person. Sincerity is a feature not of selves but of what selves can compose, can clarify from the desires for personal expression. The poem, in other words, must be without wax, and thus open, controlled, and self-interpreting in all its rhetorical manipulations:

> In sincerity shapes appear concomitants of word combinations, precursors of . . . completed sound or structure, melody or form. Writing occurs which is the detail, not mirage of seeing, of thinking with the things as they exist, and of directing them along a line of melody. Shapes suggest themselves, and the mind senses and receives awareness . . .
>
> This rested totality might be called objectification – the apprehension satisfied completely as to the appearance of the art form as an object. . . Its character may be simply described as the arrangement, into one apprehended unit, of minor units of sincerity – in other words, the resolving of words and their ideal into structure. [20]

Let us take the dream at its source, or rather at a source commenting on a prior source. This is Charles Olson:

> In any given instance, because there is a choice of words, the choice, if a man is in there, will be, spontaneously, the obedience of his ear to the syllables. The fineness, and the practice, lie here, at the minimum and source of speech.
>
> O western wynd, when wilt thou blow
> And the small rain down shall rain
> O Christ that my love were in my arms
> And I in my bed again. [21]

The impulse here is to define a mode of relatedness between words and world, and hence a model of writing and of reading, where all the energies of rhetoric are exposed and fulfilled within the poem. There is then no surplus or gap that we must fill by projecting the tawdry dramas of individual authorial lives. Where the "metaphoric" poets of the dominant mode and its transforms seek to foreground relations that evoke meanings or sites of meditation beyond the scene, Olson wants us to see how the poet in "Western Wynd" makes relational forces intensify "the detail, not mirage of seeing." He articulates a field where one can think in relationships among things as they are. The primary connections of mind to world, then, are denotative (in an imaginary world), rather than connotative or metaphoric. In order to keep the denotations intensely resonant, the poet marks his field – perceptually and musically – by a dense interplay of direct perceptions standing toward one another like planes in an abstract painting. The poetry is in the parallels between forms of desire and of energy held together in a perceptual space. Wind and desire are less metaphors for feeling than its direct equivalent within an imaginary world, so that nature and person's nature are adequate vehicles for one another, echoed again in the overt energies of the writing where the desire for concepts is constrained and directed into the plosive play of alliterating syllables and of strong vowels modulating the kinetic energies of speech from the back to the front of the mouth. Desire here takes form not by being mastered but by achieving full expression in each of the controlled, overlapping energy fields: perception, memory, projected future, and act of writing. Desire becomes a condition of energy at rest in itself, and the theological analogues in Zukofsky's poetic statement find here a perfectly adequate secular ground. The literal will suffice, provided one has learned the craft of the letter.

With Olson, as with Pinsky, the ultimate struggle is with romantic views of the mind, language, and the ways desires must be interpreted and satisfied. Consider for a moment how the wind takes form for romantic poets as they inaugurate a period Zukofsky called "the nine reigns (when) there was no literary production . . . because there was neither consciousness of the objectively perfect nor an interest in clear or vital particulars."[22] Here Shelley is:

> O wild West Wind, thou breath of Autumn's being
> Thou, from whose unseen presence the leaves dead
> Are driven, like ghosts from an enchanter fleeing,
>
> Yellow, and black, and pale, and hectic red,
> Pestilence-stricken multitudes . . .
>
> Scatter, as from an unextinguished hearth,
> Ashes and sparks, my words among mankind!
> Be through my lips to unawakened earth
>
> The trumpet of a prophecy! O Wind,
> If Winter comes, can Spring be far behind?

and here is Coleridge:

> Hence, viper thoughts, that coil around my mind,
>   Reality's dark dream!
> I turn from you, and listen to the wind,
>   Which long has raved unnoticed. What a scream
> Of agony by torture lengthened out
> That lute sent forth . . .
>   What tell'st thou now about?
>   'Tis of the rushing of a host in rout . . . [23]

These are very different poetic acts of mind. They are not the only form of romanticism, nor do they warrant careless modernist charges of egotism and vagueness. Shelley and Coleridge introduce new sources of perceptual and philosophical energy into English poetry. But in making the act of the interpretive mind, rather than the measuring mind, the poem's central focus, they also make central and inescapable some very serious problems. In their pursuit of dialectical symbolic structures capable of reconciling discordant elements into satisfying conceptual wholes, these poems simultaneously produce too little and too much meaning. On the one hand, the mind enacts only a mirage of seeing because it thinks about rather than with things. The wind has little objective status: What details the poet attends to are significant only as tenors for stories or spiritual metaphors like "pestilence stricken multitudes." On the other hand, as the mind moves over, rather than among, the particulars of its world, it leaves itself no place to rest that is not dependent upon the "trumpet" of a prophetic ego whose metaphors are its only authority. The pursuit of abstract synthesis through metaphoric processes is at best tenuous; the mind is always threatened by the possible return of self-consciousness insisting on the merely conceptual and fictive grounds for its orders and driving the self back into a despondent, passive relation to the natural energies its interpretations displace. Unseen presences, nature become metaphoric words, and story-telling winds all too easily return to the deadness of mere appearances that resist metaphor, words that lack natural grounds, and stories revealed as only mirages in reality's dark dream. Moreover, by so insistently dramatizing the efforts of mind locked into a single lyric space, the poem's craft is subject to the same alternations as its desire for meaning. At one extreme, lyric exaltation becomes the melodramatic tone poem of Shelley's opening trumpets, and at the other, the verse slackens into prosaic analogues whining the poet's passive surrender to external forces. Composition verges on losing its ground in composure, and poetic modes of relatedness come dangerously close to echoing the frenetic dualities of the culture they try to resist.

Shelley and Coleridge are great poets, but the modes of relatedness on which their greatness is based may be no longer accessible, or desirable, for our culture. Threatened by Enlightenment intellectual and social forces calling into question all they treasured, these poets had as their only line of defense the ability to make the sublime serve metaphysical purposes. The sublime enabled them to accept rationalist critiques of the limits of empirical propositions while creating a space in which the empirically unreal could remain imaginatively real, albeit indefinable except through the vehicle of symbolic imaginative dialectics. By increasing the distance between the empirical and a realm of imaginative values, these poets purchased a Miltonic exaltation and tragic intensity no objectivist poet but Pound can rival. But the price of this nobility may be too high – in the psychic torments it creates no less than in the poetic postures it encourages. And even this question may be irrelevant, because the sublime too is a faith that may have died. The symbolist vision may not be one we can make new without the various ironies of Stevens and of Ashbery. This at least seems to be the case in a time when Shelley has become Ginsberg and Coleridge's wind speaks as it does in this stanza by Robert Bly:

> The strong leaves of the box-elder tree,
> Plunging in the wind, call us to disappear
> Into the wilds of the universe,
> Where we shall sit on the foot of a plant,
> And live forever, like the dust.[24]

We find, in short, the enervated state of a desire no longer congruent with resonant particulars, and so lyric emotion depends on the person and the person on such perils as Strand exemplifies.

It is no easy task to find relief from the cramp of the mind and the feelings caused by viewing emotions so long from essentially the same position. So even though objectivism is still better in its principles than in its poets – an aesthetic in search of someone to fulfill it – its achievements deserve intensive study. I take as my first example a fairly simple poetic landscape that affords useful comparisons not only with Strand's sense of memory but, more important, with the mode of perception Wright and other scenic poets offer. This is Ron Loewinsohn's "Ovingdean Church":

> The photograph
> – if there had been
> a photograph, stopping
> the motion of the trees – would

have shown three stone crosses and
the churchyard wall, made of
flint set in mortar, from
Norman times and still
standing, above that,
two trees and a thick branch
from a third jutting in from
the right, beyond them,
the green line of a hill and
above that a single star
in a grey sky.[25]

The opening lines create a remarkably complex space. Simply on the physical level, an idea of motion is set against figures of solidity, in space and over time. There are obvious echoes of Christian meaning, but they are subordinated to the scene by the starkness of detail and by the way the lineation makes physical in the poem similar principles of relatedness between motion and stillness. The emphatic lineation and syntactic patterns allow Loewinsohn to avoid Wright's preciosity of detail; the materials here are simple and stark. More important, the details require no metaphors and no reliance on a personal condition because the relational field they create is sufficient to charge the stillness with intense energy. The visual scene is rich in complex motions created by the push of prepositions emphatically placed in the lines. The "still standing" crosses and wall carry energy from the past, and distribute them across a visual space made virtually tactile by the dance of lines of force moving above, beyond, and from the right, until all resolve into a moment of quiet unfolding of the star in sky. Endurance in time is at once a vehicle for the motion of mind and physical properties and an echo of another permanence that holds all in stillness.

Yet movement and stillness are not simply conditions of the described scene. The mention of the photograph is a marvellously indirect way to introduce the pressures of memory, without the easy personal emotions that make memory, with its capacity to unite nature and mind, so common a subject in contemporary poetry. Here the pressure of memory delicately suggests personal urgency while objectifying the forces elicited. The movements of mind between inner and outer, between stillness and motion, and between containing a scene and being contained by it, are all made to play across the same abstract features of concrete properties in the landscape. Mediation requires no metaphor or symbol and involves no mystification because the act of mind is rendered so densely in physical, visual, and aural equivalents, while the presence of mental urgency transforms all the motion so that it balances between physical and spiritual. All this comes to ultimate fruition in the final image of "a single star in a grey sky." Taken in isolation, this is the stuff ancient undergraduate sonnets are made on. But Loewinsohn refuses any easy symbolic content because the thematic and alliterative emphasis is all on inner relations of containing and being contained, not on dreams of infinity. The grayness then modulates over the whole poem, echoing film and the stone crosses but also again framing and preserving the very expansiveness time makes possible as it defines and enriches our isolation. Stillness moves, and in moving opens on endlessly receding depths that contain all motion and demand it as their sustenance.

The strongest contrasts to Strand and rhetorical scenic lyricism occur in a second, more problematic objectivist mode that tries to synthesize Williams's poetics with the subject matter of individual psychic life. Early Creeley remains by far its best practitioner. This is "The Rain":

> All night the sound had
> come back again,
> and again falls
> this quiet, persistent rain.
>
> What am I to myself
> that must be remembered,
> insisted upon
> so often? Is it
>
> that never the ease,
> even the hardness,
> of rain falling
> will have for me
>
> something other than this,
> something not so insistent –
> am I to be locked in this
> final uneasiness.
>
> Love, if you love me,
> lie next to me.
> Be for me, like rain,
> the getting out
>
> of the tiredness, the fatuousness, the semi-
> lust of intentional indifference.
> Be wet
> with a decent happiness.[26]

The magic of objectification appears here primarily in two distinctive uses of poetic force. A scenic context is continually insisted upon as literally impinging on the mind rather than metaphorically establishing an interpretive parallel for an emotion. The urgent speaking voice then carries out the literal action by running through registers of diction. Writing and experiencing are made coextensive, so that the poem's rhetoric is less a way of manipulating the scene or the audience than a way of displaying psychological energies in motion. The rain begins as too insistently itself, and hence in its otherness an insistent pressure on self-consciousness. The only way out of the tension is to find a different context, one where a form of care softens the hardness. This is why the fifth stanza is so dangerously simplistic: The choice of an awkward sincerity becomes a self-conscious way to resist and socialize self-consciousness, as if Creeley were redoing "Dover Beach." But the appeal does not involve enough of the speaker or of the medium. So the last stanza takes on the task of making release from oppression a moment of self-conscious liberation purely on the level of the author's action, with no appeal to deep discoveries or heightened sensitivity. Instead, the poem shifts registers, playing three kinds of diction against one another as indexes of psychological states. From the extreme simplicity of his appeal to the lover, the poem shifts to a series of polysllabic abstractions that richly render what they denote. Such abstraction is intentional indifference in two senses – indifference to the forms of attention not paralyzed by self-consciousness, and indifference that is a defense against the vulnerability that occurs when the self has only its own self-consciousness as its principle of definition.

Having so built a linguistic stage for one kind of self, Creeley can return to simplicity, now with a resonant sense of surprise. "Decent" echoes the latinate features of the abstractions, but as an understatement at once alive as wit and relaxed as speech. The man, now, uses poetry as testimony (not poetry about testimony) of what the lover can establish. Completing the play of mind is a lovely return to the flesh. First the wit makes good on the speaker's desire to have the lover be a figure for, or, more precisely, become the power of, rain's cleansing energies. Then our own sense of this decent wetness is allowed to spread over sexual connotations that extend both the act of understatement and its metaphoric power to suggest the recurrent role of sexual pleasure in allaying anxieties without a direct confrontation. The poem objectifies a process of deflection that ultimately celebrates the force of spirit inherent in our ways of accepting the decent happinesses that keep us full intentional beings. The dramatized life of consciousness absorbs the allusive aura sought by suggestive metaphors, and the flexibility of plain speech makes resonant, solipsistic lyric silences seem an ideal dangerously close to "the semi-lust of intentional indifference."

VI

From such diverse examples, we have a small but I think sufficient basis from which to generalize about what is most distinctive and
most promising in objectivist poetics. The dream is to make an object in
which construction and concrete perception form a complex blend: Perception takes form in construction, and construction is fulfilled in perception. Poetry, in other words, can share the spiritual force and physical
presence of abstract art, while continuing its dream that we can free ourselves from the traps of illusionism. For literary purposes this means
constructing modes of relatedness and forms of self-presence that are not
tied to dramatizing the process of attributing meanings to perception by
means of metaphors and symbols. For once these disguised semi-allegorical
gleams attract us, Zukofsky tells us, "poets put on singing robes to lose
themselves in the universal."[27] Or, as those of us reacting against Strand
might put it, once poets lose faith in an objective order where the mind
can rest and achieve resolution, there is only the triumph of will singing
out of its own incoherence, the louder for every self-conscious tatter of
its fictive, half-believed metaphoric forays into the universal.

Objectivism, then, is first of all a discipline of poetic will and a critique
of the forms of subjectivity descending to us from romanticism. Again
Zukofsky is a precise spokesman: "No predatory manifestation, no im-
position of a will not completely responsible in the poem for its acts –
Yet a manifestation making the mind more temperate because the poem
exists and has perhaps recorded both state and individual."[28] Objectivism
is not merely attention to objects: It entails the construction of aesthetic
objects in such a way that the conditions of desire are themselves dramatized and the agent is forced to take responsibility for their productive
energies. This demand for lucid self-consciousness, however, creates serious constraints on the poet. As the imagist phase of objectivism makes
clear, the impulse to avoid romantic tendencies to let reason pander to
will can tempt poets to discipline the will virtually out of existence. Insisting on objectivity establishes a pressure that easily leads to collapsing
the energy of poetry into an energy of description, with no room for the
full play of human emotions, little sense of active spirit, and a terrifying
repetition of the fact–value dichotomy that induced poets like Rakosi and
Oppen to give up poetry for politics. The poet's challenge, then, is to
make evident this power, as Oppen put it, "to construct a method of
thought from the imagist technique of poetry – from the imagist intensity of vision."[29]

Loewinsohn and Creeley, I think, meet precisely this challenge. Both
poets make the medium a central feature of the message, because the
import of the poem is equated with the specific choices that go into the

making. Then what emphases on local choice do on a temporal level (with the range of registers they introduce), a sense of collage construction provides with respect to larger compositional units. Loewinsohn describes this principle of construction as "the layering of frames of references." [30] This layering can consist of the elaborate cultural units characteristic of Olson or the delicate alignment of perceptual and syntactic units we have observed in objectivist nature poetry. In all these cases, collage allows a direct series of discrete objective notations fused into complex dimensions of interrelatedness not dependent on the interpretive will to dialectical synthesis. Consequently, poets need not submit to principles of dramatic order that encourage the pursuit of intensity by theatricalizing the poet's self-conscious stances in quest of sublimity.

We have terms for meeting the challenges Eliot and Pound defined as basic to modernism because we have a framework for exploring fresh ways of articulating emotions and acts of mind. It becomes possible to justify Oppen's equation of a phenomenological poetics with theology and Zukofsky's attacks on the epic sensibility. "The accomplished fact," as Zukofsky put it, might carry "the maximum of the real." [31] And, most important, by defining the maximum of the real in terms of perception in discrete yet intensive relations dependent upon compositional acts, the poets reinterpret the nobility of acts of mind. Nobility inheres not in transcending facts but in constructing relations among them into immediately satisfying wholes. Because the real is "accomplished," not simply given in perception, acts of disclosure and formal composition demand all those energies which romantic poets often felt could be expressed only in apocalyptic vision or in dramatizing one's awareness of the dilemmas inherent in pursuing that vision. The choices are not entrapment within the regresses of the prison house of language or the quietly heroic quest for tangible silence. Language has something to do: It makes orders that transcend description because of internal force and intelligence, not simply because it brings us to evocative depths.

Much of the most interesting objectivist work, in theory and in poetry, consists of attempts to give content to the forms of thought and images of mind that are dramatized in this layering of frames of reference. A brief analysis of two concepts – field and measure – should indicate the relevant paths of possibility. Measure is the concept for elements that mutually define one another, like the relations among church, sky, and desired photograph in "Ovingdean Church." The expanse of measure, the extension implicated by the relationships, then constitutes the field. Mind itself, as an objectified form of attention or desire, can become an element of that field. Then "person" and "self-consciousness" stand revealed as somewhat limited and anachronistic concepts. So long as language remains essentially denotative and the energies of mind can be

maintained within the compositional lines of force that the field establishes among the layered references in the poem, there need be no residue
of unnameable desire or shaping will behind the poem, and there is no
need for universals beyond it. There is nothing that can return in self-
consciousness to haunt one with the fear that one's fictions evade or must
transcend empirical conditions. The mind's need and activity can be as
present as the objects brought into relationship, so that the writer can
conceive of an intensely personal freedom while imagining the personal
as itself measured in the how and the what of its objectified engagements.
Self and mind require neither a myth of inwardness nor symbolic supplements to what they perceive and do. Presence, not nostalgia, is the
obsession of the poetry, and attributions of presence are justified because
the poem offers itself simply as a constructive act whose being consists
in its power to focus the "the" as it takes form in the measuring process.
Objectivist poetics creates an instrument sufficiently subtle to make attention and care – to the world and to the corresponding energies the
world elicits – ends in themselves.

Such dreams, at their finest, produce their own lyric mythology. At
one pole we find renewed the ideal of poetry's resistance to time precisely
articulated by Carl Rakosi:

> There is the raw data
> A mystery translates it
> into feeling and perception;
> then imagination;
> finally the hard
> inevitable quartz
> figure of will
> and language.[32]

And at the other we find celebrated the possibility that poetry need not
be conceived primarily as overheard speech or awkward public address
because in measure there is space for pure self-liberating song:

> Let's start over. *Logopeia* is the dance of the syllables with the
> whole shebang which . . . prehends them, which dances with
> them, the complete consort dancing together.
>   To dance, of course, is to touch in a particular way, to articu-
> late yourselves in touching and moving in relation to some other
> who is also touching and moving, declaring between you a shape,
> like gold to ayery thinnesse beate, drawn out from you both as
> you tend toward one another and draw apart, bending close while
> pulling apart together, your bodies swayed to music with a

brightening glance . . . The shape you are making is a *choros,* which is the place where you dance, a place defined by the use you make of it, as you define yourselves in dancing: you are the choros dancing there . . . But the choros is yourselves dancing busily in it, and *technique* is what you use to discover that place, that dance, by paying attention: now you may need a net, now you may need an elfin pinnace, now you may need to gash gold vermillion, you may need a bell to toll thee back to thy sole self.[33]

VII

When we turn to aesthetic positions that consider themselves revolutionary, we find innumerable difficulties in making judgments. Our condemnation may be proof of our corrupt tastes. Less radically, there is strong probability that, coming to a mode like objectivist poetry with demands for conventional lyric emotion, we will remain dissatisfied. It is only as we learn to appreciate the way relations are sustained and fluid emotions are formed that the mode's plainsong will be heard as intellectual and affective music. The two poems we have considered will, I hope, make it clear that objectivist poets cannot be easily dismissed and may have a good deal to show us. Yet it is hard to ignore the limitations one sees when one looks from a perspective shaped largely by the traditions of Renaissance and romantic lyricism. Most apparent is the price poets pay when they feel they must eschew generalized speculation and hence all discursiveness. If objectivist lyrics are less precious than standard academic fare, they remain on the margins of contemporary life. And if their aim is to make a place of rest for the consciousness that otherwise flows over into subjectivism, few, I think, will renounce the complexity of the self for the intricate music of such restricted compositions. There are, we must not forget, significant affinities between these poems and the spare constructivist space of noniconic abstract painting in the twenties. Neither art, I think, has been fully incorporated into the mainstream of contemporary work, nor have their implicit images of man been sufficiently explored. These may be the guides we need for a poetry and a world that can preserve a sense of reason without the theater of lyrical selves.

But the writing produced up to now leaves objectivism as at best a fruitful and interesting antagonist without the depth or complexity to spawn and sustain a range of "strong" poetic presences.[34] As testimony, I want to turn now to criticism of objectivism from within the mode. I shall ask why Robert Creeley's recent verse shifts so radically to what he calls a poetics of conjecture. Creeley certainly does not join the mainstream, but his change has interesting affinities on the one hand with the shift in Williams's late work to a more expansive personal style and on the other with the poetics of thinking as a process in John Ashbery. Measured against Ashbery, Creeley fails – this I am sure would be the verdict of most readers. The probable reasons for that verdict will lead us to reflect on how poetry can resist a self-preening emotional theater without surrendering intense lyrical emotions.

5

Robert Creeley's poetics of conjecture: the pains and pleasures of staging a self at war with its own lyric desires

I

It is possible to argue that full modernism in the arts begins with "Les Demoiselles d'Avignon," a work that turns in lucid and brutal disgust on the dimensions of self-delusive idealization inherent in the tradition of illusionistic representation. But even though very few writers have fully incorporated this lesson, I think we must take the roots of this war on representation somewhat further back. Plato is an obvious candidate, yet his opposition between forms and appearances was too simple and static to be of much relevance for modernist poetry. Rather, the central figure is Hegel, because he formulated in dynamic and secularly appropriate terms the distinction implicit in some Neoplatonism between a logic of the activity of thinking and one based on analyzing the forms of coherence present in what are offered as completed acts of thought. The distinction is crucial because it creates a new sphere of poetic action born out of the failure of our myths and lyric moments to resist the abrasive analysis of empiricist forms of lucidity. If our specific images no longer bear much authority in preserving a distinctive sense of human value, artists can hope to find a full life of spirit in the immediate qualities of acts of mind in the process of grappling with the pressure of reality. If the language for analyzing propositions has become increasingly the province of demystified modes of thought, there remains an appeal to locate the place of poetry and poetic logic in the dialectical possibilities that arise when we reflect upon our own processes of thinking and writing.

Such a mode of attention produces the most complex forms of contemporary discursiveness. More important, its imperatives place this poetry within a larger romantic project of inventing rhetorics capable of expressing and interpreting the opposition between thinking and thought. This quest links Wordsworth's shift from contiguous to symbolic thinking in "Tintern Abbey's" self-reflexive structure, Shelley's effort to mirror nature's motion in spirit's action, and Wallace Stevens's concern not for supreme fictions but for the energies and powers of concentration focused by our pursuit of them. These rhetorics project imaginative demands that go beyond the stances articulated by the scenic or emotive imaginations, and they require a sense of person different from that developed by poets like Dennis, Hass, and Pinsky. Person cannot be equated simply with a mode of responsive sensitivity or with the judgments embodied in a poet's choices and voices. As John Koethe implies, instead of a self positioned in the world, the poetics of thinking explores a transpersonal self virtually coextensive with the world's existence *as* an object of concern.[1] Instead of defining the self by its specific images, poets in this mode seek ways to escape and transcend dramatic roles that tie them to fixed or fixable positions. If there is to be a relation of person to source, the relation depends on working through and against all the rhetorical temptations poetry holds out. The ideal self-reflexive poet must be able to distance this transpersonal activity from all the structures on which the empirical self relies in order to represent itself in lyrically satisfying ways.

Robert Creeley is not Hegel (a fact not all to his disadvantage), but he presents a clear and intriguing drama of attempting to come to poetic terms with the problems and possibilities of the Hegelian imperative in modern guise:

> Conventional order tends to break up towards the end of the nineteenth century, a sense of serial order that obviously was a part of the experience of that time and the dominance of history and the sense of progress. Many of the conceptions that underlie human experience up to that point, at least in a Western context, tend to yield when we shift from a Newtonian to a Gibsonian concept of the universe. So that serialogy – one thing finding its place with another – becomes a far more complex situation in writing as elsewhere. John Cage is a brilliant instance of this new

sense of how things come together, how they find place with one another.

> Just towards the end of *Words* I had a sense of a use of poetry that would not always be the situation that I would want to call a wrap-up or a set piece, so that each poem becomes singularly complete . . . I found, okay, you read this poem and turned the page, here's another poem, that kind of patterning really got very dull for me.[2]

If we take Creeley at his word, in order to read him properly we must see what he hopes to put in place of this traditional form of patterning and the interpretive styles it requires. This is where Hegel comes in. Creeley makes the activity of thinking, rather than its results, the defining trait of "serialogy." Rendering that activity poetically significant requires new conceptions of the relationship between lyric self-expression and the workings of form.[3] Creeley's poetics of conjecture, then, requires difficult, abstract, often sterile experiments in making art of immediate self-reflective acts. There is little in Creeley's later work that most readers would cherish for careful attention or commit to memory as a special moment of intense lyric experience crystallizing a representative experience. Nonetheless, Creeley's demands for authenticity and his powerful control of the medium during his earlier work suggest that we may ignore a significant condition of the poetic imagination if we fail to give equal scrutiny to these later writings.

The later work is especially interesting to me because I think my critical stance illuminates the pressures driving him to such experiments and offers some plausible ways of appreciating the nature and possible importance of his enterprise. At one pole Creeley establishes a model of the mobility of self, the duplicity of writing, and contexts for lyric structures contaminated neither by the scenic mode nor by the ideological commitments of deconstructionist work on the same problems. In this respect Creeley creates a poetic universe engaging in itself and useful for articulating experimental strategies that we can employ in reading a wide variety of poets, from Diane Wakoski to Charles Bernstein. But I am equally concerned with another pole of his work, the reasons why it may be said to fail or to be extremely limited when compared to the work of the two poets, Rich and Ashbery, who I think provide fuller responses to many of the same imperatives. Because Creeley is so honest and probing a writer he in effect creates a demonic alter ego whose pains and problems provide an index of what it may take to respond successfully to the artistic and cultural pressures on contemporary poets.

II

The problems and possibilities are perhaps clearest in "Thinking," a poem explicitly concerned with pure self-consciousness:

> Had not
> thought
> of it . . .
>
> Had nor thought
> nor vacancy –
>
> a space
> between. Linkage:
>
> the system, the
> one after another –
>
> Though the words
> agree? Though
>
> the sounds
> sound. The sea,
>
> the woods, those
> echoing hills . . .
>
> Even in a wood
> they stood –
>
> even without sound
> they are around.
>
> Here and there, and
> everywhere.
>
> All you people
> know everything!
>
> All you know you know.
> Hence nothing else to do?
>
> – Laugh at
> that dichotomy.
>
> E.G., the one again
> from another one.
>
> Hold it –
> to unfold it open
>
> He wants to sit down
> on a chair

he holds in the air
by putting it there.

He wants to sleep in a bed
he keeps in his head.[4]

Perhaps the only feature Creeley's poem shares with the progeny of the dominant mode is its participial title. Yet even here the participial action is not qualified by a phrase placing it in a specific dramatic context. Thinking appears as an act whose basic place is simply in a given process, so the poem begins with a series of negations refusing the placements any single or simple context might afford. In this quest for freedom the poem also denies all that might get it approved in a typical creative writing class. It does not seek evocative power through developed image and metaphor; it plays with rather than relies upon fixed formal properties; and above all it does not produce the specific imaginary situation or dramatic context that in most good poems provides an exemplary concrete focus for the reader's affective energies. In fact, Creeley here is so concerned with playing off parodic and lyric aspects of his consciousness that the poem only occasionally offers any sensuous appeal.

But all these refusals become in Creeley's hands a form of counterpressure on easy lyric emotion. Shorn of illusionistic drama, the poem can achieve significant meaning only by exaggerating the internal movements employed by "The Rain." Here the meaning is almost entirely in the motion of mind as it thematically and stylistically reflects upon its own productive activity. Instead of developing an illusionistic drama, the poem literally exemplifies its subject matter: The poetry resides simply in the way Creeley calls attention to the nature of thinking. At one pole the poem becomes one of many notations fixing for a moment an aspect of Robert Creeley's "condition." As thinking, certain aspects of the self appear in as unmediated a form as possible. There is no deflection into a staged rhetorical situation that doubles the self it purports to reveal in performance. At the other pole, the immediacy takes us beyond the person to a very general abstract and transpersonal dimension that serves as the ground on which the person's activity can appear. Creeley's poem recalls Mallarmé's demand that the mind's action at once make and become a place sufficient unto itself.

The poem has four basic movements. The first shows Creeley in his finest philosophical mode. It begins tentatively, groping through enjambments, through a rich play between "thought" as fixed noun and as verb, and most important, through a series of negations. In the beginning, if it is to be genuine beginning, activity must locate itself primarily in negation, because thinking is precisely the effort to negate what is already "thought" so that the mind can reach fresh perceptions. The mind desires to occupy a "space between" objectified thought and the vacancy of pure desire or "want." This space between has a complex relationship to the idea of "linkage," at least as I read the third and fourth stanzas. On the one hand, linkage is necessarily a function of system, wherein one becomes conscious of being placed among other ones; and on the other, linkage can trap thinking if it merely repeats a linear serial model in which one merely follows other ones.

We need this double reading of linkage to make sense of the next, somewhat problematic and disappointing section. Part of Creeley's charm is his willingness to parody parts of himself, but the disgust is often heavy-handed. These six stanzas use pronounced parodic rhymes to contrast the two different possibilities of linkage. In the first three, rhyme plays off the differences between empty abstract connection and the possible emergence of distinct particulars that thinking brings into focused relationships almost in spite of the words that must be employed. (This focusing process I take as developed in the movement from unmodified nouns to the indefinite article in stanza 3, to different references of the definite article – first to verbal elements and then to perceptual objects – and finally to the demonstrative "those" which places the hills in a context of memory and expectations.) Then the ensuing three stanzas present a desperate moment where the thinker finds his particularity absorbed into the internal echoes of the linkage systems that he must use to express his acts.

Caught in a vacuous self-hatred, the writer attempts to generalize about the activity taking place. But this attempt only further distances the subject from experience and the "I" from the "you". There is only a dichotomy between empty frustrated desire and a sense of tautological repetition ("all you know you know"). Now, however, a return to self-consciousness can be more than a simple negation. Laughing at the condition allows a new sequence in the form of a new sense of sequence: "the one again / from another one" both explains the dichotomy and becomes a means for escaping it, by suggesting that the ones can combine in endlessly varied ways. The crucial fact is that thinking can concentrate attention, can momentarily halt movement ("hold it" or "stop") in order to allow speculation on the unfolding openness of relationships. Here, as so often in Creeley, mind's activity has erotic analogues. Mere repetition gives way to engaged and accepting attention, and the "it" literally unfolds to refer to the dichotomy, to a possible object of thought, and to the process of thinking itself.

The Creeley of *Words* would have stopped here, once thinking has provided a lyrical sexual analogue momentarily resolving and giving value to its quest for meaning. In this poem, however, Creeley seems to suspect that the logic of lyric closure simplifies and distorts the more diffuse logic of thinking and the perverse motives informing the need for thought. For at this moment of possible resolution the poem makes its apparently most arbitrary leap, a leap whose meaning I can only guess at. Indeed, I think that the fact of this leap and the difficulty of interpreting it in effect become the content, for the primary point here is the need for thinking to keep moving, to prevent the poem or the self from stopping in celebration of itself. One must be generated continually from another one. The presentational act becomes extremely complex, because even insisting on this need can produce the collapse into precisely what thinking must resist. The poet faces the tendency in thinking to seek objectivist rest and to become only thought. Thus the last lines present the states of tautology he has feared throughout the poem. The rhyme and the balancing of sense and verse contrast sharply with the opening negations and enjambments. Similar traps dominate the thematic level as typical contexts for sexual desire become merely abstract mental objects. Thinking here reduces its own activity to content – openness becomes only a concept of openness – and as the thinker recedes into sheer mental space, the sexual echoes of holding and openness lead to a parodic masturbatory solipsism – sleeping in a bed one keeps in one's head – so that one remains untouched and untouchable. Thinking extends desire, but thought can trap it in a state where desire is only its own object, cut off from other relationships. What closure the poem finally has suggests that thinking does not breed resolution but moves in continual polarity between moments of vision and returns to empty abstraction and tautological rhyme.

Both the form and the content of this poem enable us now better to understand how and why Creeley is bored with traditional lyric models and rejects the constraints of the well-made mimetic utterance. His is a poetics of conjecture rather than closure, a poetics I see as one whose aim is not so much to interpret experience as to extend it by making a situation simply the focus for overlapping reflexive structures, "one again / from another one."[5]

> I like those poems best, in a way where you posit a problem and see how much energy you can generate for it to survive as a question . . . Conjecture is a great word. Olson really dug it. I wanted a situation where you could speculate or kind of brood on – not in a depressed sense – but where you could sort of play with something in your head that couldn't be resolved in any simple manner. . . I'm interested primarily in questions of thinking, if that's the way thinking creates questions a "condition of speculative wonder" and also if that's the way it tries to

articulate what it feels as real. This way of thinking, conjectural, is a very curious and provocative mind-set.[6]

The only evaluative criterion for this conjectural mode is the degree of the poet's "activity," in terms of "energy of thought" and density of things happening. This standard, then, supports an opposition between what Olson called an "optative" method of writing and a field poetics devoted to the writer's sense of what comes of the "moment of possibility." The optative mode is characterized by an author's "particularized determined choice among possibilities" when they are subjected to the external constraints of plot, theme, verse form, metaphoric pattern, and so on, which, once chosen, dictate or at least greatly limit further specific choices.[7] The author has a purpose independent of his specific momentary engagements.

In field poetics, or the poetics of conjecture and extension, on the other hand, purpose is rejected in favor of simple "paying attention," on all levels, to possibilities of thinking that emerge as the poet opens up what is folded into some initial subject or condition. The poem is less a well-made object than an opportunity, a play of energies created by what Duncan calls the passages and crossings of mind, text, and world. Such a method has as its corollary a vision of the person that idealizes restless intensity (or intense restlessness) and scrupulous honesty. Creeley's style cannot coexist with scenic stasis because all artifice must become subject to explicit self-reflection. But then self-reflection is constantly endangered by finding as its contents only what is in one's head. The very processes that are intended to free the person from covert narcissism may become a prison.

Creeley, thus, leaves us with a perplexing challenge. Clearly one can be ascetic and scrupulous enough to avoid all the options we have so far considered. Even sincerity can be separated from scenic self-staging, and discursiveness can be absorbed within the intense movements of an anxious dialogue with the self. But the rewards may not be worth the effort. Intense self-reflection and radical lucidity may purchase self-knowledge at too high a price, perhaps even a price one need not pay.

III

For Creeley the price must be paid. His goal is not only self-knowledge but awareness of the possible grounds one must recognize if one is to speak of a self at all. Locating this ground requires that one find a way of adapting the intensity of the solitary lyric to the endless processes of self-qualification (in both senses of the term) that constitute "poetic thinking." This undertaking leads Creeley to explore the possi-

bility of treating writing as a process of elaborating and exploring sequences. The desire to create complex poetic sequences is by no means
distinctive to him. But his way of approaching the problem certainly is,
for even with sequences he is not content with some illusionistic model
of time and change. To his abstract mind poetic sequences must ultimately be about sequencing, must make the activity of seeking order the
principle of order and of meaning. His recent series of poems as travel-
ogues provides a clear example. The volumes are in effect held together
by the emotions basic to travel, by a quest to balance on every level two
fundamental tensions. A need for rest must be reconciled with a peren-
nial restlessness that is for him the source of creativity,[8] and learning to
let go from the hold of the past must coexist with a need to preserve the
forms and memories that still define him, shape his experience, and help
structure his desires.

These themes have as their aesthetic analogue the necessity of defining
a satisfying relationship between ground or base and free variation. In
developing poetic sequences, Creeley wants to "let what world I do have
be the world,"[9] so that he can establish a ground for recurrence without
having that ground too narrowly dictate what can be let go and what
experienced in the present:

> one possible, something
> not in mind still as
> my mind, my way I
>
> persist only in wanting
> only in thinking, only now
> in waiting for that way
>
> to be the way I can
> still let go, still want, and
> still let go, and want to.[10]

The movements here from "want" to "want to," from "still" as temporal
adverb to "still" as condition of timelessness, from absence to possibility,
and above all from the desiring "I" (beautifully dangling at stanza end in
its persistent wanting) to an "I" who lets go out of desire rather than
necessity, all in effect dramatize what is available to a self that tries to
align itself with a field of thinking. To "let go, and want to," is to find a
place in the very process of traveling, is ultimately to find momentary
peace within what "Later" poses as a terrifying sense of death everywhere imminent and immanent.

This relationship between traveling and place, or, more abstractly, between thinking and possible grounds of intelligibility and value, enables
us to connect Creeley's distrust of optative poetics with his concern for

a new aesthetic relational space based on non-Newtonian serialogy. Value – both aesthetic and personal – has always been for Creeley a function of content or measure and not a property established by either interpretive generalizations or the pure particularity of things in themselves. Thus as early as the 1965 Berkeley poetry conference we find him insisting that Williams's and Olson's ideas of measure entail fixing particulars in terms of "relational qualifications."[11] In his early poetry the active, writing self established these relationships. His recent work embodies these qualifications in poetic structures capable of capturing multiple forms of relationship and shifting degrees of relevance among particulars. The interplay of letting go and still wanting becomes a model of coherence the age demands:

> I know that Williams, in his later life particularly, began to be very dismayed and depressed and in some ways even confused about what were the actual possibilities of coherence within this context of free verse. The very term to me indicates a reaction to a previous sense of order . . . that which we call a poem. One could use set modes of coherence, a sonnet or whatever the mode might be, and could gain a very lovely articulate patterning within that structure. But again, you see, our times, so to speak, have really confronted head on a very altered conception of how the world seems to be . . . Music, probably, at least in the arts, led the way into that problem and began to make the most articulate solutions . . . Senses of duration . . . senses of the modality being a diversity instead of one containment. . . I did want to know what did the possibilities of coherence have other than what was previously the case.[12]

In traditional poetics, specific systems – both formal and conceptual or dramatic – establish a single, general overriding structure of relationships. In a poetics of conjecture, on the other hand, systems are allowed to overlap: Their task is not to define but to place by composing the particular in terms of the difference and similarities with other objects, events, and thoughts occurring in a process of thinking. Each relationship presents one possible use for the particular, and as relationships expand we begin to get some measure of how the specific detail attains significance (or significances) within the multiple contexts constituting an agent's human condition.[13] As Creeley puts it, in one of the passages connecting his existential and aesthetic concerns, "take / everything I know / and put it out there, where it's got to go."[14] What one knows must be allowed to go – all things pass away – and yet ideally as they pass they also find an imperative defining their placement in a larger field.[15] "There" is finally not completely alien to the self; on one level at least, it becomes the precondition for recognizing "here," because "there" is the structure of relations by which, as in a mirror, we know that and how one is here. "If one's still / of many, / then one's not alone"[16] applies both to the ego and to the contexts establishing the coordinates by which one takes a fix on oneself.

IV

Placing is necessarily a dialectical process. As Eliot indicated in his remarks on tradition, the attempt to relate poets to their historical groundings also entails redescribing those grounds. In Creeley's case, the process of establishing the historical forces generating his obsession with system and relationship also requires us to reconsider how we might best describe basic post-modern imperatives. Consider, for example, the significance of Creeley's concern for "relational qualifications" as an extension of post-modernism. It tempts us to draw one of the boundaries between modern and post-modern poetics according to changing views of the nature and role of grounding structures. If I might put the case baldly and omit necessary qualifications, modernist poetics can be seen as stressing the presence or absence of a single privileged system of explanation giving meaning and purpose to particulars, whereas self-consciously post-modern writers have become increasingly conscious of the multiple systems that all have equal explanatory power in appropriate circumstances.[17] In the high modernism of Yeats, Eliot, Crane, and aspects of Stevens and Pound, the central fears were nausea and narcissism – the former a sense of the meaninglessness of objective reality and the latter a corollary fear that one's values might be mere fantasies of a desperately solipsistic ego. The way beyond these dilemmas, the way to what Olson called the other side of despair, was to find, through the imagination and high-cultural tradition, metaphysical principles or ethical visions that might order experience and create an organic community. The ideal of system, as Yeats put it, was to hold reality and justice in a single thought. And when his and Eliot's metaphysical visions would no longer suffice, the Auden group sought other privileged explanatory systems in Marxism and psychoanalysis.

Objectivist quests for rest and the scenic poets' desire for moments of personal composure can be seen as ways of preserving forms of lyric order not dependent on such problematic unities of vision. It is individual constructive acts or emotional states that suffice to resolve poems. But whether such resolutions derive from a sense of personal voice or from form, they earn only atomistic glimpses of order not themselves connected or connectable to recurring patterns and energies (except for vague traces of belief in deep levels of shared natural forces). A fully capable post-modernism, for Creeley and Ashbery, at least, cannot withdraw into momentary solutions but must engage explicitly in dismantling the modernist sense of order and constituting plausible alternatives. Hence they preserve the demand for "system" (as *Three Poems* puts it) while suspending its and their compulsive dimensions. A sense of system serves as a provisional measure, suggesting links between lyric moments but with no interpretive authority over them. The effect is a very different dialectic from that of modernism. The pressure of a terrifying and empty meaninglessness becomes the pressure of a world and a self caught up in the play of overdetermination and underdetermination that results from the uncontrollable interplay of overlapping signifying systems. In Joyce, in middle Stevens, as well as in O'Hara, Ashbery, Pynchon, and contemporary French theory and practice, the writer's project is to dramatize that multiplicity, to suffer its instability, and finally to construct imaginative means for living and creating meaning and value within these shifting frames.

The quickest and most pronounced way of marking the general difference I am describing is to reflect upon changes in the philosophical climate of our century, for I do not think that writers have yet fully worked out the possibilities of the provisional, conjectural stance. Early in the century the two dominant traditions in Europe were Hegelian and analytic, each in its own way committed to the priority of a single synthetic mode of discourse and each equating truth with a specific version of scientific reason. (Their anthropological analogues might be Frazer and Malinowski; their psychological ones, Jung and Watson.) Now Hegel has passed through Heidegger's distrust of all a priori metaphysics to Derrida's deconstructive version of *Aufhebung* as the endless, nondialectical play of supplements. And logical atomism has given way to what the later Wittgenstein termed an emphasis on methods of projection by which meaning is roughly equated with use (not with reference to a fixed ontological realm of facts) and context determines the appropriate predicates to be employed in specific descriptions.[18] Metaphysics yields to measure, and interpretation to conjecture or to play, depending on whether the writer does or does not accept probabilistic criteria for provisional explanation.

These generalizations will lead us back to Creeley by way of Williams, whose career most clearly manifests the pressures on poetry, especially on objectivism, arising from this shift in sensibility. In his earlier objectivist writing, Williams found an alternative to inclusive systems in a poetry that contented itself with metonymic concentration on the multiple forms concrete experience might take when measured by the compositional activity of the poet.[19] Williams sought neither systematic ex-

planation nor metaphysical ground for his activity but located its value
in the energies it disclosed and put in relation: In the activity of composing the poet constructs an object that at once presents and measures a
specific interaction between mind and concrete situation so that linguistic
and perceptual orders intensify one another. Here measure is reconciled
with traditional expectations about form and closure because the parameters and structure of the poem are coextensive with their counterparts
in the concrete situation evoked. The mind's recognition of its own dependence, for example, is completely expressed in its mode of apprehending a wheelbarrow or an elm tree. Early Creeley adapts this poetic.
In fact, Creeley may have been the most original of Williams's many
followers, because he altered the objectivist aesthetic from emphasis on
concrete perceptions of objects and events to emphasis on concrete renderings of complex movements of the self-reflexive psyche. *For Love*
blends objectivist poetics and the confessional lyric ego, disciplining the
latter by analytic attention to the fundamental building blocks of discourse while extending the former to include a fuller sense of personality
and the pressures of the desiring, speaking voice.

Creeley's synthesis, however, is an unstable one, because the energies
and desires he works with cannot be as easily focused or limited to specific dramatic situations as can the energies of perception. Creeley, in
short, discovered quickly what came to Williams only near the end of his
career and, if I am correct, has not yet come to most contemporaries:
Discrete metonymic poetic objects cannot give full expression to the
energies that seek rest in them or create space for reflecting on the relationships their coherence and power depend upon. Modes of relationship
must become the direct subject and field of poetic reflection. The result
is not a simple poetics of free play and attention to surfaces but the exploration of modes of expression that might allow the lyric subject to
recognize how its multiple facets come to bear on specific situations.

In his objectivist lyrics Williams sought two fresh dimensions of poetic
experience that are difficult to integrate. He wanted to escape traditional
forms of lyric emotion and exalted discourse (or the satiric consciousness
of early Eliot and Pound that results from an ironic distance between
what one sees and what one feels can satisfy traditional lyric desires), so
that the poem might articulate acts of attention more closely linking the
poetic imagination with conditions of ordinary experience. And he sought
in these acts a more expansive realm of authorial activity and engagement not constrained by either dramatic or interpretive ideas about the
subject or the object of poetry. However, his painterly model and insistence on the poem itself as discrete measured object maintained too sharp
a distinction between personal and aesthetic space. The well-formed poem,
no matter how experimental its structure or uses of colloquial language

and situation, still focused energies centripetally rather than centrifugally. Objectivist lyrics could achieve intensity and precision only at the price of limiting the range, variety, and complexity of materials they could handle.

It is in this context that I think Williams's later experiments with the variable foot (and the confusions about measure and coherence that Creeley notes) can best be understood. The variable foot places the burden of structure on units of discourse rather than on the constituent units of a single concrete scenic space reinforced by dramatic illusions. Thus it offers the poet the promise of expanding the poem in both subject matter and the variety of feelings and thoughts that might be expressed – while preserving a sense of measure and structure. Consider the changes that occur in "The Desert Music" and "Asphodel, That Greeny Flower." For perhaps the first time since the romantics, a major poet relaxes in his work, really takes off his stilts or drops his ironic defenses and responses to experience without overtly imposing lyric and aesthetic intensity upon it. The burden of being poetic, a burden that almost destroyed Victorian poetry and helped lead Eliot first to despair and then to religion, is allowed to fall simply on the direct speech of the poet, with all its wanderings and repetitions (and unfortunate pretensions). Consequently, what the poems lose in virtuosity and focused meditation, they sometimes gain in immediacy and a sense of direct confrontation with the pressures demanding poetic speech: All the elements of content and structure appear as measures of a specific existential condition. The poem becomes, as Creeley puts it, simply a process of tracking one's life.[20] The poet overhears himself reflecting directly on his experiences as they unfold in the thinking of writing, and poems come to appear as results of situations, or of a condition, rather than as the deliberate creation of imaginary worlds; poetry perhaps comes as close as it can to a zero degree of imaginative projection.

Once poetry approaches radical naturalness and brings the lyric voice within domestic experience, however, it produces the need to create a space where it can take responsibility for its rhetorical energies. When they ignore this need, Williams and Creeley are reduced to poets who work like cameras, fixing brief moments that compel attention. But it is in fact because of this problem that both poets place such emphasis on pure constructive energy as a form of thinking that keeps attention a fully active state, without the risk of displacement inherent in poetic efforts to impose elaborate metaphoric interpretations on the events rendered. In rejecting the forms of ideality endorsed by modernist pursuits of "nobility," these poets put enormous pressure on themselves to correlate the empirical immediacy with a continual sense of the powers that can remain active in such a constricted world. Creeley has gradually been coming to recognize that the most direct response to the problem could be the best – concentrating on a dialectic between "here" and "there" that may be essential to the life of thinking.

When the goal is no longer to make single structures for experience, it becomes possible to shift one's emphasis from the coherent structures the mind can make to what is available to the mind on a given occasion. The poet can devote attention to the ways in which an experience raises multiple structures of concern and interacts with complex sets of interpretive predicates, from life and from art, which members of our literate society are likely to bring to bear on them. As Robert Duncan puts it, the poet need not simply present a lyric state but can reflect upon the structures of concern which that lyric state is reflection of. And because the structures the poet reflects upon are not simply dramatic projections, consciousness of self in a situation is more a matter of placing the self amid forces than of recovering some original source of expressive energies. There is little imperative to the endlessly regressive symbolist quest to unearth (or make earthly) an angel or daimon or Major Man. Once one accepts the containing conditions as a set of multiple systems in continual play, it is possible to treat principles of relationship as concretely present in the actual processes of experience.

This is the lesson of the later Wittgenstein and the example of Williams's last work. For Williams the structures of imaginative concern do not reside in the inner, often transcendental, recesses of the mind but are manifest in the enduring qualities of one's perceptions and one's interactions with other people. In "Asphodel," for example, the further poetry goes toward plain speech, the more fully the poet recognizes that it is the fundamental nature of ordinary language to contain structures that, like love and like memory, enable us to double back on the nature of our relationships and see them as generating the basic energies in which we live and think. When we can attend to and affirm these relationships we can understand how natural desire passes over into the civilized human form of profound concern:

> You have forgiven me
>   making me new again
>   So that here
> in the place
>   dedicated to the imagination
>   to memory
> of the dead
>   I bring you
>   a last flower. Don't think
> that because I say this

> in a poem
>   it can be treated lightly
> or that the facts will not uphold it.
>   Are facts not flowers
>   and flowers facts
> or poems flowers
>   or all the works of the imagination
>   interchangeable?
> Which proves
>   that love
>   rules them all, for then . . .

This folded flower – fact and fiction – is constituted in the poem's doubling back both on Williams's past and on his acts of remembering, so that poetic space and imagistic echoes disclose existential aspects of love and memory. Poem and descriptive content each create a space of relationships that is the expression of love figuring forth the "interval" that "gelds the bomb."[21]

V

From Williams's casual conversational tones to Creeley's obsessive confrontations with solipsism, however, there is a large gap that puts considerably more pressure on the possibility of creating a relational space within which various levels of discourse and personal experience can find places. Williams, after all, manages even in his most relaxed poetry to retain and make significant the aesthetic role of formal coherence. His poems continually double back in their wanderings and, most clearly in "The Desert Music," make the doubling testimony to a single pervasive unifying theme or property like the nature of love and the metaphoric role of music. Creeley, on the other hand, desires to continue exploring more complex subjective states than Williams, with, paradoxically, a much greater commitment to the loose multiplicity inherent in his poetics of conjecture. Condition and conjecture are necessary but difficult complements of one another. Thus Creeley still confronts the demonic cry, "Narcissist, I want,"[22] and still faces a desiring self dogged by emptiness and a self-conscious distrust of the forms of expression the self depends upon. Desire keeps repeating its demands in the same forms and yet is never satisfied.

Nonetheless, these dilemmas reach a partial resolution in his more radical adaptations of Williams's relaxed mode. Once the tension of the short lyric is escaped, it seems possible to allow the patterns of unsatisfied desire their play. If desire cannot be satisfied, at least its occasions can be

partially understood and the energies these desires release accepted on
their own terms. With an expanded space for poetic conjecture, and with
a form that allows reflection without the push to symbol or mimetic
coherence, Creeley finds ways of distancing himself from his insistent
need for connection with and support in others. What he sees as solipsism becomes a condition one can adjust to, even expand, in the recognition that it cannot be escaped. It may be, in fact, that with acceptance
of isolation one arrives at a state something like Wittgenstein's image of
a solipsism properly seen becoming coextensive with a pure realism.[23]
The key to this shift in Creeley's sensibility is his realization of how
multiple the individual ego is: Narcissus, in effect, can see himself fully
only by learning to coordinate his gazes in several pools, in some of
which his image may not be congruent with those in others. The echoing
of these visions constitutes an agent's place. Thus if "myself am system
of an endlessly proliferating consequence," then "I can accept its imper-
manent form and yet realize the energy-field, call it, in which it is one of
many, also one."[24]

Creeley's *Pieces* initiated the process of defining this "one" in terms of
other ones and their systematic interplay. Abstract numerical structures
form a compositional space where the self-reflexive ego finds itself at
once grounded and dispersed. However, the number system is too discrete, impersonal, and inflexible (or internally coherent) to allow expression for the full play of energies and forms of relatedness characterizing
the complex self. Thus much of Creeley's recent work seeks less artificial
contexts for illustrating freedom within "a pervasive emotional field."[25]
Experimental prose reveals to him "an insistent relational possibility of
grouping" that serves as container and resonating ground for moments
of free expression.[26] In this interplay of field and creative activity, the
writing can account for the capacity of the "I" to become one, many, and
again one. "You don't know what I is except as you says so,"[27] but within
the single yet shifting field "I" and "you" are grammatical persons or
stances within a coherent activity. The "as" linking "I" and "you" suggests the interplay of time, space, and modality by which Narcissus can
continually locate and reflect upon his own shifting reflections.

Creeley manages, then, in theory at least, to define a literary space in
which he maintains Olson's distrust of the lyric ego while transcending
purely objectivist or perceptual constructions of the poetic field. In the
discrete well-formed mimetic lyric, reflective space is created by some
form of concrete universal: Abstraction is tempered and focused by a
concrete mimetic situation and the particulars are given interpretive and
affective coherence by the presence of abstractions. For Creeley this ideal
is a procrustean bed, usually producing either a boring bad faith or a
wanting self-consciousness painfully aware of what each role lacks. The

post-modern dream of immediate objective lyrics renouncing conceptual universals for a perceptual sense that anywhere is everywhere avoids these oppositions, but only by imposing the constraints Williams came to recognize.

In his recent work Creeley denies both alternatives in order to retain elements of abstraction and particularity. He incorporates both, but only by stretching each role to limits that cannot be organically reconciled in a single lyric object. He tries to make the abstract contexts of literary space even more abstract than usual and to play in and against literary forms by relating widely divergent particulars on the model of collage. The abstract aspects of his writing no longer function as interpretively controlling given particulars. Instead, they construct a virtually self-contained space consisting of recurrent themes and situations, often drawn from the concrete dramatic contexts of his earlier poems. These abstract factors do not so much interpret particulars as generate them by continually opening up further relationships and memories. In Creeley, themes disseminate rather than gather, but the project is not a Derridean one because deconstruction is not central to it. Creeley wants to replace the conventional symbolic space of particular poems by a kind of notational space that, as in jazz, invites variations and at once gathers and disperses energies as they play off a set of grounding resonances. Or, as he summarizes this dispersing interplay of past themes, memories, and several levels of particulars, one "must walk / all the things of life about which one talked."[28]

The closest analogy I can find for the space of his more recent work is abstract expressionist painting. Throughout his career Creeley has invoked Pollock's view of composition by immediate engagement in a field as a model for his own creative activity. And certainly his lineation offers a drama of intensive choice similar to what one experiences from Pollock's line. But the best general analogies are to painters working with simple, stark relationships. Rothko, for example, exemplifies a principle of form in no way reliant on narrative or dramatic elements. The power of thinking in his characteristic work stems from the way patterns and colors create a field of energies, as if the brush stroke were a means for inhabiting the implicit life and light in the color. This play of energy and form establishes what I take to be the most evocative paradox in modernist art: The more abstract the aesthetic frame is, the more concrete and sensuous are both the details of the painting and the traces of the painter's activity in choosing the particulars.

In Creeley's case, the repeated abstract themes focus multiple relationships among particulars without restricting any given particular to an illustrative symbolic function or to serving an aspect of a constructed dramatic scene. Meaning and coherence in his later work are extensive: The repeated concerns create resonance for particulars while allowing them to be simply what they appear to be in the flow of the writing. The analogue between concept of self and concept of literary particular is a strict one: In both cases there is a need for an objective sense of place and ground for them to be meaningful, yet the more abstract and purely functional that place is, the less bound either is to a limiting single set of concepts and relationships. Prose is Creeley's exemplary medium for this project because it allows abstract contexts and particularity to pull further apart without losing their linkage. Indeed, each pole becomes literal, and each moment evidence that we can accept pure prose without losing all reverberation and succumbing to Sartrean nausea. Multiplicity of relations can replace the attributions of depth that justify scenic, metaphoric styles. This is why Creeley is careful to separate the surreal images in his work from any claims to capture deep natural or psychological forces. Rather, the surreal is one of the ways in which the full play of energies takes us beyond the logic of thought to modes of literalness appropriate to the processes of intense thinking focused within a field:

> With no intention they occur at times, but again they come out of literal states of feeling. They are found in a literal circumstance rather than a fantasy. This book that I've written for Marisol has many surreal situations in it that are literal . . . I was again thinking of Bacon, Francis Bacon, the presences of the images that one finds in his painting are surreal, to put it mildly, but their impact on consciousness comes from the fact that they are a literal reality. They're not about something. It has to be actual . . .[29]

VI

If both self and poem are distributed across these multiple levels, it may be that we cannot rely on traditional interpretive practices for producing coherence in either domain. We do not need interpretations that produce hypotheses about motives in an act, because everything that matters is simply present. The self or the text are within the process of attention displayed (as terms of action, not as rhetorical reactions to a staged situation). There is nothing beyond that field that one can fix as determining meaning. Even when we examine overall patterns there is no place for traditional interpretation, since the abstractions do not create a controlled synthetic grasp of the particulars. Underlying patterns only foster and intensify processes of dissemination. Under these conditions,

Creeley's complex recent work is hard to discuss without either tedious particularity or the generalizing about poetics I have been indulging in. Yet I must demonstrate my points. The best I can do is offer remarks that are more like commentary than interpretation.[30] I shall describe the flow of energies in some particular passages of the later work I find most interesting, the "prose" piece *Mabel*. For the prose reveals both the freedom of conjecture and the constant danger of a medium of lucidity that will become so free from all traces of traditional lyricism that it only denotes, without emotional reverberations for the reader. This is Creeley's version of the dilemma of combining self and a rhetoric of self: He must find a rest that is not literarily dull or repetitious, yet he must be as honest as possible about the specific, nontheatricalized features of his ordinary life as it is lived in the mind.

The first part of *Mabel* consists of the prose from *A Day Book*. It introduces once again all of Creeley's basic themes, now not as urgent discoveries but as aspects of a contemplative field. In order to stress the new tone of his writing, this text is the most abstract and programmatic of the book's three parts. Amid the overlap of familiar themes and various specific scenes exhibiting their place in Creeley's experience, we find several methodological passages like the following:

> Like this – writing – "fitful tracing . . ." No copies, nor intent, nor much at all – but phases . . .

> Phasing. System again, really – or wanting some information as to the context, call it, in which language is being experienced . . . One of the people in the so-called class remarking Beethoven's means of working, not "linearly" as, now this is done, now done, now that is to be done, now that – but in a situation almost spatial (he was speaking of the drafts of the 5th symphony, of B/s taking this from that, and putting it in there, then taking that out, putting in something else, so that the material was both an accumulation and a collection variably possible, i.e., could be "shifted around" in a various formal situation, etc.[31]

Two specific scenes clarify how this spatial field becomes at once accumulation and collection. The opening paragraphs of the text require close attention to the play of reflexive energies:

> He is waking to two particulars. One, that he is to make, before sending it, a copy of the letter, and then realizes the letter has been mailed. And two, that all the assumptions involved in what has happened to himself and his wife, in their so-called fantasy,

are literally assumptions. They are not right or wrong. How is the intersection possible? The light is faint in the room. Overhead he makes out the long beams of the ceiling . . .

The descriptions are such that he cannot trust them or rather, would say, fucking is fucking. Having said that, what to say. She lifts her leg. It sounds like a cow. All the tone is wrong . . .

The letter leads only to further complications. He will pay the money if required to . . . He has never met nor seen him. There is only a somewhat vast emptiness of sentimental assumption to make reason.

We begin at a ritual waking, a beginning that is one among myriad beginnings and a coming to consciousness that has none of the symbolic overtones often attributed to it. Here, within a cycle of beginnings and repetitions and in a literary order where lyrical theatrics and symbolism give way to tentative, unsatisfied, self-conscious scrutiny, is the affective space of Creeley's writing. As particulars emerge they also dislocate consciousness, forcing the agent to self-reflection and to attendant discomforts with the empirical self. In abstract terms, one wakes to encounter two, and a concrete doubleness breeds a variety of tensions – between intersecting demands, between assumptions or inadequate expressions and underlying realities, and above all between what the self desires to be and the many inadequate attitudes this self sees itself assuming with respect to various particulars. (Later these self-parodic attitudes will be associated primarily with Creeley's relationships to women.) Here the two particulars introduce public and private aspects of Creeley's life, and each in turn breeds the pressure to get things right and to negotiate the poet's own errors and uncertainties. Particulars involve proliferating relationships and questions, each with its specific tonal quality and each requiring coming to terms with what wakes in self-consciousness. Moreover, the particulars manage to create affective dimensions without accruing anything so heavy as symbolic meanings and without the sense of imposed congruence that I find in poets like Stafford. The first paragraph manages to set a mental attitude in which the shades of light and the vertical details of window and door retain their distinctness as description and yet evoke objectively the dominant sense of entrapment. Atmosphere does the work of symbol without the strain.

The form of these paragraphs, however, assumes the burden of resisting this entrapment, while at the same time deepening our sense of Creeley's anxiety. By the simple device of reversing the order of the particulars as objects of reflection in the second and third paragraphs, Creeley sets the aesthetic space of writing against the existential pressures presented. Unable to trust descriptions, he still insists on the freedom of mind to present itself groping and conjecturing amid attempts at description. By the end of the third paragraph, the two fields created by the particulars blend in an uncomfortable surreal equation of ego, self-disgust, and muted violence toward his wife. Here, as in much contemporary writing, posing the problems as field for reflection becomes the only mode of resolution, and thinking itself becomes theme and refrain ("Whatever he thinks of seems to twist away, like a fish turning," and "It is all somewhat too linear as if thinking were, he thinks, a line to be followed"). This doubling of thinking – positioned in relation to a world and looking on itself as positioned – demands a writing where linearity gives way to unfolding extensional space. The stage is set for the succeeding entry, which, without explicitly referring to its predecessor, returns to the same themes and images on different levels of generalization and different spheres of dramatic experience. The text has its own ways of waking as the writing mind attunes its self-reflexive capacities for attentive conjecture.

A better example of how the critic must track the relational energies of given fields of experience occurs in a sequence that moves toward momentary satisfaction and resolution. The sequence is the narration of two days,[32] which begins as a summary of the previous senses of discomfort and uncertainty ("All the day has seemed echo after echo of previous condition"). Creeley then gives the description (previously quoted) of his quest to know "what it is to be specifically myself" and from this ground shifts to a series of positive reflections:

> I think the most useful truth I've been given to acknowledge of others, as a man, is that in one's own experience another's is not necessary [sic] denied nor increased . . . one could love *two* – or myriad, as I now find, either in myself or in another, and the relation to *one* is not of that fact lost. Will it be that someday we come to some relation . . . that what they do is more relevant to all their lives, one by one or all in all, than what they didn't. I feel such trust in life, once I stop all that previous qualification – just that I know I'm alive, and witness it with such pleasure in others, *we are here* – I'm happy, in the most simplistic of senses.[33]

The final assertion here captures both the pathos and the power of Creeley's experiment. The prose is as simplistic as the happiness. The ideas are quite elementary and the insistence on making literature of their direct statement almost embarrassing. Yet that simplicity involves substantial risks which in turn establish a contrastive base that dignifies the emotion. Creeley's gesture is as unliterary as Malevich's "White on White," and by the same token, it becomes a complex simplicity because of all the rejections entailed in creating the appearance, the pain, and the vulnerability of an honesty that entails facing oneself when one is not in moments of heightened sensitivity. Such gestures perhaps cannot be offered more than once because negation is not a strong or expansive rhetoric, but here, at least, the shock redeems pathos by art without the perhaps hapless gesture of attempting to transform the self.

Instead of transformation, in fact, Creeley makes of this simplicity a different kind of transitional gesture. Simplicity functions as a condition of permission, an invitation to fill out by a new lyric attention the familiar spheres of experience the writer makes literary by his refusal of literariness. Notice how he expands this moment. Immediately after these abstractions produce a sense of radical concreteness, there follows a quite different kind of abstraction very rare in Creeley. He turns to a sequence made entirely of quotations from writers such as Keats and Defoe. Having reconciled his personal life to experiments in multiplicity, he can explore other forms of echo where diversity thrives without the elements' canceling one another out. The past for Creeley becomes here simply an extension of his present condition: "One path only is left for us to speak of, namely, that *It is*. In this path are very many tokens . . . for now *it is,* all at once, a continuous one."[34]

Then we move from past to a directly rendered personal memory of a sexual encounter between Creeley, another man, and a woman. The unity and multiplicity theme now takes the form of three contented lovers, and the scene (framed again by the windows and French doors of his bedroom) plays off against both the earlier sexual confusions and the tone of tired dissatisfaction. The scene partakes of a recurrent motif in *Mabel,* a demonic view of sexual experience as pure extension of the ego or as pure tautology ("fucking is fucking") where human sexuality is reduced to purely biological functions.[35] But in this context the vitality of the writing enables Creeley to escape these reductive traps. Yet he manages also to avoid the standard symbolic or abstract attempts to dignify sexuality by sublimating it and interpreting it in moral or psychological terms. When the proper context is composed and the mind is clear, sexuality can be celebrated simply for its capacity to occupy a person's full attention.[36] The sexual encounter here becomes fully human and yet resists sublimating metaphor because of its concrete intensity and fully satisfying immediacy. Three can also be one because they can so fully share one space. Ultimately the space depends on the writing because it can integrate those previous acts of thinking which lure feelings and energies to the sexual scene. Creeley's summary makes explicit his dream that pure attention suffices to render a scene a place where imagination can rest: "On the bed, he watched, felt his own cock tense with it, could not see the eyes facing also toward the sight, hers, erotic, lovely, tight with interest, his own, fucking, fucking in knowledge of animals, in delight and permission of animals, gravely, sweetly, humans without fear or jealousy, but intensive increasing provocation."[37]

Moments like this free the other two parts of *Mabel,* "Presences" and "Mabel: A Story," to engage in more intensive and many-faceted trackings of Creeley's personal condition. "Presences," a text playing off Marisol's equally obsessive variations on a set of recurrent themes, is Creeley's most relaxed and meditative work, ranging from personal memories to surreal narratives and purely abstract reflections on spatial relationships. "Mabel: A Story," on the other hand, confines itself essentially to the women, real and imaginary, in Creeley's life and the various stances, fears, and conditions of possibility they produce for him – again on several levels of reality. Both sequences differ from *A Day Book* by virtue of their preference for a purely psychological space, intended to be literal without the mediation of empirically concrete situations. Creeley's condition becomes more fully an internal set of dramas, sustained only by reflection on other memories and fantasies. The basic mark of this difference is a shift from a diary form of notation to a purely abstract set of formal structures based on groupings of three episodes, each of one, two, or three pages.[38] The dream here, I think, is that in abstraction lies freedom, for to be a secure egotist one wants to require no external or dramatic justifications for the mind's attending to what it constructs from what comes before it. All the mind's energies can be released to concentrate on images and thoughts immediately present, with other questions simply bracketed.

Again analogies of collage and abstract expressionism are relevant, especially because depth becomes a function simply of how surfaces fold back upon themselves, and the poet makes no claims to capture any latent realities. For example, the three meditations of the first grouping in "Presences" each deal with discrete imaginary worlds on different levels of psychic reality, yet they overlap and fold upon one another by a repeated theme of the problem of imagining a decent order whose fluidity is measured by different qualities of water imagery. Yet the themes allow no summary; their role is presenting the series of places one comes to dwell in as one pursues recurrent concerns. The echoes among these concerns then free the themes from dramatic urgency and give them the solidity of Marisol's shapes, with also the same capacity to elicit further variations. "Here" and "there," "one" and "many," by virtue of the quotation marks they have come to bear, are no longer contrasted indexes of joy and terror but simply coordinates for an order through which experience can flow.

VII

The very success of these folds as enclosures for the flow of experience also proves a serious drawback. For when the self becomes only a set of abstract relations, the expanded field of play becomes like a flexible cage. Everywhere the world seems to yield, but always the bubble keeps one returning to the particulars of Robert Creeley. In fact, his most recent volume, *Later,* seems to recognize that his concerns for occasions and condition trap him within an inevitably denotational style hard to reconcile with the freedom of thinking. Creeley, in effect, accepts both halves of the Cartesian *cogito* as he concentrates on echoing the style of his earlier work, but in a more reflective mode. Organization here is simply by recurrent themes (which grow somewhat tedious, despite some very moving poems) – the idea of aging, what one can make of the accumulations we call a self, and the will to keep being Robert Creeley. On the one hand there are many lovely lyrics based on the refrain "That's it," which expressses a will to synthesize the particular with a sense of totality so that the poet has an alternative to the pressure of time. But the return to the old style proves a painful burden because the moments of present attention cannot suffice. Duality oppresses:

> "I feel faint here,
> "I feel faint here,
> too far off, too
> enclosed in myself
> can't make love a way out.
>
> I need the oldtime density, . . .

But Creeley has only the old-time will and an asserted heroic solipsism that seems to have slipped by the ironist Creeley – so great is the pain:

> All who know me
> say, *why* this man's
> persistent pain, the scarifying
> openness he makes do with?
>
> Agh! brother spirit,
> what do they know
> of whatever *is* the instant
> cannot wait a minute –

will find heaven in hell,
will be there again even now,
and *will* tell of itself
all, *all* the world.[39]

I emphasize Creeley's withdrawing from his most experimental work, with somewhat mixed results, because I think it indicates a fundamental weakness in his ideas of the conjectural mode. If we can specify this weakness, we may deepen our sense of the pathos in Creeley's work, and we should be able by contrast to indicate why Ashbery's version of a poetics of thinking and Rich's model of selfhood seem more successful styles – for art and for life. One significant clue is the final section of "Presences." Formally the passage returns us to the single unit that also marked the beginning and center of the work. But how are we to take this return? Does form allow materials for free play, or does the very structure that produces resonance by putting facts in contexts necessarily condemn Creeley to a solipsism whose only realism is its absorbtion in his own condition? His tone seems at once celebratory and bitterly self-parodic:

> I began to make self-portraits because working at night I had no other model. Thinks that the world is little. Weather walking, in rain. I used myself over and over again. Sees green. Passing people, goes forward, goes green, goes white. I would learn about myself . . . You are your own best friend.
>   I put things where they belong. I return to reality. People should think of themselves. Walks streets at night, working at night. I had no other model. I used myself over and over. I see you.[40]

Creeley can conclude only with banality, with the slogans of popular psychology, and with a will to find ways to use the banal without being embarrassed by it. A poetics of thinking can at least free us from the structures that must take such truisms, or their evasions, as climactic rewards for heightened sensitivity. But it replaces them only with a sense of variations that remain uncomfortably close to banal repetition. Creeley's aim, I think, is to collapse "The Poet" into the man who suffers and needs, yet who retains sufficient imaginative energy to construct a field for those needs that in its range of affects keeps our and his attention. In this field we find a reflective space where parody is not an end in itself but a means for accepting the various forms of foolishness and inadequacy that are a large part of what one is. If the artist can no longer wield an imagination that Coleridge saw as analogue of God's creative power, he can still learn to move freely and energetically in the space of relatively empty creation to which the solipsist is condemned. Yet there is one sense in which he may succeed too well. The poet threatens to appear only as someone who suffers and needs, and the space he creates for motion seems often to close in on itself with a terrifying repetitiveness. However diffuse the levels of ego, Creeley's poems offer to an audience the specific conditions of a single person who becomes representative only on very abstract levels.

Rich and Ashbery each reveal by contrast what may be unnecessary problems in Creeley's version of poetic thinking. If Creeley must concentrate on the personal self as the source and measure of poetic energies, that self need not be confined to private concerns, nor must it imagine itself as essentially passive, essentially a victim of forces that at best produce conditions that engage one's emotional attention. Creeley confuses a necessary antitheatricalism with a problematic distrust of all self-assertion. Rich, on the other hand, dramatizes a way to contextualize thinking as a process of self-creation for a community firmly rooted in a sense of history. And Ashbery adapts a more complex conjectural mode that also handles a second problem in Creeley: his objectivist equation of lucidity with a spare language suspicious of all excess even when the field for the self is generated largely out of linguistic invention.

Radical invention is incompatible with Creeley's need to keep the conjectural self positioned – if not in dramatic scenes then in clear relational frameworks. Invention then must be confined to fixed patterns that define at least a clear abstract place. Ashbery, on the other hand, never lets the active self and its context become entirely separate realms. Self and context continually interpenetrate, so that invention is both a positing of self and a way of escaping or extending it. This means that his poetry can remain fully conjectural, can praise in the intransitive mode (as David Lehman puts it), and, above all, can make self-consciousness an inherently transpersonal force. Ashbery is not without his disgust at the banalities we have to live by, but he can keep the burden collective. And, more important, when one is not locked into equating the banal with the entrapped specific self, Ashbery can allow himself to treat the existential self as simply one element for the imaginative play of consciousness as it tracks its intricate journeys. For Ashbery the significant "I" is a condition of imagination, not primarily a specific indexical sign, so that he is free to allow himself to enter all the positions of self – as need, as self-delusion, and as lyric celebrant – that are in effect equally as real for anyone in his audience. Moreover, once the "I" is seen as imaginary, several of the problems we saw plaguing other writers about rhetoric and audience become fields for lyric play among the roles of "I" and "you" and the dialectics they impose on each other. Freedom from the documentary impulse of objectivism and its personalist extensions allows Ashbery to explore all the duplicity inherent in discursiveness, in its relation to the world, to the dynamics of language, and to other people.

The corollary of Creeley's sense of self is a narrow drama of self-consciousness. He vacillates between self-disgust and the freedoms of attention and pure thinking. But he cannot introduce into his reflections much sense of history or a broad enough range of concerns to keep the conjecture a complex philosophical movement. So on the one hand he shows the need for the stage of self-making that Rich makes an imperative of poetic thinking, and on the other he cannot create a range and surface richness for his conjecture that compares with Ashbery's. In his poetics of thinking Creeley becomes a victim of what had been his greatest strength: his taut, ascetic language. In short personal lyrics the spare style both intensifies emotional concentration and twists drama toward abstraction. But when the abstraction becomes the site of poetic activity, that same asceticism inordinately narrows the field and impoverishes the sense of self we need to connect the abstractions to experience. Because it lacks conventional modes of concentration and creates its own world, the rhetoric of conjecture must be a lush one. Thinking matters in itself primarily as a generative force, whose full range of effects and affects Ashbery's metaphoric magic introduces on the new nondramatic stage.

Thus Ashbery and Rich each turn on its head a different feature of the myth of lucidity that traps Creeley. Ashbery asks why it should be the case that an ontology of surfaces requires a language whose highest role is to focus attention in intense acts of naming. Perhaps the very fact of reducing reality to surfaces puts the demand on us to invent ways of folding or eliding those surfaces in interesting ways. Perhaps one ought to be able to write Barthes's patient an intricate and evasive note self-consciously unexpressing condolences and thus expressing positively some edges of the subject we would not see at all within our conventional social rituals, or even within our conventional dramatic understanding of what disease and cure are. If, as Novalis said, the only cure for self-consciousness is more self-consciousness, then our most desperate contemporary need may be for means to make a world of surfaces become Stevens's revolving crystal. In that play of light we may in fact find new ways of locating something beneath or within their interactions that requires and rewards the efforts of imaginative expression.

Rich takes the radically different tack of accepting the demand that one concentrate on the denoted historical self. Without that demand a consciousness as capacious and intransitive as Ashbery's may swallow everything and leave no room for the sense of struggle we need to struggle against melodramas of struggle. But one must then construct a self willing to risk melodrama as the price of having something to struggle for and powers of self-staging to struggle with. It may be a mistake to separate conjecture from dramatic scenes. It may be only by working through scenes and by engaging in explicit critical reflections on the temptation of passive narcissism that one fully measures the poet's power to dramatize thinking and thinking's power to make concrete differences in public life.

6
John Ashbery: Discursive rhetoric within a poetics of thinking

Like Creeley, and indeed like all the poets who recognize the need to transform lyric modes in order to save them from their own indulgences, Ashbery struggles to find an attitude by which one earns and explores a self-conscious rhetoric in reaction against rhetorics that claim naturalness. In this respect, at least, romanticism must die. There is no dream of a purified language. In fact, impurity of language becomes a mark of authenticity, since it registers the poet's awareness of the duplicity of discourse and the complexity of intentions. In impurity is our freedom and our salvation. For Ashbery this is a good deal more than a slogan, and ultimately it comes to involve a good deal more than rhetoric. In the muddiness and muddledness of language he finds grounds for recovering the philosophical ambitions of high modernism. Concern for rhetoric becomes a meditation on rhetoricity, on what is involved in our being thrown into a language that on the one hand corrupts all it touches and on the other keeps promising to take us beyond its corruptions to some still point where all nouns are verbs and all metaphors what Frye calls literal assertions of identity:

So I cradle this average violin that knows
Only forgotten showtunes, but argues
The possibility of free declamation anchored
To a dull refrain, the year turning over on itself
In November, with the spaces among the days
More literal, the meat more visible on the bone.
Our question of a place of origin hangs
Like smoke: how we picnicked in pine forests,
In coves with the water always seeping up, and left
Our trash, sperm and excrement everywhere, smeared
On the landscape, to make of us what we could.[1]

I shall concentrate here on what Ashbery makes of our making of us
what we can.[2] This means first of all recognizing the averageness of our
violins and thus taking a critical stance on those rhetorics – public and
private – which promise release from "our trash . . . smeared / On the
landscape" into a theater of noble roles and symbolic depths. Only then
does Ashbery's greatness and cultural significance fully emerge, for out
of this critical self-reflexiveness he creates terms for a new lyricism. I
want to trace some of the basic strategies and thematic emphases characterizing this project, first in his radical transformations of conventional
lyric subjects, then in two ways he builds upon the sense of person and
language established by those transformations. Ultimately, I hope to show
how he creates a form or site of poetic thinking where we can imagine
the life of Major Man become available in our minor keys.

Ashbery's recent work can be seen as an increasingly ambitious dialogue with modernism. How, he asks, can poetry serve significant cultural roles without asserting special powers of poetic integration that in
fact blind it to its own impotence and conceal the powers it does have?
Thus where Eliot seeks to fill out the vision of Tiresias, Pound those of
Odysseus, Malatesta, and "hosts of an ancient people," and Stevens that
of the humbler but equally exemplary stance of an ordinary citizen of
New Haven, one of Ashbery's most characteristic speakers is "Daffy Duck
in Hollywood." Daffy is obviously a figure of the paralysis inherent in a
world where there is neither force nor authority in high-cultural traditions, but he is equally a figure of the new freedom such a vision brings,
because it enables us to stop dreaming of cures for our anxieties. Daffy
shares Hass's concern for building personality through a strong sense of
"the limits of imagination," but he captures the inescapable imaginary
role playing that is an active function of acknowledging these limits. It
seems somewhat ridiculous to hope for salvation in high culture, since
that culture has produced us as its ony heirs and has left fantasies where

we expected syntheses forged by a Coleridgean "poetic logic." But the multiplicity of those traditions and the inventiveness that kept producing in order to avoid looking very hard at its progeny remain a testimony to a kind of strength, once we learn to look with eyes not clouded over by nostalgic melodramas. Parody brings its own forms of passion and compassion, a lesson Creeley's objectivist vision could not handle:

> There were to whom this mattered not a jot: since all
> By definition is completeness (so
> In utter darkness they reasoned), why not
> Accept it as it pleases to reveal itself . . .
> The pattern that may carry the sense, but
> Stays hidden in the mysteries of pagination.
> Not what we see but how we see it matters; all's
> Alike the same, and we greet him who announces
> The change as we would greet the change itself . . .
> No one really knows
> Or cares whether this is the whole of which parts
> Were vouchsafed – once – but to be ambling on's
> The tradition more than the safekeeping of it. This mulch for
> Play keeps them interested and busy while the big,
> Vaguer stuff can decide what it wants – what maps, what
> Model cities, how much waste space. Life, our
> Life anyway, is between.[3]

Modernist poetry has characteristically concerned itself with this "betweenness" as a historical, stylistic, and epistemological condition. What distinguishes Ashbery are the diffidence and somewhat self-indulgent self-contempt with which he poses the problems and the ironic flattening he gives to the dreams of releasing the "pattern" or the "big, / Vaguer stuff" from the mysteries of pagination. For betweenness can no longer be a clear transition from corrupt surfaces to revivifying pattern. Culture is nothing else but the formation of what tradition makes of us as we try to make ourselves in it. Consequently, there are no single maps we can hope to reconstruct. Eliot's purposive burglar is himself the unwitting victim of his play because his very resistance to his culture may be one of the roles by which the "big, / Vaguer stuff" takes the forms it wants. As we continue to explore the patterns of mind released by "poetic logic," we find ourselves no longer masters of those patterns. Rather, we experience judgment itself as a vacillation between creating and being created by the poetic space it inhabits. Just as what we see threatens to collapse into who we are, only the quality of our seeing remains a viable principle for distinguishing between victimhood and vision. The poem responsive to modern history must learn to balance these desires, to share Tiresias's prophetic wisdom with the inescapable sense of oneself as a version of Daffy Duck. Our problems may be the result less of the poverty of spirit than of the poverty of representational means still uncontaminated by the spirit's sublimely destructive enterprise of attempting to know itself.

If "Daffy Duck in Hollywood" makes apt commentary on modernist ambitions, "Metamorphosis" strikes closer to home by applying analogous perspectives on the project of the personalized, naturalistic lyric:

> The long project, its candling arm
> Come over, shrinks into still-disparate darkness,
> Its pleasaunce an urn. And for what term
> Should I elect you, O marauding beast of
> Self-consciousness? When it is you,
> Around the clock, I stand next to and consult?
> You without a breather? Testimonials
> To its not enduring crispness notwithstanding,
> You can take that out. It needs to be shaken in the light.
>
> To be delivered again to its shining arm –
> O farewell grief and welcome joy! Gosh! So
> Unexpected too, with much else. Yet stay,
> Say how we are to be delivered from the fair content
> If all is in accord with the morning – no prisms out of order –
> And the nutty context isn't just there on a page
> But rolling toward you like a pig just over
> The barges and light they conflict with against
> The sweep of low-lying, cattle-sheared hills.
> Our plight in progress. We can't stand the crevasses
> In between sections of feeling, but knowing
> They come once more is a blessed decoction –
> Is their recessed cry.
>
> The penchant for growing and giving
> Has left us bereft, and intrigued, for behind the screen
> Of whatever vanity he chose to skate on, it was
> Us and our vigilance who outlined the act for us.
> We were perhaps afraid, and less purposefully benevolent
> Because the chair was placed outside, the chair
> No one would come to sit in, except the storm,
> If it ever came. No shame, meanwhile,
> To sit in the hammock, or wherever straw was
> To see it and acclaim the differences as they were born.

And we were drunk as flowers
That should someday be, or could be,
We weren't keeping track, but just then
It all turned the corner into a tiny want ad:
Someone with something to sell someone
And the stitches ceased to make sense.
They climb now, gravely, with each day's decline
Farther into the unmapped sky over the sunset
And prolong it indelicately. With maps and whips
You came eagerly, we were obedient, and then, just then
The real big dark business got abated, and I
Awoke stretched out on a ladder lying on the cold ground,
Too upset and confused to imagine how you
Had built the colossal staircase in my flesh that armies
Were using now, their command a curse
As all my living swept by, the flags curved with stars.[4]

Here a discursive poetry is set against both the mode of restrained lyrical judgment and any discursive project for getting beyond such romanticism. Confronted in the epigraph to *Praise* with a somewhat similar, although more generalized, beast, Hass finds an imperative to praise him. Ashbery, instead, disarms him by absorbing him into the conditions of awareness and opportunities for language he makes possible. On the one hand the beast is a complete demystifier, "with maps and whips" tormenting us for our vanities and ultimately reducing our dreams that identity can be a "long project" to the "tiny want ad" that emerges as identity's ultimate text and pretext. Yet in acknowledging the banality and inevitability of our temptations to lyric song, the poem makes its awareness of our duplicities itself a field for lyric exuberance and remarkably precise public statement. By refusing the vain poses of definite thoughts, the poem produces a self-consciousness capable of moving from perception to reflection, from immediacy to self-criticism to the opportunities for linguistic play that the multiple folds of consciousness allow. The very poses we cannot escape dramatize the infinite capacities of the mind and language "pretending to resist but secretly giving in so as to reappear / In a completely new outfit and group of colors once today's / Bandage has been removed."[5] Thus the spirit of discursiveness, a refusal to indulge in the traditional temptations of lyricism and literariness, becomes the basis of a new lyrical theater. One can have one's lyrical self, without devouring it too, so long as one employs critical self-consciousness to preserve a distance sufficient to keep us from even dreaming we can equate the self, or selves, we stage and the empirical agent caught up in existential demands.

II

Distance, however, is not enough. We need to see what becomes of the existential self and its relation to lyrical emotion in poems less concerned with parody than with passion. this is where Ashbery's version of the poetics of thinking opens new alternatives to conventional dramatic ways of presenting and understanding the forms of relatedness and patterns of unfolding central to our emotional lives. Given the distrust of depth evident in both the content and the voice of "Daffy Duck," Ashbery must define an alternative to the assumption that the quality of poetic imagination resides primarily in its powers to interpret actions or situations. He subjects the normal concentrative focus of the lyric imagination to a series of self-conscious dispersals over apparently diverse associations, so that his work has at least the appearance of basing value on the capacity to engage fully in continually shifting degrees of emotional intensity.

Dispersal among motives, then, will be my central theme, itself motivated by Ashbery's rationale for a different way of locating the interface between aesthetic and existential qualities:

> No longer is there any question of adjusting a better light on things, to show them ideally as they may never have existed, of taking them out from under the sun to place them in the clean light that meditation surrounds them with. Youth and happiness, the glory of first love – all are viewed naturally now with all their blemishes and imperfections. . . The proper perspective is not to exaggerate the importance in the general pattern of living of the disabused intellect, whose nature is to travel from illusion to reality and on to some seemingly superior vision, it being the quality of this ebbing and flowing motion rather than the relevance of any of its isolated component moments that infuses a life with its special character.[6]

It is important to notice that Ashbery, like most experimental writers, interprets his rejection of idealizing representation as a gesture toward a more complete mimesis. Life and character itself lose their character when they are too quickly submitted to any simple logic dictated by representational or interpretive desires. To confirm this fact, we need only recall the reduction of spirit in the service of putative psychological depths we find in deep-image poetry or the trap imposed by the use of single identities in confessional poetry, in Creeley, and in those transformations of the scenic mode we have discussed. For Ashbery, mimesis entails multiplicity, entails capturing the many levels of diction and explanatory possibilities (each involving a different modality of self-consciousness) that "reflect the maximum of my experience when I'm writing."[7] The motive here is not to represent confusion but to dramatize qualities of mind, shifts of emotional levels, and possible structures of coherence among dispersed particulars and interpretive codes:

> The shape filled foreground: what distractions for the imagination, incitements to the copyist, yet nobody has the leisure to examine it closely. But the thinness behind, the vague air: this captivates every spectator.

> There were so many things held back, because they didn't fit into the plot or because their tone wasn't in keeping with the whole . . . The rejected chapters have taken over. For a long time it was as though only the most patient scholar or the recording angel himself would ever interest himself in them. Now it seems as though that angel had begun to dominate the whole story . . . one can almost hear the beginning of the lyric crack in which everything will be lost and pulverized, changed back into atoms ready to resume new combinations and shapes again, new wilder tendencies, as foreign to what we have put in and kept out as a new chart of elements on another planet.[8]

Perhaps the strongest, most resonant of these polyphonic possibilities is the blend of naturalism and idealism in Ashbery's often-quoted description of how pronouns function in his work as dispersals of the dramatic. The mild self-irony does not cancel the sense of intriguing new directions:

> The personal pronouns in my work very often seem to be like variables in an equation. "You" can be myself or it can be another person . . . and my point is also that it doesn't matter very much, that we are somehow all aspects of consciousness giving rise to the poem and the fact of addressing someone, myself or someone else, is what's the important thing at that particular moment rather than a particular person involved. I guess I don't have a very strong sense of my own identity and I find it very easy to move from one person in the sense of a pronoun to another and this again helps produce a kind of polyphony in my poetry which I again feel is a means toward greater naturalism.[9]

Dramatic person gives way to the qualities of acts distributed over grammatical persons, so "person" can be defined only in terms of roles in a rhythm of consciousness reflecting on and in its ongoing activity. Then, once the idea of person is transformed, the attendant loosening of specific lyrics introduces the possibility of taking all a poet's utterances as workings and tracings of a larger poem, not beyond but distributed over the particular acts through their multiple relatedness.[10] Thus poetry becomes coextensive with the vagaries of the thinking self, a dream sought by poets as diverse as Hass, Pinsky, and Creeley, without any need to denote that self in specific contexts. The point is that self is imaginary, or comprises selves in positions, and thus the solipsist is a realist because he can play all the functional roles in dialogue.

As we shall see more fully in a few moments, the contemporary need for and difficulty in projecting specific audiences here finds a striking solution. Aware that "We too are somehow impossible, formed of so many things / Too many to make sense to anybody,"[11] Ashbery constructs a thinking self that absorbs dialogue into its own condition. Within its various modes, levels, and rhythmic interchanges between lucid criticism and lyric effulgence, this self affords a solipsistic, yet precise, solution to Wallace Stevens's basic challenge to poetry: "The measure of the poet is the measure of his sense of the world and of the extent to which it involves the sense of other people."[12]

There are, however, a great many concerned and sensitive readers of poetry who consider Ashbery representative only of a decadent philosophical surrealism and of the kind of poetry that becomes important because it gives academics something complex to write about.[13] I have many obvious reasons for hoping to change their minds – or, to put the same point in terms better suited to contemporary thought, for wanting to get them to occupy a somewhat different reflective and affective position. I shall therefore try to show how an Ashbery lyric, "No Way of Knowing," constitutes a complex fabric of "decreations" that expand our sense of lyric emotion.[14] The work and play of reading begin, and ultimately end, with the title. For here Ashbery initiates the process of unmaking and remaking the traditional love lyric, primarily by its way of at once suspending and extending the personal. "Way" picks up a metaphor central to *Three Poems* and basic in contemporary poets like Olson, Snyder, and Creeley; it combines traditional Eastern and Western religious associations with concrete conditions of place, method (how = Tao), and motion. The title also balances between concrete and general, while offering several ways of reading the force of its negation. Is the title simply a statement that the particular experience to be presented is not a good way of knowing? Or, if we take the title generally, does it suggest that knowing is impossible, that there is not a way but ways of knowing, or that there is a way but it is not accessible to one seeking knowledge? Then there are various ways of knowing how the title relates to the poem. The title may be, as Ashbery suggests is the case with most of his titles, simply a way into the poem,[15] or it may suggest a comprehensive idea or paradigmatic set by which internal coherence can be given to the whole poem.

It is crucial to insist that these multiple possibilities are neither frivolous nor aspects of a purely arbitrary exploration of permutations or patterns, as in the case with many *nouveaux romans*. Here the very multiplication of questions becomes a kind of remark, pointing to the complex interrelation of meta-languages that makes it so difficult to feel any secure knowledge about the nature of our acts of knowing. For Ashbery the mind stands toward its own knowing in the condition of infinite regressiveness that Derrida shows is the dilemma inherent in trying to know about the language we use in describing our knowledge. The difference between these figures, however, is equally significant, because for Ashbery the problematics of relation are not primarily of sign to signified but of act to other acts as the mind tries to identify secure resting places.

The poem's opening passage requires equally thorough scrutiny:

> And then? Colors and names of colors,
> The knowledge of you a certain color had?
> The whole song bag, the eternal oom-pah refrain?
> Street scenes? A blur of pavement
> After the cyclists passed, calling to each other
> Calling each other strange, funny sounding names?
> Yes, probably, but in the meantime, waking up
> In the middle of a dream with one's mouth full
> Of unknown words takes in all of these:
> It is both the surface and the accidents
> Scarring that surface, yet it too only contains
> As a book on Sweden only contains the pages of that book.

"And then?" is an enticing lyric opening. Its counterpart is Prufock's "Let us go then, you and I." But where Eliot, late Victorian that he is, decreates plot to express an obsession with transcending a blocking and inadequate present into the future, Ashbery, late aesthete that he is, poses his speaker standing just beyond a present wondering about the possible extensions of that moment, both for the desiring self and for the mind. This opening establishes a crucial question of how transitions are made, understood, and emotionally survived. It expresses a muted yet anguished cry of belatedness that works on several levels. Abstractly, the cry elliptically presents the question how a moment and a poem must depend on previous experience and discourses whose terms are always present and never clear. The past requires supplementing, yet gives only imperatives without directions. "And then?" may also be an ironic comment on the act of writing: The poem has been started by marking a blank page; experience has been disrupted, but the marks provide no coherent demand for subsequent reflections. The poet may always be facing an "And then," always starting over to finish a story whose beginnings are unclear and dispersed.

To remain on these abstract levels, however, is to miss the emotional drama of the poem. The abstract elements are there, and I shall keep insisting on them as themes, but they exist as counterpart, and often as evasion, of what the end of the poem suggests is a dialogue with a lover at the close of an affair. On this implicit dramatic level, "And then?" marks a moving reversal of language's phatic function. The phrase asserts a possibility of continuing while simultaneously evoking the paralyzing silence between two people who seem to share at most the desire to avoid embarrassing silences. Finally, "And then" signals the collapse of discourse into monologue as the speaker turns in solipsistic reverie to think about his condition after the lover leaves.

The play of abstract and dramatic levels defines the kind of problem that leads Ashbery to his distinctive form of decreation. On the one hand, "And then?" holds out the possibility of successful transition from existential loss to reflective and poetic life. Yet the question mark insists that existential and textual orders also exist as antagonists – each external to the other's desired hegemony, yet each a motivation and enhancement of the other. Poetic discourse may simply mask a cry of appeal to a specific person, himself displaced into the safe but distanced status of general poetic audience. Yet it may also be the case that the personal drama is itself primarily a metaphor for giving emotional bite to abstract reflections on the problems of belatedness inherent in all splits, even within the self, between the grammatical roles of "I" and "you." We are certainly caught up here in problems of indeterminacy, but these are means, not ends. Ashbery's purpose is probably not simply to present indeterminate discourse or even to show the inherent duplicities of language.[16] What matters is how forms of indeterminacy intensify our engagement in complex reflection on precise relations among loss, belatedness, the desire to know, and the play of transition and transference. The reader sees indeterminacy as an affective and conceptual vehicle for organizing a dense, deeply moving field of diffuse emotions implicated in a self-reflexive dramatic situation. Insofar as the poem's fluid shifting of contexts decreases easy lyrical self-delusions about interpersonal relations, it may, in fact, serve as a means for projecting fresh ways to organize our sensibilities in terms of rhythms of perceptions not confined to single theatrical roles.

"And then?" breeds at least three semantic and emotive codes at once gathering and dispersing the ensuing details. All are questions, all are versions of a problematic shift from an indeterminate event to the possible consequences and traces of the event, and, dramatically, all are infused by self-pity and a sense of nagging absence as the speaker thinks of a life without the lover while suffering from the presence of his or her absence. The details are radically contingent: pavement without action, sounds and names without presences or meanings, and throughout, dreams where all the events get summarized by words without referents, that is, words that have become symptoms of loss. Yet, in another sense, the details are not contingent enough. All sound the same note of absence, and all reduce flux to obsessive repetition – hence the self-parody of line 3, which expresses self-knowledge but not self-control, and the final images from the quoted passage. The richly indeterminate "it," referring possibly to "dream," to "waking," or to the entire condition of the preceding lines, suggests the leveling of distinctions that makes one see "all" as surface scarred by accidents, and it helps explain why the surface contains without engendering needed discriminations and directions for action. Everything collapses into one book, or, better, the pages of a book on Sweden – empty or irrelevant signs nontheless suggesting unrecoverable depth because of the speaker's unspeakable need and desire for response.

The remainder of the poem's first stanza distributes these anxieties over two contradictory levels of discourse – one the self-mocking "yep" accompanying a flattened series of repetitions of the "surface" metaphor, and the other a rich, theatrical, almost Renaissance lyric vocabulary ("the days in between grow rank, / Consume their substance, orphan . . ."). The final lines then place this opposition in the context of the head–body contrast, which thus repeats the problem of desiring intellectual control while recognizing that thinking does not conquer or know, but only displaces the pain: "The head is / necessary, And what is in doubt here." The head is "in doubt" both because one desires its power and because one recognizes the gulf between the "here" of mind and the "here" of the feeling self. We end with the head in control, but only in a flattened, parodic version of the most formal and imposing of signs, "Do not disturb."

Heads, however, have the power of disturbing themselves. Their characteristic act is the split between the lover's "Yes, but" (an echo of the nostalgic "yes, probably" of the first stanza) and the knower's sardonic, "There are no 'yes, buts'!" With this aligning of pathos against useless power as an introduction, the second stanza is dominated by a lucid head trapped in the endless supplementarity of discourse attendant upon suppression of the body. The mind wants rest by reducing the body to desires and differences, to a play of metaphors it can stand above by quiescently accepting the fact that "There is no way of knowing." Then the mind ignores its own abstractions by trying to collapse differences so that evening becomes a secure metaphor alleviating the pain and promising a future in which presence is purely phenomenal, without traces of what has been lost:

> For many this is near enough to the end: one may
> Draw up a chair close to the balcony railing.
> The sunset is just starting to light up.

By using metaphors to soothe the painful play of metaphoric transfer, however, the mind negates its basic powers and creates a new entrance for pain and doubt. The desire to make the metaphor of evening lead into a physical presence will not erase the charged, implicit features of loss because the language of "ends" and "sunsets" will not reduce to referential status. Such metaphors (however buried) make explicit the memories of absence and belatedness motivating the first stanza. Ashbery picks this up brilliantly in the progress of associations that begins the third stanza:

> As when the songs start to go
> Not much can be done about it, waiting
> In vanilla corridors for an austere
> Young nurse to appear, an opaque glass of snapdragons
> On one arm, the dangerously slender heroine
> Backbending over the other, won't save the denouement
> Already drenched in the perfume of fatality. The passengers
> Reappear. The cut driver pushes them to heaven.

Here the stoic attitude soon produces a sadly true "Yes, but." The parallel of evening with the songs starting "to go" reintroduces, despite itself, precisely the aura of romance, and hence of impinging loss, quietly prepared by the preceding metaphors. Romance is momentarily distanced by parodying melodramatic romantic desire, but the scene itself is set in a hospital context that finally allows the return of what the metaphors had been seeking to repress. The co-presence of the mind's multiple channels and its irreducible link to the body, subtly elicited by the plethora of terms for "ending" in this passage, leads to the lover's imaginative identification of himself as maimed victim. Now he is a literal victim of "accidents scarring that surface."

This unconscious identification becomes more explicit as the stanza progresses. Tone and degrees of intensity vary rapidly, often confusingly, but the dominant rhythm vacillates between maintaining distance ("I like the spirit of the songs, though") and explicit reflections on pain and the need to "push back the dead chaos" that lead to undisguised cry: "Why must you go? Why can't you / Spend the night, here, in my bed with my arms wrapped tightly around you?" The questions, along with this physical version of containment, produce slightly pathetic and parodic versions of the first stanza, allowing in turn a rueful, somewhat whimsical, ironic reflection on the gulf between desire and knowledge:

> Surely that would solve everything by supplying
> A theory of knowledge on a scale with the gigantic
> Bits and pieces of knowledge we have retained:
> An LP record of all your favorite friendships,
> Of letters from the front? Too
> Fantastic to make sense? But it made the chimes ring.
> If you listen you can hear them ringing still:
> A mood, a stimmung, adding up to a sense of what they
>   really were
> All along, through the chain of lengthening days.

Parody of knowledge on one level, however, does not preclude bodily feelings' retaining their power in memory, so that whatever "it" produces here can partially satisfy desires unable to express themselves in a fully determinate fashion. This turn, in a poem that is in many respects about transition, is deftly handled. One can say, "No, but," a partial realization of what one seeks in saying, "Yes, but." "But" reverses the insistent temporal flow and sense of loss initiated by "And then?" in order to assert linguistically and thematically the complex relation of memory to belatedness. Memory preserves only in negated forms, in the taunting mixture of presence and absence that is the corollary ironic version of this final "Yes, but." This balanced feeling of sweet preservation and nostalgic self-pity establishes a "sense of what they really were," denser and more complex than is available to the skeptical voice engaged in the poem's half-successful quest for knowledge.

All these thematic and tonal resonances may be heard in the concluding phrase, which gathers everything and resolves nothing. In essence the "chain of lengthening days" only puts in a concrete image the ambivalences contained in "And then?" – thus dramatically reminding us of the ways flux demands endless repetition while gradually determining abstract categories for clarifying, although not resolving, the nature and implications of the repetitions. On the one hand, this chain of lengthening days is a chain of necessity, an image of endless transition and increasing distance from precious objects. But the chain is also testament to the power of love and memory to forge links among the disparate elements of flux that otherwise fly apart. And as a chain of love and memory, the lengthening days are not merely natural facts, objects of external necessity, but images of a human agent's willed submission to desire and hence to the otherness of transition. The chain then captures both the pain and the power of memory, and it at least partially fulfills the implicit pastoral implications of this evening Angelus scene. But even sublated into a landscape of the mind, the pastoral setting seems to parody slightly the notes of triumphant nostalgia. What resolution there is, after all, is only a mental act making the best of a necessity and unable fully to reconcile chimes and chains. Is there not ultimately in this lyric attention to chains a gleeful awareness of one more duplicity worked by language and the psyche? For there is a faint echo of sadomasochism, ironically appropriate for the mixture of fear and anticipation folded into the lover's "And then?"

III

Although it is foreign to the spirit of Ashbery's delicately balanced complexities, I think it crucial that we attempt to understand as discursively as possible the general poetic model informing works like "No Way of Knowing." For at stake is not simply a distinctive way of extending the lyric but also a model of psychic economy that represents a significant stance for preserving lyrical dimensions of experience. Ashbery's models of relatedness derive from the same general ideal of poetry as Creeley's: "Poetry lies primarily in the fluidity of thought rather than the objects of thought." Everything hangs, though, on how that fluidity is understood. With Creeley, thinking seeks a ground of rest; with Ashbery, thinking is closer to an erotic force that moves us to explore the peripheries of the forms of consciousness engaged in practical action:

> Memory, forgetfulness, and being are certainly things that are happening in our minds all the time which I'm attempting to reproduce in poetry, the actions of a mind at work or at rest . . . My poetry is really consciously trying to explore consciousness to give it perspective . . . I never thought of myself as having a relationship to confusion; every moment is surrounded by a lot of things in life that don't add up to anything that makes much sense and these are part of a situation that I feel I'm trying to deal with when I'm writing . . . I begin with unrelated phrases and notations that later on I hope get resolved in the course of the poem as it begins to define itself more clearly for me.[17]

An old opposition between practical and poetic language gains renewed force by eliciting a bemused fascination that sustains two basic quests: "to elucidate a lot of almost invisible currents" and to record a thought process where "the process and the thought reflect back and

forth on one another" as the interplay of meaningfulness and random-
ness.[18] This is why specific clarity about a given love affair is less important than the range of associations and possibilities the event creates in
the remembering, writing, and remaking. Then Ashbery can render the
personal voice as simultaneously liberated by and trapped within the mind's
dispersals and partial integrations of desire.

The best way I know to generalize about Ashbery's poetics is to analyze the specific idea of expression that informs it. The personalism of
most contemporary poets is expressionist in a fairly simple, naturalistic
sense. The goal of poetic rhetoric is to serve two kinds of expression –
to construct qualities of apparent sincerity that create the illusion of human speech and to make the control of rhetoric itself an expression of
the poet's sensibility. These aims can conflict, although in the best poetry
of the mode the conflict is not damaging to specific lyric effects (it may,
however, weaken the poet's claims to authority). Yet neither is the conflict constructive.

The poets we have considered use rhetoric, but they rarely examine
rhetoricity, that is, the complex states of mind that go into self-conscious
manipulation of language. Such an examination need not entail an arid
metapoetics. It does entail asking what one's acts of poetic thinking or
uses of rhetoric can be expressions of. And this process, as we have seen,
brings emotional life within the intricate duplicities of "of" as subjective
and objective genitive. Personalist poets like Plumly stress the subjective
genitive, the conscious work of giving form to the formless and distinctive psychological qualities to the impersonal. However, these idealizations of poetry's power to disclose or to make real are haunted by the
other dimension in the term "expression of." If we stress the objective
genitive, linguistic acts disclose not what the agent experiences but what
is disclosed in his or her way of experiencing. "Expression of" can be
equated with "symptom of," as in Barthes's reminders of what the choice
of codes signifies beyond the intended message. In "No Way of Knowing," for example, expression is always poised between disclosing an
agent's desires and revealing essentially unconscious symptoms the conscious agent cannot master. Similarly, the patterns that symbolist poets
use to clarify qualities within experience become elements that in effect
decide what they want and indicate symptomatic aspects of a discourse.
A writer like Eliot, seeking to define his age historically and psychologically, becomes himself a defined historical and psychological object.
Ashbery changes the status of poetic patterns in order to make this duality of expression the field for aesthetic discourse. The oscillating, abstract
fascination needed to negotiate the terrain of such a field constitutes the
naturalism Ashbery aspires to when he is writing.

If we consider this greater naturalism in epistemological terms, it demands rethinking the ideal of dialectical synthesis in poetry; if we consider the naturalness in psychological terms, it leads to undermining and complicating the readerly and ethical ideals of identification. In order to dramatize the consequences of such shifts, it is worth the slight exaggeration of claiming that the dialectical idea in philosophy is parallel to (and has often supported) the organicist ideal in art.[19] Both models emphasize the act of synthesis as the primary figure for the mind's powers, for in that act relations are constructed that allow the mind to negate, preserve, and surpass the partial nature of its particulars. But for Ashbery, as for Derrida, only two features of dialectic can be accepted – that is, negation and supplementation. There is no synthesis whose completeness is not a delusion, although there is also no way of quite dispelling the dream of totality. Thus the poet's task is to manage in engaging ways the processes, not of synthesis, but of repetition and variation, processes that emphasize forms of relatedness and of attention very different from those traditionally prized in our essentially idealist literary traditions.

In *Three Poems* Ashbery makes his central theme the need to reinvent terms capable of revealing poetic powers that will fulfill Stevens's dream of the nobility of imagination. Ashbery's theme is the same as Hass's, the presence of value in phenomena lustered by human use, but his sense of the light's source and way of working is far more sublime:

> The way is narrow but it is not hard, it seems almost to propel or push one along. One gets the narrowness into one's seeing, which also seems an inducement to moving forward into what one has already caught a glimpse of and which quickly becomes vision, in the visionary sense, except that in the place of the panorama that used to be our customary setting . . . a limited but infinitely free space has established itself, useful as everyday life but transfigured so that its signs of wear no longer appear as a reproach but as indications of how beautiful a thing must have been to have been so much prized, and its noble aspect which must have been irksome before has now become interesting, you are fascinated and keep on studying it.

> "Whatever was, is, and must be." These words occur again to you now, though in a different register, transposed from a major into a minor key. Yet they are the same words as before. Their meaning is the same, only you have changed: you are viewing it all from a different angle, perhaps not more or less accurate than

the previous one, but in any case a necessary one no-doubt for the in-the-round effect to be achieved.[20]

Instead of seeking vision, poetry is the technique of fascinated re-vision, and its goal, its pursuit of an ultimate in-the-round effect, demands of us the flexibility to move from carousel to comic-strip balloon, to convex mirror, to several variants on Stevens's revolving crystal. Nothing would be more foolish, under this dispensation, than to construct poems in order to give special impact to resonant concluding images, because conclusions have very little special status. If they claim to resolve matters, they probably oversimplify and choose a form of blindness. The world will not change. Change depends on our shifting angles of vision. At the most, conclusions may serve as provisional changes of key allowing a change in perspective that eventually makes them further questions extending the linguistic web: "So one must move forward / Into the space left by one's conclusions."[21]

The psychological correlate of closure, I have argued, is the dream of a coherent and satisfying representation of the self, either as an individual or as someone in full possession of the terms by which he or she identifies with other people. These are our small want ads. In Ashbery's world, such identifications are the stuff lyric self-delusions are made on. They tempt us to let the imagination ignore the process of dispersal inherent in any effort to impose closure on emotional fields. The psychological analogue of repetition and variation, then, is an insistence that the desires we mobilize in our quest for conclusions in fact overdetermine any self-representation the resolution might allow. The concept of motivation links the overlapping domains of psychology and linguistics that we need in order to recognize what Ashbery makes of these overdeterminations. In traditional poems, a plausible hypothesis about motivation derives from a sense of the whole. Once we can hypothesize intention, we can produce coherence for the overall linguistic structure. Conversely, we begin to trust notions of intention when we see them explaining relations between parts and wholes.

When we turn to Ashbery, it may be impossible to dispense with this model of motivation as our guide for reading a text. But at the very least, we must recognize how complex the idea of intention is and how so much of modern thought locates forces within intentional acts that are not contained by or available to rational consciousness. So the overall intention we attribute to an Ashbery poem must be posited in terms of constructive activity rather than of projecting interpretations on experience. Our hypothesis must be at a very abstract level, where we must be attentive to very untraditional ways of locating motivations. Because the manifest level of the text seems to deny both immanent design and traditional notions that specific plans inform specific choices, the dream of ideal, consciously controlled motives gives way to something like the materiality of motive stressed in discussions of *ecriture*.[22] But Ashbery is neither philosopher nor ideologue; he resists any reduction of motive to single theoretical constructs. Dispersal in his work makes motivation shift among a variety of psychological domains. Dramatic scene and linguistic scene breed a rich interplay among the free actions of consciousness and the determining forces that express themselves as resistance to and qualification of that freedom. Qualification is the sine qua non of quality. Thus, as scenes multiply, overlap, and come in and out of focus, the speaking subject also becomes multiple. But the stage is not Creeley's underlying abstract patterns. In Ashbery the stage appears only through the condensations and displacements that we recognize in the transitions among levels of scene. The more complex and difficult the transitions, the fuller the interplay between motives: We are asked to participate in acts of mind that attribute motives for acts and invite analysis of the motives for the attribution of motives. The "motives of motive" is Ashbery's version of "the meaning of meaning."

This concern for multiple levels of motivation invites a Derridean vocabulary, but it cannot be reduced to Derrida's characteristic themes. In Ashbery the complexity of motives derives from the interplay between the voices of a writing self and the presures on the empirical self in a concrete situation it cannot control. By rendering this complexity, Ashbery creates a dramatic field where he can explore the ironic combination of creative freedom and existential pathos. The surface of repetition and variations demands a corresponding psychic rhythm of identification and dispersal, so that where one stands and what one observes become simultaneously functions of one another and dispersing supplements of one another. The logic of syntactic connections diffuses into multiple logics, whose internal principles of relatedness never become sufficiently clear to allow a single coherent interpretive structure. Transition becomes the central, perhaps the only, definable principle of structure in Ashbery's psychological version of Heraclitean cosmology.

"Transition," in turn, is a final duplicitous term for describing Ashbery's poetics of variation and repetition. "Transition" has both temporal and logical meanings: As a temporal index, transition points to constant change; and as a logical function, it suggests the presence of a general pattern of relationships giving coherence to the temporal movement. "Transition," in short, reflects the facts that time demands change, but change within consciousness depends on structures of repetition that allow languages to make sense.

"Transition" is transference across gaps, so the process of metaphor, whose full duplicity Ashbery richly captures, is its literary figure. In his work metaphor retains its traditional function of clarifying events by submitting them to complex paradigmatic sets, while also reflecting a contemporary sense of dispersal because the codes metaphors invoke depend upon and produce their own psychological and linguistic possibilities. Traditional metaphors, like Yeats's "The soul is a bride who cannot in that rag and tinsel hide,"[23] suppress multiplicity because they are controlled by a central passionate argument. But as soon as one suspends that argument over two or three possible plots for which traces exist in the text, one invites readers to reflect upon the various implicit features of the metaphor not motivated by the single argumentative structure. For example, it is possible to attend to the psychological and stylistic qualities of the self-theatricalizing in Yeats's metaphor, or, if the complicated sexuality of the figure can be connected to other strands in the poem, one is invited to distribute its force across elements not explicitly invoked in its dramatic context. But in so emphasizing psychological or deconstructive strands of the text, one clearly would not be responding to Yeats's intentions and probably would not be reading the poem on the aesthetic terms it invites. Yeats's intention is that we know where we are as masters of our language.

Ashbery's multiple motivation of metaphor as act as well as content of the poem, on the other hand, suggests problems in the concept of mastery that simultaneously render the mind a diminished thing and exalt its powers to play with the historical and psychological forces that diminish it. The motive in metaphor, then, is an urge not to interpret experience but to extend it by inventions and elaborations. A mind continually in pursuit of the motives informing its craft no longer views Narcissus as trapped within a hall of broken mirrors. We now find him playing the role of Menelaus grappling with Proteus and aware of the erotic energies released by this struggle. The most surprising feature of this struggle is that by learning to accept defeat and adapt what Barthes called a mood of speaking lightly, Menelaus wins some astonishing victories. There is a good deal of Auden in Ashbery, but it is an Auden who must, and can, pass through Raymond Roussel. When it does, as in "Daffy Duck," Ashbery's very freedom with metaphor produces an uncanny precision of phrase. By altering angles of vision, Ashbery becomes at times a poet with all the discursive skill of the best neoclassical writers.

IV

We have seen Ashbery's motives for metaphor. Now we must measure what he makes of them in his poems that self-consciously extend their lyric strategies into attitudes provisionally exploring the effects of a new philosophical orientation. I shall therefore concentrate on two poems, each of which extends the lyric model of "No Way of Knowing" toward a very different realm of inclusiveness. In these explorations, Ashbery earns the right to be seen as continuing the highest ambitions of modernism while adapting himself to our culture's deepest needs for coming to terms with a self that can neither escape nor accept the rhetoric, the inevitable otherness, that makes acts of identification possible. In each realm the two poems take up, that of cultural history and that of ontological speculation, Ashbery's distinctive achievement is to make processes of thinking significant even though he can promise no depth of dialectical concentration. He is precise and fluid enough so that our minds can be fully engaged simply in the qualities that emerge as he engages reflectively on a chain of thinking. Thus he recovers Stevens's and Pound's sense that poetry must be extensive, must achieve sublimity by its scope of attentions, while he transforms the romantic constitutive imagination into a more casual, but equally powerful, ideal of the lushness of invention, not simply as a principle of style but as a condition for understanding our nature as beings who suffer and dream and wonder.

My first choice is inevitable. One simply cannot ignore "Self-Portrait in a Convex Mirror,"[24] because even if it is more traditional in focus than most Ashbery poems, it stands as probably the greatest American poem since the work of late Stevens. In this poem rhetoricity and conditions of identity become close correlates – each dependent on rhythms of vision and revision, identification and dispersal, and each achieving a modified transcendence by self-consciously luxuriating in the mind's inventive powers. Close attention to Ashbery's introductory passage will indicate how these analogies get established as principles of force that reflect the dual properties of intentionality and self-reflexiveness basic to the life of thinking:

> As Parmigianino did it, the right hand
> Bigger than the head, thrust at the viewer
> And swerving easily away, as though to protect
> What it advertises. A few leaded panes, old beams,
> Fur, pleated muslin, a coral ring run together
> In a movement supporting the face, which swims
> Toward and away like the hand
> Except that it is in repose. It is what is
> Sequestered. Vasari says, "Francesco one day set
> Himself . . ."

The opening "As" is a brilliant epistemological variation on the epic "In medias res." It functions here to set us immediately within an action that is a temporal, psychological, and analogical transition among speaker, painting, and the multiple contexts each elicits. Temporally, the "As" brings the energies of the portrait into the present, allowing a rich psychological identification of the speaker with the gestures, and then with their expressive meaning. The tension between self-projection and self-protection establishes the basic meaning of the painting as a state somewhere between the painter's intended effect and the intentional stance of the observer, and it articulates what will unfold as the basic rhythm of the observer's meditations. This blending of internal and external is intensified by the analogical thrust of the "As": The painting's expressive energies serve as the vehicle of a metaphor whose tenor will be the various ways the speaker sees himself in the picture and tries to stand outside it in order to register the meanings and motives in his acts of identification.

Notice, for example, how the movement from identification to attention to surface details shifts immediately to tensions between the ambivalent hand, figure for the complex need and defensiveness of both desiring selves, and the reposeful face, sequestered in its identity. A stage is set for the complex play of desires in relation to that face, a play that will demand continual dispersal of the mind's loose edges in a variety of perspectives and voices. Even casual metaphors like "swim" will lead later to more intense meditations on water as an image of deep repose and constant movement. "Swim" serves as one key signature for unfolding patterns, significant less for their descriptive meaning than for their status as nodal points for intersecting strands of the meditation. Similarly, the "It" of "It is . . . / Sequestered" will prove a densely packed shifter. It will refer not only to the face but also to the vague yet pressing desires sequestered within the face by a speaker who identifies with these depths and yet recognizes them as alien to his reflective acts.

The ensuing details call attention to the mysteries of what is sequestered in the portrait and in the implicit motives of the speaker's act. Three external perspectives construct the painting as essentially surface – Vasari on the painting's creation, the relation of the portrait to shifting conditions of light and time, and a brief mention of the painting's reception by Pope Clement. Each reminds us of tensions between the repose of an artifact and the need even of artifacts to find another to complete them, to bring to them "the intricate evasions of as" afforded by a responding consciousness. Here both speaker and painter find momentary identity in the tension each seems to feel between the self as it is portrayed and the desire for the portraying self to be known through its expressions. Yet each of these modes of responding to the painting's charged surface appears in a different tonal key; and tonal variety itself becomes a sign of how complex and multiple are the terms for identification and distance, doubled again in the persons of painter and speaker.

First, the problem of identification is abstract: The portrait in a mirror is a literal reflection serving also as metaphor for the duplicities of self-reflection and reflection of self in another. Thus the portrait figure and, implicitly, the identifying speaker appear simultaneously in contradictory past participles. They are at once embalmed or fixed in the poses they assume and projected as unfilled toward some potentially completing otherness. The poem moves rapidly from a completely flat mention of how the changing light keeps the painting alive to a moment of deep identification, motivated more by the return to the linguistic code of swimming than by a need for scenic development:

> The time of day or the density of the light
> Adhering to the face keeps it
> Lively and intact in a recurring wave
> Of arrival. The soul establishes itself.
> But how far can it swim out through the eyes
> And still return safely to its nest? The
> Surface of the mirror being convex, the distance increases.

The arrival is of two souls, one in the painting, the other in the responding act. Thus the identification allows a brief lyrical cry immediately caught up in abstract understanding. The compression here is remarkable. The lyric effect is literally a result of the convexity of the mirror, which both projects the image out to the observer and imposes a sense of infinite distance that remains between the two (a distance repeated in the shift from lyrical to analytic tones).

Finally, the third contingency, Clement's reception of the portrait, ironically reverses the distancing by preparing an extended, intensely lyrical motivation. But again the transition is essentially linguistic, as Ashbery suggests that transition itself is a complex blend of casual surface and deep potential to motivate identification. Here the key term is "materialized," a rich pun on tensions between contingent events and the nature of self-portrait, which traps what it expresses of a soul posing and posed in a place and a medium. Since the self-expressive portrait has no power over the actual details of its reception and is reduced to an object of economic exchanges, spirit here is dangerously close to mere surface, or matter. Yet this very reduction (matched by the surface contingency of the transition) is immediately transcended because of the way the power of attention can be fixed by mere surfaces. The speaker's language shifts from describing the matter of the painting as abstract "soul" to seeing it as a gaze: "There is in that gaze a combination / Of tenderness, amusement and regret." (The list of qualities here transforms the triad of past participles earlier used to describe the poem's surface.) The moment in which the speaker's fear of reductive surface is most directly stated constitutes also the richest moment so far of lyrical identification with the imaginative sufferings of the subject. At the moment of negation words fail, but a tune beyond the speculation of the words takes shape in this empathic duet. The lyric passage resolves itself finally in the return of the figure of the hand. Now the hand looms large because the surface is charged with consciousness: Aware of his own solipsistic globe, the speaker sees the hand as symbol of both the trapped expressive desire and the need for release that he shares with the figure in the portrait. ("One" in this poem is often two – pyschologically and semantically.)

The next descriptive passage ("There is no way . . .") considers surface details as aesthetic choices and thus prepares for the climactic passage of the poem's first section. Identification with the trapped soul, and therefore with the ironies of its condition, produces a series of perspectives for addressing the portrait – from face, to soul, to gaze, to the quiet intimacy of "Francesco." The hand becomes a figure expressing the latent violence in the way both artists resist the surfaces of their media (where both weave "delicate meshes that only argue its further detention"). But because hand and eye can be seen as expressing an embodied person, they elicit also a momentary solution within the tensions. The violence merges with a sense of identification, so that the speaker can take as an affirmation his ability to get his problems stated in a simple opposition of "pathos vs. experience." But the balancing remains trapped on a self-referential surface, so the affirmation becomes here little more than gesture that "doesn't affirm anything."

For a fuller affirmation, the lines of relational force between painting and world must become more explicitly determined, a process requiring that the speaker begin to explore contexts apparently contingent to this state of satisfied repose. One must break out of the circle of self-representation, if not by entering some deep self then at least by engaging the multiple folds created by relations among surfaces. The second section of the poem employs quick transformations in order to initiate this process of submitting the painting to contingent otherness: from the globe of the painting to the balloon of comic-book thinking, then to dispersing clouds that are momentarily echoes of the balloon popping. In the popping of the balloon and the transitions it breeds, the focus shifts from the painting as finished object to the painting as an object being constructed amid the flux of events. Now any affirmation of identity must depend not on self-enclosed self-representations but on what the artists share as makers. The shift to genetic conditions is marked by multiple transformations, as balloon and clouds shift into "turning seasons" and "carousel":

> How many people came and stayed a certain time
> Uttered light or dark speech that became part of you . . .
> until no part
> Remains that is surely you . . .
> Whose curved hand controls,
> Francesco, the turning seasons and the thoughts
> That peel off and fly away at breathless speeds.
> Like the last stubborn leaves stripped
> From wet branches.

Here a contradictory aspect of surfaces threatens not the collapse of meaning into tautology but its dispersal into the chaos of "leveling." Change on the outside, multiple identities and influences within, leave the empathic artist aware of how difficult and necessary it is to achieve the repose of the first section. The leaves are no longer emblems of a "longing to be free" but figures of nostalgic resistance to change. When the curved hand and globe get equated with the turning seasons, self-enclosure seems no longer a trap but an ideal, an exemplary image for accepting what this more powerful creative force imposes. Negation and contrast offer fresh ways to value Francesco's repose. But even this realization collapses under what Ashbery sees as the implications of change: a sense of distance in time and pyschological space from the artistic powers that come to seem only anachronistic taunts intensifying one's sense of flux. Indeed, in the light of these turning seasons, the appeal of Renaissance idealizations that permit the figure's repose becomes the greatest illusion entrapping the artist.

We need read only one more section of the poem fairly closely before offering a quick summary, for by the conclusion of the third section the basic themes and strategies have all been indicated. "Self-Portrait" is unique in Ashbery's work because the different motivations emerge more slowly and fully than in other poems, each being subjected to a variety of tonal perspectives. But the effect of variations amid repetition remains constant. Thus the third section here, like the synthetic passages in *Three Poems,* proposes a momentary resolution of the opposite perspectives on identity posed by the first two parts, only to make the resolution a motive for new permutations of idea and tone. The section begins with another casual, merely verbally motivated transition, but it immediately shifts to an intensely compressed series of metaphors that start to bring together the themes of flux, possibility, and the uses of painterly repose:

Tomorrow is easy, but today is uncharted,
Desolate, reluctant as any landscape
To yield what are laws of perspective
After all only to the painter's deep
Mistrust, a weak instrument though
Necessary.

The previous section had reached momentary peace by contrasting the "uncharted" today with the inevitable loss brought by thoughts of tomorrow. That easy acceptance of today breeds a fresh challenge, making it possible to come to terms eventually with the complex presences and absences of the painting as work in history. The quoted lines enact the complexity of today as a matrix of possibilities by refusing to allow the chain of thought any secure resting place. Each phrase calls out for a conventional reading and then subverts the ordinary phrases we are tempted to provide in order to complete the metaphors. Instead, metaphor breeds further metaphor, decreating today into potentials for fresh chartings. For example, we can be comfortable with an easy metaphoric equation of the present with a landscape reluctant to be divided according to laws of perspective. But Ashbery works at least three permutations on the ground metaphor. Laws of perspective become as multiple as the landscape, become only provisional and ambivalent features of the painter's art. (The pause after "deep" invites our filling in supplementary phrases that are exploded by the surprising "mistrust.") Then the ensuing phrase nicely qualifies "mistrust," because both "mistrust" and "laws of perspective" are possible sources of the modifying apposition. Both principles of order and skeptical doubt are equally weak instruments, yet both, by a further surprise, are irreducible necessities of the act of understanding.

Ashbery has introduced this meditation on possibility by posing it delicately between possibilities and by counterpointing it with the second section's negative attitude toward change. Here possibility balances between a continued sense of loss and a renewed sense that forms are possible, even inescapable, so that change supports the desire to "ramble back home." Moreover, the instrument of such balancing is a return to identifying with the painter's art, now as a general metaphor for the conditions of knowledge. Change itself, in the following lines, takes form in visual images of a landscape covered by plant growth and of the bubble chamber and containing room seen in the portrait. Generalization, however, is no release from nostalgia. Only when the feeling of absence leads to a causal "focus sharpening towards death" does this string of painting analogues allow the shift in emotional valence that produces a momentary resolution of the themes of repose and change. With the ironic, unfulfilled promise to speak more of death later – a gesture at once defensive and indicative of the empty futurity thoughts of death produce – the poem brings into focus a summary equation of change and emptiness. This equation expresses the way works of art exist in and out of time. Emptiness and change simultaneously destroy dreams and clarify their significance in artistic visions:

> . . . What should be the vacuum of a dream
> Becomes continually replete as the source of dreams
> In being tapped so that this one dream
> May wax, flourish like a cabbage rose,
> Defying sumptuary laws, leaving us
> To awake and try to begin living in what
> Has now become a slum.

Dreams collapse into slums and serve as the diacritical opposite allowing the definition of "slum." Thus, although dreams die (and are already dying in their quixotic appearance as cabbage roses, not Dante's visionary rose), dreaming itself is a force that alters a purely horizontal surface of flux into pyschological contrasts between value terms and mere appearances. This relation of dreaming to slum takes on witty overtones in the ensuing contrast between Sidney Freeberg's academic language and Ashbery's lyrical extension of that language to account for "importance if not . . . meaning." Under the dramatic impetus of lyrical identification, dispersed themes accumulate as artistic expression itself becomes the dynamic middle between "the vacuum of a dream" and "the source of dreams." The holes dreams leave "were to nourish a dream which includes them all, as they are / Finally reversed in the accumulating mirror":

> And we realize this only at a point where they lapse
> Like a wave breaking on a rock, giving up
> Its shape in a gesture which expresses that shape.
> The forms retain a strong measure of ideal beauty
> As they forage in secret on our idea of distortion.

To remain posing in one's place is to win the only possible victory over time, to take as the source of meaning and strength one's active involvement in the distortions of time and perspective. The convex mirror is an ideal figure for the ontological status of figures, just as involvement is an active submission to the endless circlings and convolutions insisted upon in Ashbery's figurings.

Yet the lyric voice allows its moments of vision to mask its own involvement in complex distortions and changes. After this passage, the section concludes by flattening out into another, highly qualified attempt to achieve affirmation. Even the triumphant image, after all, is "codification" and linguistic representation: Words and dreams remain only "something like living." And the linguistic qualifications here are further qualified by the dramatic fact of repetition. Each of the first three sections has turned in its conclusion to qualified forms of acceptance, from an affirmation that does not affirm anything, to "it doesn't matter," to "Why be unhappy . . . ?" The terms themselves suggest an implicit motive for the entire meditation, the obsessive desire to find some kind of peace and release from the burdens of thinking. When all the reflections keep returning to the same note, and this note does not seem required by the content of each section, we are invited to see the thinking as motivated not only by the painting but also by some unstatable need in the subject. This need seems at once relieved and intensified by the encounter with the painting, as if the speaker's own mental hand were divided between the desire to identify and a desire to break out of the balloon of his own endlessly circling monologue. The purest abstractions remain complex emotional acts dramatically grounded in a rich sense of thinking as an act balanced between idealizing power and the pathos of distortion. This poem has now become like the painting: As we know it better we find it enticing as a form of repose, yet the very condition of repose threatens to become a trap, not for its peacefulness but for its capacity to enclose consciousness in an endless pursuit of the very terms that entice it.

If I am not to make this essay its own, less interesting, form of trap, I must assume that the poem's general rhythms of thinking and specific motivational forces are by now fairly clear, so that I can conclude by briefly summarizing the rest of it. The fourth section begins by dramatizing the third's abstract realizations about the ways the portrait takes on meanings by virtue of its life in change and its contrast to personal and social slums. This section is the poem's most relaxed, often discursive, rendering of empathic connections among poet, portrait, and the selves both try to capture. The fifth section, then, in effect breaks the balloon once more and urgently faces up to a sharpened sense of contingencies – both of the painting's place amid historical events and of the speaker as agent within his historical setting. The pressures of the city, the implicit background for both acts of self-reflection, transform earlier abstract meditations on change into demonic concrete forces, and the wind becomes now a figure for all contingent impersonalities (as it echoes and reverses Eliot's *Ash Wednesday*):

> This wind brings what it knows not, is
> Self-propelled, blind, has no notion
> Of itself. It is inertia that once

> Acknowledged saps all activity, secret or public:
> Whispers of the word that can't be understood
> But can be felt, a chill, a blight.

By now, however, the rhythmic nature of this meditative stance is sufficiently obvious to raise immediate counterbalancing thoughts: Even the blight of an unintelligible word continues the tune because the very awareness of loss makes one notice life and return to new recesses on the surface of the painting. History is precisely the medium for preserving the energies of Francesco's act of resistance to it:

> . . . Since it is a metaphor
> Made to include us, we are a part of it and
> Can live in it as in fact we have done
> Only leaving our minds bare for questioning
> We now see will not take place at random
> But in an orderly way . . .
> Like the concentric growing up of days
> Around a life: correctly if you think about it.

The momentary assertion of order here is the poem's most confident so far. Yet the "if" and the ambiguous references of "it" make me wonder if the overtones of cliché in the final phrase might be intended to limit the realm of the concentric to the abstract space of thinking.

What guarantee do we have, however, that even thinking can remain concentric? Able to preserve itself against a leveling wind, the mind yields its powers of focus before the more subtle otherness of a "breeze." The final section, then, begins by awakening the mind to the complexities of a present doubled between self and portrait. Because it insists on its own presence, the portrait forces the self to recognize the object of attention as ineluctably other. The portrait in its otherness becomes pure ideality, a "porch" onto another castle, which the poet's abstract thoughts ("But it is certain . . .") cannot prevent from dispersing into the emptiness of a history that had momentarily given it life. To identify with the painting, "the darkening opposite of the present," reduces the life of consciousness to various aspects of existence in a museum where "all time / Reduces to no special time." Throughout this section Ashbery allows the speaker's mind to ruminate in a kind of self-indulgent haze among discursive speculations and personal circles, like the attack on mirror games. The point, I think, is to match abstraction by abstraction: As the portrait recedes into its history, the responding mind loses focus and dwells only in the slum of its own loose opinions. The "will to endure" masks and enervates itself.

Partial reversal occurs again only when Ashbery breaks out of what seems the speaker's own version of the whispered-phrase game, in order to state directly the nature of the problem motivating the line of discourse.

> Once it seemed so perfect . . .
> This could have been our paradise: exotic
> Refuge within an exhausted world, but that wasn't
> In the cards, because it couldn't have been
> The point. Aping naturalness may be the first step
> Toward achieving an inner calm
> But it is the first step only, and often
> Remains a frozen gesture of welcome etched
> On the air materializing behind it,
> A convention. And we have really
> No time for these except to use them
> For kindling. The sooner they are burnt up
> The better for the roles we have to play.

In stating this negative position, Ashbery also begins to gather many of the relational patterns dispersed throughout the poem, a gathering that prepares for the final muted image of what a contemporary paradise can consist in, beyond all nostalgias. We begin to hear "whispers out of time" as images of fixity, like the "frozen gesture . . . etched / On the air materializing behind it," play off against the perverse light implied in seeing conventions as "kindling." Also, "frozen etching" is picked up in the recognition that waking dreams remain palimpsests, diagrams "sketched" on the now domesticated wind as emblems of desire for a self-knowledge that can transcend history. To say that "it was all a dream" is to posit a knowing, or at least desiring, stance outside the generalization, just as the flood of repetitions – dream, wind, city, radiance, mirror, balcony – all point beyond their literal utterance to forms of relatedness articulated in the dialogue between speaker and painting. An idealized relation to a specific content can no longer be our paradise. We are exiles from all explicit forms of coherence, but in an artist's dreams there remain forces that occasionally provide moments where the tune (or as *Three Poems* puts it, "the idea of the spectacle as something to be acted out and absorbed") remains "in the air":[25]

> The hand holds no chalk
> And each part of the whole falls off
> And cannot know it knew, except

> Here and there, in cold pockets
> Of remembrance, whispers out of time.

"The hand" collapses Francesco and the speaker into a metonymy for all artists, now working virtually against the repose of established media. The knowledge that can motivate and direct the hand, once the wave has crested, exists only in fragments and doubling, in forms that cannot represent their knowing. "Here and there" becomes the precise instance of that doubling. The phrase explodes cliché into vital, though muted, moments of presence and thus into an evocative sign of a continuity between past and present, other and self. The form that union takes is oxymoronic: Cold pockets of remembrance yield intimate whispers as art and thinking simultaneously retain their abstractness and reach through it to an almost sexual summary vision of the dialogue whose rhythms constitute the meaning of the poem. These same oxymoronic suggestions that knowledge is manifest in fragments that can only intimate their source reach a climax with the blend of static and dynamic in "whispers out of time." The whispers emerge out of the past, are given form by their relation to time's contingencies, and constitute a state of identification that momentarily transcends time. The waking dream materializes by eliciting desires that pose the self at once within and beyond the history that encloses it.

V

Not a bang but a whisper: The past may be dead, useful only for "kindling," but in that kindling there is a diffuse light dancing across our inventions and casting shadows that project the possibility of a steadier, more constant source to whom we relate, as we do to Francesco, only by a constant circling. "Self-Portrait," in other words, demonstrates that Ashbery has ambitions for his form of discursiveness that are perhaps grand enough to put Pinsky's to shame and almost grand enough to justify the critical effusions of Harold Bloom. In these whispers out of time, Ashbery locates a version of Stevens's Major Man, but his approach is cautious because explicitness may erase more than it exposes and because the image limned in his book may not be quite "man" as we know him. The poetics of thinking leads Ashbery to dream of glimpsing "the other side of knowledge" where the conditions of our knowing become themselves metaphors of our state for one who can learn to take the appropriate stance. By "Litany" (1978), "I" and "you" are no longer simply positions in an endless discourse but figures for two conflicting and yet necessary grounds of identity and of freedom. Now his solution to the problem of audience becomes constructing a place on which to stand in order to understand whom and what we seek in our efforts to speak. These are the poem's opening lines:

I

For someone like me
The simple things
Like having toast or
Going to church are
Kept in one place

Like having wine and cheese.
The parents of the town
Pissing elegantly escape
    knowledge
Once and for all. The
Snapdragons consumed in a
    wind
Of fire and rage far over
The streets as they end.

So this must be a hole
Of cloud
Mandate or trap
But haze that casts
The milk of enchantment

Over the whole town,
Its scenery, whatever
Could be happening
Behind tall hedges
Of dark, lissome
    knowledge.[26]

At one level it is simply a linguistic truism that the indexicals "me" and "this" are not fixed and hence apply to all possible selves and places. But Ashbery turns semantic facts into philosophical metaphors. The openness of the indexicals fits perfectly with the simplicity of the details because they extend the domain of someone "like me" to cover virtually any "me." Where in Creeley the objectified "me" is terrifying, here it liberates the self to merge first- and third-person perspectives. This simple positioning of the self also raises a more complex possibility: Perhaps the self is primarily a function, not an entity – a function that is manifest in our assertions of desire or our investments in things. Then the left column's easy statement includes all selves because it captures the fundamental force of self, the taking as mine a shareable relation to a field of objects.[27] Both the objects and the functions are common to all selves, yet the imaginary act of saying "mine" allows the self to assert a sense of individuality while recognizing its existence as an object among objects.

The self here finds something like Creeley's condition of rest, but the rest has profound philosophical sources and hence creates extremely simple possibilities of emotional resonance. At one pole of poetry, of our inventing thoughts and selves, there is a radical freedom within contingent banality. There is nothing to question or deny the self's pure mobility. But the "this" of the right column also introduces a very different condition of freedom requiring a very different sense of self. Because of the associations with "haze," I take "this" as referring not to the empirical "me" but to the condition of self-consciousness about the "me," hence to the poetic voice itself. In this position for the mind, self, and voice, it is not enough to be "like me." The dream is of something ideally "me," although that "me" may not be the empirical self. And this dream has its own forms of freedom, but they initiate a constant fear of traps because the ideality opens a romance of endless attempts at definition that will constantly cross and unsettle the empirical stage. This romance, this pursuit of the doubled self, gives the "tall hedges of dark lissome knowledge" their mysterious fascination while breeding a desire to understand that state of desire. This play of desires, in turn, produces an aura of both enchantment and void. Reason becomes a seducer by virtue of the vanities he or she so proudly displays.

Much of Ashbery's best poetry becomes, then, a strange erotic dance of seven veils: The forces of discursive synthesis like reason or the demands of the empirical ego are suspended from their immediate objects and contemplated from premises that are never so good as in the promising. Poetry becomes "the extreme austerity of an almost empty mind / Colliding with the lush, Rousseau-like foliage of its desire to communicate / something between breaths, if only for the sake of others."[28] Or, to put the case more abstractly, poetry is the endless qualification of both the desires acted out by this passage. Yet in this endless qualification, one begins to glimpse almost unimaginable conjunctions of empirical freedom with the abstractness of Stevens's Major Man, now relocated in traces left by the process of dissemination. This vision depends entirely on the poet's power to stage his imaginative acts as both immediate and extremely general. In that site one need not quest for "truth," because the mind achieves a point of view that includes the nature of points of view and captures the movement of their living one another's life and dying one another's death as they play out the motives within our meanings.

Once the poet can so position himself, "no way of knowing" can be transformed into "the way the songs shadow as you bend over it,"[29] so that the shadow shares with the haze of enchantment a power to fascinate us into ideal spaces reason has no reason to inhabit. Thus in "Flowering Death" Ashbery turns self-reflexiveness into a metaphysical poetry where discursiveness embodies a sense of the elemental only gestured at by the scenic deep image:

> It is their collective blankness, however,
> That betrays the notion of a thing not to be destroyed.
> In this, how many facts we have fallen through
> And still the old facade glimmers there,
> A mirage, but permanent. We must first trick the idea
> Into being, then dismantle it,
> Scattering the pieces on the wind,

So that the old joy, modest as cake, as wine and friendship
Will stay with us at the last, backed by the night
Whose ruse gave it our final meaning.[30]

Instead of building toward emotional fulfillment in the natural metaphor
of night, Ashbery has night serve as a "ruse" for capturing "our" conditions of meaning. If man does not invent death, he does invent out of
his sense of death a framework for appreciating both quotidian values
and the space figured forth by the casual exchanges of "I" and "you."
The final joy is contemplating the ground those exchanges engender as
they define the essential equation of meaning within meaninglessness and
become an abstract figure for the desire informing that absurd and sublime process.

7
Self-reflection as action: the recent work of Adrienne Rich

If some quantitative measure of self-consciousness were the basic norm for poetry, there would be no question that Ashbery is our most important poet. But my claims about lucidity do not entail such conclusions. Self-consciousness is a means, not an end. And its presence or absence matters less than the particular qualities of it a poet employs. Charles Wright, Hugo, and Merrill are extremely self-conscious poets, but their treatments of self-consciousness tend to weaken their poems. Wright's poems subsume it into craft and subtle sensations, Hugo's revel in reflecting on himself posing in roles he never takes responsibility for, and Merrill's are so conscious of his own position that they offer only attitudes to strike, not significant things to say, with regard to the topics flowing through his mind. Conversely, there are several significant alternatives to Ashbery's way of positioning the self-reflective mind. I think, for example, of Robert Duncan's recent speculative meditations linking the processes of mind to basic natural forces, of David Antin's experiments in creating a community around a casually self-reflexive narrative voice, of Derek Walcott's penetrating uses of his ambivalence about

165

America, or of younger poets like Charles Hartman, who try to adapt Ashbery to an artful discursive style that echoes High Renaissance lyricism. Nonetheless, for a distinctive imagination, for the power of a style others can adapt, and for engaging many of the basic problems of our culture, the most significant alternative to Ashbery is the recent work of Adrienne Rich.

If Ashbery refines "fence-sitting / raised to the level of an esthetic ideal,"[1] Rich shows how poetry can become a challenge to fence-sitting and in large part a redefinition of aesthetic ideals. At her best this "woman sworn to lucidity"[2] develops a discursive lyric speech strong enough to absorb and transform the passive qualities of the scenic style into figures for a poetic will reconstructing the mind and forming a self committed to political identity. Her way of conquering the scenic mode refuses both the defenses of irony and the consolations of craft. Instead she manages to project poetry as a force within social life, a force that literally exemplifies a woman's capacity to integrate subjectivity and community, memory and potential, self-reflexive mediation and believable speech. Such an enterprise risks idealizing itself almost as much as I am idealizing it, but Rich eventually comes to terms with the excesses in her programmatic work and makes that awareness an index of the values one can create as a discursive and political poet. Full of longing and sick of passivity, she makes poetry a way of resisting contemplative states where the collapse of will passes as the triumph of intelligence. Self-consciousness becomes the dramatic vehicle for self-definition.

Rich's concern for exemplary acts of self-definition leads to a critique like Pinsky's of contemporary poetry as enervated romanticism. But her reasons differ from his in much the same way as do her ideas of how poetry must be discursive. For Rich, contemporary poetry fails because it has lost touch with any significant source of energy. Expectations about the medium are less at fault than expectations about life. Poets work in the last stages of a culture characterized by an exhausted, but still dominant egotism that has "misconstrued energy not as Eternal Delight but as pure Will": "I have thought that the sense of doom and resignation to loneliness endemic in much masculine poetry has to do with a sense of *huis clos,* of having come to an end of a certain kind of perception."[3]

Keen as this criticism is, it also betrays some of the most problematic elements in Rich's work. Her explanation seems at once too simple and somewhat blind to the nature of her own achievement. If the weaknesses she describes derive largely from an oppressive sense of what counts as lucidity, vague ideals of a feminine source are not likely to restore writers' or readers' confidence in the speculative poetic imagination. And if the main emotional problem is passivity, the logical solution is less a cultivating of sheer delight than a return to using the imagination as an instrument allied with the struggles of will. Most important, Rich seems to me to belie her own greatest strength. Hers is hardly a poetry of "Eternal Delight," but it is a masterful exercise in adapting artistic skill to the processes of defining and taking responsibility for an identity.

As the example of Rich's criticism indicates, it is not always easy to concentrate on her strengths. So a good part of this chapter will be as concerned with how to read Rich as it is with her specific concerns. In my view some of her ideas are little more than slogans, and others seem to me unnecessarily confined to female subjects. On the one hand she can be too general, on the other not general enough. The latter problem is relatively easy to address, although my proposal may prove controversial. If we are to appreciate fully the general import of Rich's poetry – that is, if we are to let males identify with what they overhear – we must read her explicit themes on two levels: as particular responses to woman's plight in our time and as instances of general human concerns for identity and community.

Treating her ideas and the occasional awkward or shrill attitudes they elicit is more difficult, especially since there are already sharp critical dichotomies about her recent work.[4] I think it is clear that we cannot ignore her assertions or treat them as donnés that allow her to create engaging aesthetic objects. Commitment to her ideas is a crucial feature of Rich's poems and, as we shall see, a basic factor in understanding the depth and originality of *A Wild Patience Has Taken Me This Far*. Instead of ignoring the commitment, we must concentrate on the qualities of consciousness and grasp of contemporary experience it produces. This orientation will not justify all her ideas or save all the poems, but it should get us beyond discussions that bog down in overt ideology – hers or ours. Her positive qualities emerge most clearly, I think, if we treat Rich's ideas not as abstract generalizations about the world but as instruments within a general project of making "the woman in the poem and the woman writing the poem become the same person."[5] The project, then, is primarily ethical, a matter of ethos. Ideas are one of the ways Rich tries to produce and to test a set of character traits exemplifying a woman's power to create an identity in touch with plausible sources of strength and capable of responding forcefully to an oppressive sociopolitical order. Her poetry is less an assertion of ideas than a quest "to live / in a clearheaded tenderness."[6] Ideas are dialectical features of that quest, as significant for the adjustments in self-understanding they produce as for the general stance toward experience they simultaneously describe and warrant. Finally, this poetic project must be measured not on aesthetic terms but by the existential consequences of poetic craft – by whether or not we can respect the poetic persona produced and the model of community she hopes to produce through the witness she bears.

Describing the poetry in and of this project will not require another tracing of Rich's development from the author of well-made lyrics to radical feminism. We know what she says and the stages in her learning how to say it. We need, nonetehless, ways of describing the force of what she says, especially as it creates an alternative to the dominant mode. Thus I shall concentrate on three basic qualities of her work: its processes of defining and testing personal identity, its capacity to make private states serve as public political testimony, and her elaborating a discursive style that absorbs scenic moments into a dynamic process of self-consciousness capable of linking the poet to her community. For my purposes we need to focus only on her last two volumes, *The Dream of a Common Language* and *A Wild Patience Has Taken Me This Far*. It is here that she fully recognizes how to achieve what her earlier volumes sought. Poetry can become an example of character and the ground of community by making its mode of speech an index of powers of consciousness affording possible stances toward experience. Personal voice can be active, flexible, and compelling in its engagements. Minimally, this model of voice prevents poetry from becoming a delicate instrument for playing nostalgic harmonies. Ideally, personal speech becomes the vehicle for a form of presence that requires no elaborate rhetoric of the numinous. Voice in context is "self-delighting, self-appeasing, self-affrighting" because its energies and permutations are direct, virtually literal expressions of how the poet might encounter experience beyond the text. With Rich we can stress the poetry of and as her politics.

Rich's poetics of the speaking voice has as its basic task a need to overthrow the constructed, illusionistic drama of perceptions one finds in the scenic mode. Drama must remain, but now as an image of poetic construction under the constant pressure of the self's need to understand her world and to share that understanding: "There must be ways, and we will be finding out more and more about them, in which the energy of creation and the energy of relation can be united."[7] This is not simply the poetics of process she had worked out by 1969. Then she thought of process largely in epistemological terms, that is, as a means of gaining access to fluid and contradictory feelings that one suppresses if the poem is too consciously controlled. With *The Dream of a Common Language,* she develops a sense of process emphasizing the connection between composition and constructing a responsible self. Writing is more than a process of self-discovery; it is taking a stance as one absorbs a life into linguistic forms and imagines the social roles those forms can play. Instead of providing tactile substitutes for action, Rich wants poems to test what language can achieve in a world made of more (or less) than pure texts:

If from time to time I envy
the pure annunciations to the eye

the visio beatifica
if from time to time I long to turn

like the Eleusinian hierophant
holding up a simple ear of grain

for return to the concrete and everlasting world
what in fact I keep choosing

are these words, these whispers, conversations
from which time after time the truth breaks moist and green.[8]

The final metaphor exemplifies the conjunction Rich seeks. Language
may seem abstract and mediated in comparison with the other states of
vision in the poem. But "these words, these whispers, conversations" in
fact recuperate and extend natural powers because they satisfy "the drive
to connect," thus fulfilling our deepest natural desires to know and feel
that our knowledge is shared. That is why we care about truth. Rich's
specific truths also claim to return women to their nature in another,
perhaps deeper, sense. Speech is a radical political act cutting through
cultural traditions and refusing the self-pity of victimhood that ties women
to imposed definitions of their nature. Even their resistance has been
appropriated as a mark of frustration and failure. But now Rich hopes to
dramatize models for "choosing ourselves   each other   and this life":

What kind of beast would turn its life into words?
What atonement is this all about?
– and yet, writing words like these, I'm also living . . .

And how have I used rivers, how have I used words
to escape writing of the worst thing of all –
not the crimes of others, not even our own death,
but the failure to want our freedom passionately enough
so that blighted elms, sick rivers, massacres would seem
mere emblems of that desecration of ourselves?[9]

II

This is poetry of sheer assertion. Its success depends on two sets
of factors: internal ones that illustrate the poet's power to control experience by intelligence and external ones that determine the depth and
quality of that grasp of experience as she defines her processes of choos-

ing. Will must be able to master language, and the language must give significance to the will it expresses. Readers are likely to demand this interrelationship, and consequently the poet is likely to demand of herself that she continually scrutinize the grounds and consequences of her assertions.

In discussing Rich, then, I shall proceed in three steps. First I want to demonstrate how well she handles the internal factors in her best assertive poem, "Transcendental Etude," which serves as a coda to *The Dream of a Common Language*.[10] Here she gathers the volume's tensions between natural and unnatural (or metaphoric syntheses and metonymic gulfs between emblems and their referents) within a celebration of the power of grounded voice to transform the passive, scenic self into full political identity. After exploring the nature of Rich's achievement in this mode I shall try to provide two kinds of contexts. Assertions are only as good as their capacity to engage problems requiring assertion, so I shall try to indicate how this successful political poem comes to terms with problems basic to Rich's poetry since about 1968. Assertions, however, are not to be appreciated solely by their relation to the past. Part of Rich's greatness is her refusal to be satisfied by such assertions. She makes them points of departure, or the creation of new sites for imaginative inquiry. Indeed, her best work in my view is the process of dialectical self-reflection in *A Wild Patience* through which she tries to understand exactly what her assertions commit her to and the emotional price she must pay in remaining faithful to them. In these reflections she finally wins her battle to subordinate aesthetic questions to simple human concerns for the ways in which poems might express a life and offer it to a community.

"Transcendental Etude" begins in the scenic mode, one more foray in poetic deer hunting. The scene, however, releases energies that cannot be contained within the meditative lyric mind alone. They require the speaking voice to become conscious of its powers by adapting private memory to public contexts. Then memory presents an imperative to spell out the relation of "the fertility and fragility of all this sweetness," won in a moment where nature breaks through a debased language, to the social problem of women needing to rescue their lives from analogous demonic forces:

> No one ever told us we had to study our lives,
> make of our lives a study, as if learning natural history
> or music, that we should begin
> with the simple exercises first
> and slowly go on trying
> the hard ones, practicing till strength
> and accuracy became one with the daring.

Rich is careful to acknowledge the distinction between nature and culture Pinsky insists upon, but primarily in order to insist on the possibility of their complementing one another. Poetic will is woman's way (and, I insist, a basic human power) of extending natural fertility to cultural domains:

> No one who survives to speak
> new language, has avoided this:
> the cutting-away of an old force that held her
> rooted to an old ground
> the pitch of utter loneliness
> where she herself and all creation
> seem equally dispersed, weightless, her being a cry
> to which no echo comes or can ever come
>
> But in fact we were always like this,
> rootless, dismembered: knowing it makes the difference.

Such generalized memories build to a final challenge:

> two women, eye to eye
> measuring each other's spirit, each other's
> limitless desire,
> A whole new poetry beginning here.

Rich's response to that challenge mounts slowly, from a quiet sense that "vision begins to happen in such a life," through a catalogue of the domestic features of life a woman can will as her own, to a final self-conscious integration of all the descriptions and metaphors:

> Such a composition has nothing to do with eternity,
> the striving for greatness, brilliance –
> only with the musing of a mind
> one with her body, experienced fingers quietly pushing
> dark against bright, silk against roughness,
> pulling the tenets of a life together
> with no mere will to mastery,
> only care for the many-lived, unending
> forms in which she finds herself,
> becoming now the sherd of broken glass
> slicing light in a corner, dangerous
> to flesh, now the plentiful, soft leaf
> that wrapped round the throbbing finger, soothes the wound;
> and now the stone foundation, rockshelf further
> forming underneath everything that grows.

There are no small want ads here. There is a good deal of Yeatsian idealization, but it is sustained by the flexibility of self and the capacity to treat metaphors as simple, just extensions of natural, descriptive speech. The will to metaphor need not be a will to rhetorical, "poetic" effects, nor must the poet choose between self-consciously parodying her imaginative exuberance or concealing that exuberance by subordinating will to grounds where there reigns only a carefully wrought evocative silence. Metaphor is simply the basic vehicle for composition. It makes available for public thought the many-sidedness of woman's potential, while allowing the poet to recognize the naturalness that moves her to realize her powers. Her mastery does not depend on paralyzing both the self and the lover with Gluck's cold control. Mastery for Rich derives directly from the intensity of care, which demands as its expression and fulfillment metaphors responsive to fostering "everything that grows."

III

This relation between natural and cultural orders is more than a thematic ideal. We might say that it is their integration in her speech that gains authority for the poems. She manages to combine rich, rhetorical cadences and public themes with a sense of concrete, personal passions. Such authority is very difficult to maintain. It is threatened on one side by a temptation to heroic self-projection, to Yeats's crowing about the solitary will's triumph over incoherence, and on the other by temptations to valuing the self primarily in terms of the pathos to which its project submits it. It is perhaps only by recognizing how fully she recognizes and addresses her temptations that we learn to relax our suspicions when the poems achieve confident and plausible resolutions. So I want to concentrate here on locating in Rich's political poetry the basic problems that one can say are overcome in poems like "Transcendental Etude." At the core of these problems is Rich's need to maintain a stance at once realistic and idealized. She must then defend the idealization while locating the authority within concrete encounters. However, the most accessible poetic models for gaining authority in this way in fact contradict her project, deriving emotional intensity and personal integrity from the poet's capacity to register pathos in a dramatic situation. Rich must retain enough of that capacity to engage us in her troubles but not so much that all she offers is another example of noble victimhood. This necessity leaves her with two dangerous options: that she take as her vehicle of poetic emotion a version of the states of pathos by which our culture has trapped women or that she overcompensate for such emotions by strident assertions that in fact undermine the identity she claims. Instead of building a self, such poems appear vehicles for escaping into the fantasized roles of heroine or martyr.

We have seen that for Rich silence is less a means to transcendence than a condition of powerlessness imposed both by the blindness of others and by one's own fears of having nothing of consequence to say or of having too much to say that is all bitterness and invective. Thus she must resist the scenic mode, but clear needs are not necessarily easy to translate into practice. Consequently, many of the most moving poems even in *Diving into the Wreck* are emotionally at odds with the powers they would generate. Their intensity lies in a scenic pathos that often substitutes for images of possible action. For example, "When We Dead Awaken" turns on finding an adequate language for women's social plight. Metonymic details set the scene, but then in summary the poem reaches for metaphors like those of "Transcendental Etude":

> – tell it over and over, the words
> get thick with unmeaning –
> yet never have we been closer to the truth
> of the lies we were living, listen to me:
> the faithfulness I can imagine would be a weed
> flowering in tar, a blue energy piercing
> the marred atoms of a bedrock disbelief.[11]

However, "listen to me" betrays a deep uneasiness. The metaphors are so figurative, so tied to an old language of evasive fantasies, that they in fact call attention to gulfs between the poetic and the true. Rich offers not the truth about lies and a concrete example of fidelity but the transformation of actual problems into figurative solutions that make disbelief harder to dispel. The best one can say for these lines is that the images present an ironic, pathetic state where the imaginary and the effectual prove incompatible. But revealing the temptations of the imaginary is not the truth the poem seeks.

A similar escape to the imaginary becomes even more problematic in the conclusion to "Incipience," a poem about denying the dreams of men and "imagining the existence / of something uncreated / this poem / our lives":

> Outside the frame of their dream we are stumbling up the hill
> hand in hand, stumbling and guiding each other
> Over the scarred volcanic rock.[12]

These images are a long way from new creation. They make me think of the illustrated cover to a cheap paperback romance, *After the Disaster: Love and Freedom in the Wasteland*. The images seek to produce both strength and pathos. But in the lyric mode, without extended dramatic development, and, here, without any form of action except imaginary gestures, those qualities breed only melodrama. And melodrama contradicts all the hopes the poem asserts. The speaker remains, despite her will, trapped in dreams that for centuries men have imposed on the female imagination.

These endings may well be only symptoms of a deeper problem inherent in the style Rich chooses as her vehicle to escape well-made poems and made-to-please psychology. At the end of the sixties her will to change led her to explore a variety of free-verse forms structured by implicit juxtapositions among diverse scenes. This style could capture the fluid, fragmentary aspects of experience while multiple threads of coherence might disclose the unconscious realities and forces relatively free of the oppressive patriarchical orders that determine discursive intelligibility. Yet for Rich the style was probably a mistake.[13] It did not give enough play to her remarkably precise intelligence and capacity to control syntax and cadence. (Compare the quotations given here to the state of concentration that is both the subject and the experience of early poems like "An Unsaid Word," where the single sentence and delayed verb dramatize Rich's power to hold in a single thought quite divergent materials.) More important, the juxtapositional, notational style was so successful in capturing the flow of consciousness that it could not produce any of the counterpressure by which one establishes individual identity. The overlapping scenes and reflections present a deep vision of a personal plight; they even give mythic and historical dimensions to the plight. But they do not have the power to transform plight into active personal choices. The style's passivity is part of the poet's lament, not part of her solution.

Because I sound like Yeats on Pound's being only a mirror of the flux in his mind, I must be cautious. Yeats did not see that Pound's form of juxtaposition was also an attack on scenic self-indulgence or passive submission to events. For Pound, juxtaposition was radical selection, the result of powers of concentration to dwell almost exclusively within luminous details. Rich does not have Pound's options. He could rely on details because he accepted the historical energies and imaginative orders they transferred to the present. There is for her no resonant background not shaped by an oppressor. She must render the scenes and the strength to absorb the scenes into her own definitions of luminous details. Yet her means often fail. Series of scenes become an invitation to contemplative passivity or even to the self-indulgent fantasies of the lines I just quoted. The style will not translate pathos into an effective ethos.

In her most effective renderings of pathos Rich seems to recognize this link between her frustrated powerlessness and the only style available in which she can even render the pain. Consider another concluding segment, this time to "The Burning of Paper Instead of Children:"

> I am composing on the typewriter late at night, thinking of today. How well we all spoke. A language is a map of our failures. Frederick Douglass wrote an English purer than Milton's. People suffer highly in poverty. There are methods but we do not use them. Joan, who could not read, spoke some peasant form of French. Some of the suffering are: it is hard to tell the truth; this is America; I cannot touch you now. In America we have only the present tense. I am in danger. You are in danger. The burning of a book arouses no sensation in me. I know it hurts to burn. There are flames of napalm in Catonsville, Maryland. I know it hurts to burn. The typewriter is overheated, my mouth is burning, I cannot touch you and this is the oppressor's language.[14]

The forces of oppression ultimately reduce the poem to prose and prose to obsessive repetition among associations. Rich becomes Creeley without his self-irony, but with the self-hatred the irony can relieve. Most terrifying is the collapse of all time into the present and hence all community into solipsism. Even the lyric moments within the poem leave only these unconnected traces. The pure present manifests itself as a metonymic perversion of spirit – the composing mind reduced to phrases, scene absorbed into a language divorced from touch, and the self become only an anxious cry trapped in its own needs.

Given such pressures, it should not be surprising that Rich often overcompensates. If passivity continually frustrates, the obvious alternative is to seek some means to project idealizations that at once disclose and justify certain courses of action. Yet, as my brief contrast to Pound indicates, idealization is extremely difficult for someone with Rich's beliefs. She simply has no models. There are no contexts for indirectly giving dignity to the self and no roles into which the self can be subsumed, no mind of Europe that rewards impersonality by embracing its constructions. Even the great women writers found ways to sublimate or ignore their anger, so they provide sustenance but not guidance for Rich's project.[15] So much for her relation to the past. Her relation to the future then becomes extremely problematic. Lacking models yet desiring change, she cannot just do without ideal images. She must turn herself into a representative figure, at once victim of an oppressive history and the necessary emblem of plausible alternatives to it.

But the role of self-created model is a dangerous one, the more so in proportion to her sense of its private as well as public necessity. The features that serve as exemplary are selections from the experiencing self. When one makes such selections while resisting private anxieties, there are obvious and powerful temptations to conceal – from the self as well as others – basic aspects of one's actual emotions. It is all too easy, as Tennyson and Yeats show, to see the self largely in third-person, public terms. There are then numerous possible vacillations between the actual self and the possible selves that one's audience needs (or that the self as audience needs). Conversely, if the model is to have power, it requires a structure of sharp contrasts to other kinds of selves or to blocking social problems (for example, by blanket charges of patriarchy). This need for contrast also intensifies the temptation to exaggerate one's sense of vic-timhood in order to dramatize the forces oppressing women. Finally, all these existential problems are compounded in Rich's poetry by the desire to unite speaker and writer, for then the actual self is always responsible for its fantasies and projections – a noble moral stance but often a disas-trous poetic one, unless one masters techniques of self-irony.

"The Stranger" compresses into a poem brief enough to quote in its entirety the fundamental problems of strained idealization that occur throughout Rich's poetry:

> Looking as I've looked before, straight down the heart
> of the street to the river
> walking the rivers of the avenues
> feeling the shudder of the caves beneath the asphalt
> watching the lights turn on in the towers
> walking as I've walked before
> like a man, like a woman, in the city
> my visionary anger cleansing my sight
> and the detailed perceptions of mercy
> flowering from that anger
>
> If I come into a room out of the sharp misty light
> and hear them talking a dead language
> if they ask me my identity
> what can I say but
> I am the androgyne
> I am the living mind you fail to describe
> in your dead language
> the lost noun, the verb surviving
> only in the infinitive
> the letters of my name are written under the lids
> of the newborn child.[16]

This poem acknowledges its status as a pure construct of the imaginary, so one would think that it defuses critical suspiciousness. Yet, in Rich, states of vision must be connected to possible dispositions toward action; this is her great danger and great strength. If we are to take her as seriously as I think she intends to be taken, we must examine the qualities of person the fantasy reveals and hopes to transfer. Here the answers are depressing. The idealized figure who walks the streets could be Ed Dorn's *Gunslinger*. Or perhaps we should think of Gary Cooper suddenly attuned to "the shudder of the caves," as if Westerns could become Cocteau fantasies. Yet Rich cannot treat these associations ironically. She needs a new heroine. In a brief space dignity must be born and must have male and female attributes. The need, however, is all too evident. It is hard not to see the rhetorical strategies as dictating the mythic elements, rather than the mythic vision requiring the rhetoric. Rich's reach may negate her grasp.

Take the treatment of anger as a first example. Her concept of female anger is deep and precise. Anger cleanses the sight because it brings one to full self-consciousness and frees one from the repressive force of *ressentiment* that blocks full compassion. But must it be visionary? Does it require the androgyne as a figure unifying the anger and the mercy? The mythic reach here tends to make the discursive clarity seem as fantasized as the androgyne figure. This marriage of myth and reality is one where each partner might do better on his or her own.

If the treatment of anger were the only place where the two principles cross, my complaints would be only positivist grumpiness. In fact, though, all the problems get much more severe in the last stanza, ultimately undermining the assertion of identity necessary to Rich's project. Structurally, the second stanza shifts from streets to a room, and from external observation to claims for an identity that cannot be made or understood in the "dead language." But the inside seems terribly impersonal because it is so mystified – as if one could assert identity only in fantasy, in defensive or evasive gestures masking as heroism. The crucial problem is the relation between will and language. Once she must posit her images of value on the other side of language, Rich condemns herself to conditions analogous to those we saw in the scenic modes relying on pregnant silence. There is no determinate content to satisfy an all-too-determinate need. She goes to myth as a way of projecting beyond the dead language some alternative text, some verb that sustains the living "I" and the living mind. But no one can read that text except by self-projections. Otherwise the letters of the name remain illegible, dividing the person into an empirical actor and a fantasized vision of the self as hero. When one's name appears in this language, one can never know if the name read is one's own or an image made up in order to escape the self's actual condition.

IV

Difficulties like these persist in Rich's most recent work. Acute critics like Helen Vendler are correct in virtually all of their specific charges against individual lines. But such accuracy begs the larger question of appropriateness. I suspect that one would be as accurate in making the same charges against Whitman, and as far from the mark. First of all, both poets base their enterprise on rejecting traditional aesthetic criteria. Were Rich not to challenge these criteria, she would risk condemnation on her own terms, because it is crucial to her that women no longer seek to please, or not to displease, what appear to be essentially male cultural demands.[17] Rejection of criteria does not, of course, suffice to free one from them if the criteria are basic to values one appeals to. Rejection must be accompanied by alternative standards. For Rich, the standards are very simple. Poetry matters to the extent that it makes possible new forms of consciousness that give women "access to their own powers" – whether these be for new styles of poetry or for new ways of representing ourselves in our actions and commitments.[18] Poetry, then, is not different from other modes of discourse except for the focused interrelations it emphasizes and the emotional challenges it poses if the writer is not to appear bathetic or melodramatic. Rich hopes to meet that test by fully elaborating her concern to unite the woman speaking the poem with the woman writing it. Poetry then becomes in part a process of self-criticism, in part a process of adapting these criticisms into plausible idealizations of states of mind and stances. One earns authority not by retrospect but by the way the qualities one's acts exemplify promise an ethos for the future.

We can see Rich implicitly approaching her work with the same critical standards her critics employ, but then interpreting the problems as part of the content she must confront in self-consciousness. Rejecting traditional lyric criteria leads Rich in her recent political poetry to construct standards of self-reflexive lucidity. Poetry matters because of the ways it helps one live one's life. And one demonstrates that conviction by dramatizing the process of trying to understand that life – by recognizing one's blindnesses, by attempting to have one's recognitions lead to worthwhile goals, and by taking full responsibility for the consequences of pursuing the goals. This means, on the one hand, elaborating the ideals of a poem like "Transcendental Etude" and, on the other, idealizing the process of grappling with problems of idealization.

The mode that reaches fulfillment in "Transcendental Etude" gets established at the very beginning of *The Dream of a Common Language*. The title itself carries a strong criticism of much of Rich's earlier political work. The myth that matters is not one beyond language but one of language. The oppressive forces, then, are not ontological features of mediation, the old romantic cry, but political factors that prevent language from fulfilling functions inherent in its potential nature. Rich is to romanticism what Habermas is to Hegel: more restricted and more conceivably effective in leading to changes in our politics.

These implications become explicit in the volume's introductory poem, "Power," whose task is to reverse traditional expectations of the role of myth in poetry. The first lines echo Kore myths as the poet thinks of a bottle of medicine unearthed from a construction site. Rich, however, quickly shifts from medicine to the making of medical cures, from passivity to activity, and hence from mythic associations to a specific historical figure, Madame Curie, whose legacy can take concrete form in discursive language. Curie is not quite a model. Instead she establishes a different kind of authority. The poet need not locate single models from the past but can try to construct a sense of community with a variety of women who appear in memory. Even the differences that prevent the past from passing on models become potentially productive by demanding a reciprocal dialogue. Sympathy with another's problems can lead to understanding features of one's own condition, and efforts at self-definition can become instruments for appreciating the problems oppressing others.

In this exchange there is considerable sustenance for Rich's hopes to overcome several dichotomies, especially that between private and public lives.[19] As a community forms with the past, and as sympathy produces self-knowledge, it is possible to imagine poetry as a form of action. In poems one aligns oneself with other women and one tries to dramatize one's capacity to take power through and for them. If Curie died "denying / her wounds   came   from the same source as her power,"[20] then one can use her life to see how the two aspects might be united. And one can use one's sympathy as the contrastive term directing and dignifying the poet's quest to explore her own wounds as potential sources of power. Her project can depend not on a fantasized self but on grounding the imagination in history and then testing oneself against its realities. Once we have this historical consciousness, it is possible to give poetic voice a concrete focus. Instead of a person's being absorbed within scenes, scenes become challenges to the poet to produce a discursive poetic framework adapting them to the concerns of a society. Now Rich's greatest liability becomes an important source of strength. Her obsession with victimhood and her various forms of self-staging become states she can offer within a version of Augustine's confessional community. If she, and we, can understand her intense reactions as states of consciousness to be read dramatically rather than programmatically, they become the wounds within which lie both sources of power and tests of the qualities of a reflective poet to understand and direct her life.

We have seen where this initial project leads. But "Transcendental Etude" cannot be a stopping place because its assertions of identity have yet to meet the very tests of history that sanction figures like Madame Curie. Those tests, in turn, require Rich's articulating the inappropriateness of aesthetic criteria. *A Wild Patience Has Taken Me This Far* is her response to that challenge. Here the single norm for the person speaking the poem is the power she dramatizes that the writer can wield as a historical agent. If we are to appreciate this work fully, we must read it not by aesthetic criteria, but from the inside, as a project for exploring the interconnections between poetry and life. Thus I propose to treat the volume as a single, unified text working out the possible grounds and possible consequences of the ideals of freedom, community, and poetic speech elaborated in *The Dream of a Common Language*. I doubt that each poem was written solely with an eye to its place in a volume. Rather, I suspect that after she finished several poems she saw how they articulated the emotional curve her life was taking. She then began to use them as a record of the demands on her to change while remaining faithful to a set of principles. Indeed, how else acknowledge the difficulties of change, the slidings and adjustments one must make, and above all, the powers conferred by reflecting on the process, unless we consider individual states as elements of a larger process? In that process, moreover, Rich in effect shows that a political poet need not choose between aesthetic criteria and loose propaganda. She asks us to suspend aesthetic criteria, but only so that we can take a reflective attitude toward her capacity to make language and cadence instruments in understanding, testing, and taking responsibility for the choice of a life.

Making a self worth attending to requires demonstrating power to reflect on the problems that arise from choices, especially problems of oversimplification that breed the excesses I have been discussing. The scenic mode cannot entertain criticism of itself; Rich's recent poetry by contrast depends on a continual self-scrutiny that does not collapse into quiescent self-irony. Thus the power of the poetry resides not in the ideas, which remain somewhat simplistic, but in the poet's grasp of what it is like to try to live in accord with an explicit body of ideals and commitments. Like Yeats in *The Tower* and Lowell in his later poetry, Rich explores a form of poetry in which the work is not primarily a figurative, illusionistic construct that applies to the world as a hypothetical label for possible emotions. Rather, the poems are intended to function as literal examples of living and writing within what history makes possible and necessary. So the greatness of such poems lies less in how they structure experience than in how they dramatize capacities to reflect on and within it as the poets try to keep themselves from hardening into their ideas or using their poetic powers to create alternative worlds. Emphasizing the internal coherence of a volume, then, is not for Rich primarily an aesthetic act but a way of insisting that poems and lives can be continuous, can deepen one another when framed as a single process.

The unity of a volume of poetry is awkward to elaborate. Simply covering the scope leaves little room to get beyond thematics or to provide sufficient quotation and close commentary. So I beg the indulgence of my readers and ask them to follow along in *A Wild Patience* in order to consider my descriptions. "Images," which the compliant reader will notice is the first poem,[21] states the volume's central tension and its central fear. The tension is between images that dismember and those which allow mutual acts of remembering. The fear is that the resources available to the private self who must remember "would not be enough." The initial pressures in the volume are enough to make Rich's voice shrill, her anger vacillating between its demonic poles of self-pity and self-righteousness, and her reliance on personal relations apparently incapable of carrying the force, or even the cadence, she requires for them. I quote the most awkward moment because its overgeneralized claims reveal some of the difficulties in making the self an emblem of social victimhood:

> And what can reconcile me
> that you, the woman whose hand
> sensual and protective, brushes me in sleep
> go down each morning into such a city?

Rich must become a vehicle for rage and must register the personal consequences of public policies. But the danger of personalizing is that one treats the self as something special, demanding undue consideration and whining where one should accept reality. The streets she refers to after all are not in East Harlem or the South Bronx, where there are short vacations and often a great deal less love. So the assertive self, the self as example, easily becomes the source of blindness rather than insight and a block or a burden to community.

I cannot claim that Rich sees the problems I indicate. But the title and the position of the poem suggest that after writing it she may have seen that it could play a double function: stating themes and dramatizing the extremes to which the pressures of public life will drive the poet relying on private sources of strength and care. Certainly the first three poems of the book all offer the problems of uniting private and public, and all have very weak moments, whose exemplar is the awful conclusion to "Integrity."[22] There Rich wants to treat the power of female hands within a personal relationship as a principle for reconciling critical anger and disciplined tenderness. But the hands appear pure emblem or metonymy, that is, a figure that stands out as a fantasized wish incapable of performing the enormous public task assigned to it. All this, however, is probably prelude to the next poem, "Culture and Anarchy," which attempts to get beyond the relation of two women into a sense of dialogue with a variety of women's voices from the past. Here Rich begins to extend the new model of self-definition elaborated by "Power." Instead of concentrating on asserting herself against an oppressive world, she can base her imaginative efforts on acts of sympathy. In sympathy she must recognize the limits of woman's will, of any will, and hence must redefine commitments as essentially fealty to a community's needs and projects. In community there is solace for failure and ground for not making failure an excuse to collapse will into ironic self-consciousness.

"Transit" is perhaps the fullest emblem of this redefinition of self as learning to recognize limits. The poem constructs a relationship to an imaginary sister – she the reflective self and her sister, the skier, the emblem of worldly self-confidence – thus staging the two basic roles that Rich must reconcile as the constituents of the freedom she pursues. Both levels come together in a superb moment where self-doubt leads to a sympathetic aligning of the self with necessity:

> How unaware she is, how simple
> this is for her, how without let or hindrance
> she travels in her body
> until the point of passing, where the skier
> and the cripple must decide
> to recognize each other?[23]

This is not the triumphant woman of "Transcendental Etude." But it is triumph nonetheless, more difficult and perhaps more enduring because the poet commits herself to exploring what the earlier triumph entails. As a thematic gesture, this reconciliation takes female heroism beyond the realms of anger and assertion. In self-doubt, in the experience of the tortuous distance between possibility and fact, one comes to a knowledge that ties the self to others and establishes a dramatic basis for the model of freedom as remembering expressed by the next poem's return to origins:

> that common life we each and all bent out of orbit from
> to which we must return simply to say
> this is where I came from
> this is what I knew . . .
>
> Freedom. It isn't once to walk out
> under the Milky way, feeling the river

> of light, the fields of dark
> freedom is daily, prose-bound, routine
> remembering. Putting together inch by inch
> the starry worlds. From all the lost collections.[24]

Freedom, then, is not the solitary transcendence for which the scenic style can suffice, nor is it Lowell's skier risking death as he follows the course of his extreme emotions. Freedom is the reconciliation of cripple and skier, each aware of the power and limitation of the other.

This ideal of freedom is more than a thematic postulate. It poses imperatives for the poetic act, which in turn test the value of the model. The central section of the volume is devoted to two of these imperatives, each involving capacities and challenges inherent in the self-definition Rich articulated in her previous book. One imperative is to make explicit the forms of mental power the poet can idealize for herself. "What Is Possible" returns to Rich's earlier fascination with male energies of concentration (for example, in "An Unsaid Word") in order to expel definitively the ghost of Wittgenstein. The skier and the cripple here take epistemological forms, and scenes become images for psychological correlates. The poem's opening succinctly captures the alternatives:

> A clear night   if the mind were clear
>
> If the mind were simple, if the mind were bare
> of all but the most classic necessities . . .
> This is how I would live if I could choose:
> this is what is possible.[25]

But the "ifs," the conditions, outweigh the possibilities, demanding and authorizing a different choice. It is the mind of woman, of woman's lot if not her necessary fate, which dwells in "ifs" and the muddied history they produce. Unity with a nature one can contemplate is simply irrelevant. The task and the choice are to attend not to metaphors of clasping planets but to the signs from history that reveal nature's darker, more dangerous threats. Not what fulfills nature, but what denies it, must become the center of attention, so possibility itself becomes an ambiguous, disturbing reminder of the horrors nature may conceal for those who read it too simply.

The second imperative follows from the first. If the object of knowledge is the shifting realm of possibilities and guilts, the poet must find ways to adapt her quest for identity to the otherness and contingency of historical being. Put in stylistic terms, she must reconcile the assertive voice of *Dream of a Common Language* with the fluid, multileveled juxtapositions of *Diving into the Wreck*. She must capture the cripple in herself without losing the skier's self-possession. Her solution is to me brilliant. She makes the cripple in herself a means of access to other psyches; then she makes the access a source of self-knowledge and basis for community. The deeper the pain, the deeper the capacity to share with other conditions, which we then, through the objectification of sharing, come to recognize as partially defining our own psyches.

In order to test her capacity to accept this imperative, Rich turns to a figure with whom she finds it difficult to sympathize. "For Ethel Rosenberg" treats sympathy by dramatizing the act of remembering as a dialectic of differentiation and identification. The poem begins with Rich as the skier and Rosenberg as the cripple, but roles oscillate rapidly under the pressure of women's political plights. All the forces come together in the final lines:

> If I have held her at arm's length till now . . .
>
> If I dare imagine her surviving
> I must be fair to what she must have lived through
> I must allow her to be at last
>
> political in her ways   not in mine . . .
> defining revolution as she defines it
>
> or, bored to the marrow of her bones
> with "politics"
> bored with the vast boredom of long pain
>
> Small; tiny in fact; in her late sixties
> liking her room   her private life
> living alone perhaps
>
> no one you could interview
> maybe filling a notebook herself
> with secrets she never sold.[26]

It is these secrets she has never sold, secrets no one possesses in such a way that they can be sold, which Rich wants to understand. For precisely because they cannot be sold they may be shared, may give access to a fundamental core of pain and of strength. The poem establishes three basic sources for this pain and the consequent sense of a deep self: betrayals by family, the difficulty of reconciling ideals with political actions, and the effects of Rich's own distance from Rosenberg's awkward, confused approach to realities she does not understand. Rich cannot share any of Rosenberg's specific beliefs or choices. But the process of the poem's remembering makes it impossible to avoid identifying with her plight. Rosenberg's deep sense of failure and frustration ultimately gives her a deep self, beyond politics and even beyond language – secret in the fullest sense. Yet that secrecy can become a gift, a force for aligning the women and, especially, for giving Rich a sense of where her own political frustrations leave her. Read in the context of the volume as a whole, this is the poem where Rich has to see herself as other, her ideals as partial traps. But in that seeing, she reestablishes another, less willful principle for defining oneself as a self within history, tied to a community of women by bonds that only poetry can speak.

From this perspective Rich can write a strange companion poem on Simone Weil that uses history as an alternative to Weil's self-inflicted torment. Here the movement is from sympathy to an increasing distance, but we eventually see that the distance takes place within a deep identification. In Weil, Rich finds her own tendency to posit authenticity through imaginary visions of the self as victim, and through Weil she manages an extremely complex form of address to the "you" that combines sympathy and raw, self-divisive self-confrontation:

> What is your own will that it
> can so transfix you
> why are you forced to take this test
> over and over and call it God
> why not call it you and get it over
> you with your hatred of enforcement
> and your fear of blinding?[27]

In judging Weil and the Weil in Rich, she holds in a single thought the positive motives for her own secular project and the negative self-judgments that perhaps must accompany a necessary single-mindedness.

These specific encounters frame a set of poems exploring the two poles of identification – with those intimately involved in Rich's private existence and with essentially public figures around whom diverse women might organize their energies. "Mother-in-Law," the first of these, offers perhaps the most complex feelings in the book. Rich wants to transpose to her actual personal relations the imaginative dialogue that could create such bonds with Rosenberg. But actual persons will not stand still to have their secrets known or to sympathize fully with Rich's. Instead we get a chillingly impersonal frame that echoes the ballad form of repetitive questions. Such distance is a protective device for facing an encounter where imagination cannot bridge the distance between different kinds of women's lives. The mother-in-law seems to have genuine desire to give and receive sympathy. But Rich sees that the exchange is impossible – first because the daughter-in-law's reflexive consciousness produces a sense of difference that tempts her to various forms of righteous self-staging. Were she to yield to that temptation, however, Rich might have saved herself the pain of stating the truths that divide them. Instead she does state her secret, in a plain record of facts over the past ten years. But here facts are weapons, because Rich knows the facts cannot produce some transpersonal objectivity. Once the facts are out, once the mother-in-law's fantasies are shattered, there will be no more efforts at intimacy. So the speaker returns at the very end – half in defiance, half in depressed isolation and a sense of political failure – to the impersonal motif of asking questions. In this formal gesture she can at last establish a mode of civility that partially masks the pain and distance.

The tone of "Mother-in-Law" permeates the relationships to different groups of women in the middle of *A Wild Patience*. In effect, the two imperatives – to the confusion of history and to a poetics of sympathy – pull against one another. The more carefully Rich looks at women's lives, the deeper her sense of both the need to overthrow oppression and the difficulties of the task becomes. And this sense in turn requires her to shift her vision of freedom. Freedom becomes less an abstract ideal than a condition characterized primarily by a set of inescapable oppositions. One is torn between the possible and the actual, between lives dreamed and lives that must be lived. To insist too much on actual differences among women or the difficulty of changing lives may be to opt for a premature tragic sense of limits. Positing necessity always can be an excuse for accepting one's own privileges without any corresponding responsibility to work for others. But to commit oneself to dreams that cannot be realized is to give way to sentimentality and, worse, to court the bitter disillusion and loss of sympathy that follow. The two states cannot be integrated; this is one of the many dichotomies that Rich comes to realize will not be resolved simply by attributing evils to patriarchal culture and imagining alternative structures. But the two states can perhaps be balanced so that one learns to accept both sets of fears and both sets of pains without letting either conquer or paralyze commitments to bringing about new self-images for women.

"Frame"[28] brings into focus all these tensions. It looks back to the division and frustration of the poems preceding it, and it introduces a final sequence of poems that try to recuperate a modified basis for hope in the will founded on sympathetic acts rather than on abstract political ideals. "Frame" is not without its own delusions, at least in my eyes, but by this point in the volume the limitations of or unconscious symptoms in her acts become part of the dramatic experience. The poem is based on a complex sense of scene as Rich recounts a narrative of injustice involving a black girl. Yet the force of the poem resides primarily at the margins of the narrative, in the italic statements expressing Rich's feelings of outrage, frustration, and sympathy. The poet again seeks identification, but here under the pressures of a social order that isolates women and of a literary medium sadly tangential to the order of events. Rich's goal is to make the margin a place where identity and identification can and must be formed. The poem keeps returning us to the poet's position: "just beyond the frame trying to see" into a world where the white males do not know they are blind. As Rich recognizes the extent of their blindness, a blindness their power makes it unnecessary for them to confront, her sense of need becomes increasingly intense. Need creates a virtual litany that becomes a link to the oppressed woman.

The price, however, is considerable. As Rich's sympathies increase, the poem becomes shrill – I think because she wants to produce a sense not of fact but of the terrors facts can produce in the oppressed. Then the concluding assertion creates a resonant, complex sense of the "there" that the poet shares with the girl:

> . . . What I am telling you
> is told by a white woman who they will say
> was never there. I say I am there.

"There" makes sympathy a specific commitment, and it insists on the poet's capacity to share a social condition despite the privileged position she often laments in her prose. Telling remains a source of power and a vehicle for self-definition against a society that crops frames in all-too-narrow, self-serving ways. The poet can make a new, self-referential picture expressing and using anger. But the very assertion of identification here reminds us of all that the poet and poetry cannot do. We are brought short before the tension between the possible and the real that Rich has established and now wants to resolve. She cannot be there in the same way the black girl was. She cannot even be an "I" in the undivided sense the last lines want to assert. Poems then appear ultimately very weak political instruments, precisely because of their way of being there. Poems allow us to think we are there, to project identities, while we are in fact somewhat uncomfortably elsewhere, never quite identifying enough to pay the political price.

At best, poems leave us there and here, coming to know the other's plight within our own sympathies and necessary differences. "Frame" does not acknowledge the plight it demonstrates, but that plight informs the two climactic poems of the volume: its longest, "The Spirit of Place," which reflects on the despair of the "Grandmother" sequence; and its concluding poem, "Turning the Wheel," which summarizes Rich's engagement in the cultural echoes of the Southwest.

"The Spirit of Place"[29] is perhaps best seen as the volume's fullest interpretation of the phrase that haunts it, some variant of "it is not enough." The opening sets the basic thematic rhythm by shifting quickly from a lovely scene to a discursive reflection encountering the irreconcilable opposites one faces when one thinks of the history transacted on that scenic stage. The contrast between place and history is then extended into a sense of duality within history because this is New England, the land where the hope of pure solutions and a new freedom could not control "the old Murderous uncaring." Necessities and blindness harden around the images one uses to foster freedom, and the agents proclaim radical solutions without radical changes of heart. Even the syntax of these opening participles participates in the ambiguous duplicities of historical being. For a moment the second section can escape these ambiguities by shifting to a quieter, more personal mood where the women can remain at peace with one another and with the spirit of place. But being there together is enough only when privacy suffices, and for women that occurs only if they are able to put aside the fact or fear of a male violence that ironically seems the more imminent the more the lovers experience their separate peace. So self-consciousness cannot be reconciled to place. It must take up a distanced perspective capable of balancing what cannot be integrated:

> . . . your split-second
> survival reflex taking in the world
>
> as it is   not as we wish it
> as it is   not as we work for it
> to be.

The poem's third section has as its subject Emily Dickinson's house, a place where scene and history coalesce. Here in effect we experience the reward of reflective self-division, because now Rich can define a third world, one of words, where she can identify with the poet who most fully articulated the contradictions of New England life, so that they constitute a permanent figure for living as a stranger in any place. Sympathy becomes a complex force, eliciting a ritual performance of the three basic familial roles a woman plays and then producing a renewed commitment to the work of making places where this kind of union remains possible.

Now the fourth section can spell out from nature and from New England the spirit of accepting limits that must inform that work. However, Rich is never content with limits unless she can make consciousness of them a bridge to some larger sense of connections and possible actions. So the final section once again turns outward to place. The scene is the clear night sky of "What Is Possible," with the same sense of expansive scope casting the night as an analogue to the lucid mind. And again she chooses history, "the world as it is   if not as it might be." This affirmation of things as they are now includes the New England history of reformist idealism. Acceptance is not submission to fate; the oriole too may be a realist. The power of her vision depends on her pushing the initial scene until the stars become an increasingly evocative figure of distance and clarity recuperating all the volume's self-division:

> Ourselves as we are   in these painful motions
>
> of staying cognizant: some part of us always
> out beyond ourselves
> knowing   knowing   knowing
>
> Are we all in training for something we don't name?
> to exact reparation for things
> done long ago to us and to those who did not
>
> survive what was done to them whom we ought to honor
> with grief   with fury   with action
> On a pure night   on a night when pollution
>
> seems absurdity when the undamaged planet seems to turn
> like a bowl of crystal in black ether
> they are the piece of us that lies out there
> knowing   knowing   knowing.

Self-division here is the prologue to whatever freedom may be possible. Self-division is the path to knowing, and knowing the access to this remarkable sense of a remembering become virtually transcendental. These stars hold one another in place as they mediate between the purity of what knowing can possess and the determination to hold onto one's situation in history without surrendering to easy solutions or oppressive social systems. The stars embody a distance from ourselves that is both the pain of knowing and the sense of grounded identity that knowing can produce because it aligns us to objective conditions. Finally, knowing creates its own litany – as an act of sheer will and as a testimony to the awe that stems from finding oneself linked to situations and persons beyond the individual ego.

Even this sense of awe, however, must be challenged and qualified before Rich can end the volume on a note of acceptance and self-knowledge. This is why she concludes with eight poems reflecting on her experiences in the Southwest, where the spirit of knowledge leads to strange and disturbing senses of place. There the spirit of place goes back beyond recorded history: Its appeal is to mythic identifications with chthonic powers whose votary is the shaman priestess. This appeal places Rich back with the thematics of *Diving into the Wreck,* but now facing the temptation of succumbing to the nostalgia for mythic answers to political and psychological problems. After a rich and complex identification with Mary Colter, a woman architect who gave up her loyalties to home and family so that she could express in art the spirit of this place,[30] Rich concludes the volume with her own refusing any such journey:

Turning the Wheel

The road to the great canyon always feels
like that road and no other
the highway to a fissure   to the female core
of a continent
Below Flagstaff even   the rock erosions wear
a famous handwriting
the river's still prevailing signature

Seeing those rocks   that road   in dreams   I know
it is happening again   as twice while waking
I am travelling to the edge   to meet the face
of annihilating and impersonal time
stained in the colors of a woman's genitals
outlasting every transient violation
a face that is strangely intimate to me

Today I turned the wheel   refused that journey
I was feeling too alone on the open plateau
of piñon juniper   world beyond time
of rockflank spread around me   too alone
and too filled with you   with whom I talked for hours
driving up from the desert   though you were far away
as I talk to you all day   whatever day.[31]

Rich insists on maintaining the poetry of discourse, now with a "you" that is at once personal and general. The way of lonely authenticity in relation to the mysteries of landscape is not a necessary alternative to social corruption. She can refuse the journey without feeling she has denied herself. There need be no false heroics, because connections to living women make demands on the present and give the sustenance needed for resisting nostalgic solutions.

Distance in time cannot be bridged, but it can make us celebrate what bridges distance in space. Discourse becomes this poet's paradigm for accepting things as they are without resigning herself to what we have made of them. If she can at once accept and criticize her own stances by risking the divisions of self-consciousness, she has every right to hope society can pursue that same endless, tauntingly gradual process of self-revision. Even male poets may follow.

8

Epilogue: Criticism and contemporary poetry

I

Ashbery's "And then" is not only an emblem for awkward beginnings. He speaks equally well for the incompleteness that haunts my sense of this ending. I have tried to praise poets while criticizing our culture's dominant ideas of poetry. This approach leaves me vulnerable on both points – as minimizing the poets' accomplishments in order to shore up my general criticisms or as selectively evading my overall strictures. The vulnerability, in turn, points to a larger problem. I have argued that criticism of contemporary poetry ignores some of its basic responsibilities if it rests content with describing the work of individual poets. We fail our culture and we fail the poets if we do not seek some general contrastive basis on which to establish the significant tasks poets must perform. Without a sense of the challenge poets face it is impossible to use more than aesthetic criteria in judging their work. Yet aesthetic criteria are in themselves not discriminating enough, because despite all the differences they elicit they do not create a frame of questioning for the poets that establishes their possible claim to canonical status.

Recognizing the need for contrastive terms, however, does not guarantee one's producing adequate ones. Were the criteria easy to establish,

I doubt critics would be content with description. So we go round in a nasty circle. Lacking general criteria, we describe; in describing we reveal the need for larger frameworks; but as we produce those frameworks their limitations drive us back to more modest and definable tasks. Critics have their own ways of repeating the conservative turns our poetry has taken.

I suspect that there is no satisfying theoretical way out of this circle. The best that critics can probably do, certainly the best that I can do, is simply to recognize that even if one's generalizations stem from problematic criteria, it is better to generalize than simply to describe. It does not take accurate, impartial vision to produce at least questions that help stage the significance of a poet's work. Whether I have done so is by now a question the reader will have decided, so there need be no more justification on this score. But we are not done with self-justification. Having insisted on self-consciousness, I cannot easily leave the book without the appearance of imposing my criterion on myself. Since I have argued that these displays of private self-consciousness can lead beyond themselves, revealing both general problems and possible stances for negotiating them, there is a special obligation on me to show that my own problems as a critic reveal confusions where choices must be made by poets and those who judge poets. Our difficulties in producing clear directions for criticism may prove one useful index of the price we pay for a poetry that for the most part does not foster complex concepts of reading or invite connections with the central questions and practices we find in other intellectual disciplines. On a more general level, reflecting on the process of criticizing a position like mine might help us locate principles of agreement beneath our differences. And could we make these principles explicit, we might motivate criticism to attempt influencing the course of poetry, a task I find uncomfortably easy to claim is a compelling one.

II

My specific doubts about the critical approach I have adopted take the form of several closely related questions: Do the poets I praise fully satisfy the criteria I use; are the criteria I use the best ones by which to praise the poets I praise; do my criteria have sufficient general relevance to justify my hierarchical claims; and, finally, if my criteria are not those most relevant to contemporary poetry, is that the fault of my criteria or of the poetry or of historical conditions requiring that one distinguish how we judge contemporary poetry from how we judge earlier work? Criticism always involves seeking the provisional stance of an outsider, of one who can see the whole. But if one gets too far outside, the whole becomes an amorphous mass, and one's terms grow inappropriate to the specific contours poetic practices create.

The most probing test of my criteria is whether they allow me to generate the fullest possible terms of praise for those poets I take as our major ones. However, it is not obvious that Rich and Ashbery are as good as I claim or that the good I claim is the good they see themselves as providing. No poet can successfully resist all forms of criticism, and every poet has a limited stance. Yet Rich and Ashbery seem more vulnerable than most major writers to sharp critical pressures that I do not fully address.

I imagine most readers would acknowledge that Rich is remarkably successful in dramatizing the powers of the self-reflexive will to construct a speaking voice responsive to the needs and possible sources of strength women encounter in contemporary society. But does that suffice to constitute major poetry? There is first of all the issue of whether her explicit address to women and questions of female identity can or should be read as an instance of more general human problems. It may be that ideals of universal human concerns are an anachronism to be replaced by what Francis Lyotard calls local narratives organizing the values of specific communities. But even then it is difficult to know whether the critic must speak from within the concerns of that community or whether the poet should take up the general implications of her refusing to address a general audience. How Rich addresses the plight of women is also a somewhat problematic issue, because her model of self-consciousness may not be sufficiently involuted or flexible. She is not free of Creeley's excessively denotative frame of reference or his ascetic sense of what a trustworthy language can be. She knows that political solutions will not suffice, yet her commitment to practical freedom may keep her from exploring the dense or elegant forms of linguistic complexity and exuberance that characterize the greatest lyric poetry. In that complexity we might find the forms of freedom poetry best exemplifies.

Finally, the emotional complexity she does preserve creates a different kind of problem. She insists that her awareness of limitations is not an excuse for domesticity but a challenge to the political will to foster a sense of mutual sympathy on which a community can be formed. But in isolating women's lives and dwelling on experiences of lack and love, she may not afford that community much more than domestic roles to play and private consciousness to cultivate. Rich is our best public poet, but the better she understands what that publicness entails the more she makes us think the role itself may be a trap, capturing one within a limited world it is poetry's role to expand.

Ashbery addresses precisely this issue, offering poetry as a model of forms of consciousness that public life cannot provide. But his work can appear even more problematic than Rich's. Where she may be trapped by pressures of reality, he may resist some of those pressures all too well, only to succumb to others. All contradictions become grist for the pleasures of consciousness and peripeties of linguistic grace as the mind makes of us what it can, so that there is in the images he constructs very little that connects reflective to practical or ethical stances. As the critics writing in *Beyond Amazement* have pointed out, Ashbery dramatizes a capacity to celebrate complexity without an irritable reaching after fact and reason, provides a source of imaginative freedom from deadening forms of closure, works out an exemplary philosophical stance toward the complexities of personal identity, and elaborates a lyric stance open to the full range of modern reality (largely urban and not rooted to geographical place) in ways that no more "naturalistic" literature can.[1] Yet all these attitudes are largely passive – a far cry from the energies Milton, Wordsworth, Keats, Yeats, and Pound devote to projecting images of human capacities that can influence behavior by establishing the terms we can use in our self-representations.

Thus, there is a second perspective from which Ashbery's characteristic stances seem to give up more than they preserve because they are all too submissive to cultural pressures in their quiescent distrust of "ethical" idealizations. His lyricism, however ironized and interwoven with marvelous stylistic and conceptual inventiveness, remains based primarily on loss, nostalgia, and memory (although his recent work seems to desire a fuller sense of the sufficiency possible within the attitudes he constructs, so there is less of the almost self-parodic nostalgia in poems like "Hop o' My Thumb"). It may be that the very elegance and sophistication of his self-consciousness so creates a quiet personal sublimity that Ashbery need not seek alternatives to our culture. He dignifies what we suffer from, and frees us to take lucid pleasure in a lurid psyche we probably cannot escape. Yet it remains all too easy to rest content in a distanced and rarefied sublime, based in fact on a range of emotions surprisingly narrow in relation to the linguistic and intellectual capaciousness the poems revel in. Ultimately, most Ashbery poems idealize the sweet, quiet nostalgia of the resigned survivor savoring what memory affords rather than exploring ways to construct new worlds that are more than fragile substitutes.[2]

His poems, for example, rarely conclude with the resonance of "Self-Portrait" or "Flowering Death." Though he continually interprets the energies of his own making, the interpretation usually dissolves into conclusions like that of "Metamorphosis," where the dance of intellect still requires and produces the nostalgic delicacies of the scenic theater. For all the clever ironies shifting the tone between camp sensibility and a self-denigrating flatness, and despite the precise rendering of romantic

fears that an impersonal "you" will absorb subjectivity as thought's eva-
nescence recedes into the cold chill of otherness, loss remains the ultimate subject and resigned composure the basic stance. Decentering the
self restores a sense of transpersonal mental energy, but a transpersonal
privacy is not much of an advance on the tacitle silences of Plumly's
concluding images. Ashbery, in other words, shares an emotional economy in which most of the ethos derives from conditions of pathos.[3]
Energy is reserved for negotiating loss and limits, and character is understood by judging actions according to the reflective attitudes they elicit,
rather than the modes of action they might project.

Much more is involved here than a need to produce a more balanced
account of Rich and Ashbery. We find ourselves confronting a basic
problem in any use of "ought." Might it not be the case that our attempts
at cure are really the essence of the disease? As Wittgenstein suggested,
it is prudent to look very closely at the moves by which any criticism
invokes the authority to assert that things can be different from what
they are. Such moves may simply be ways of avoiding necessity, or they
may exacerbate problems by making us discontented with what we can
accomplish.

One example especially disturbing to me is the possibility that the
ideal of a self-consciousness capable of transcending irony may have been
only a fantasy that enabled Yeats, Stevens, Pound, and Eliot to write
beautiful poems. When we deal with works of art we cannot escape the
possibility that what are claimed as existential values may exist primarily
for esthetic effects. And aesthetic effects often delude us about existential
possibilities. But even if early modernist poets could create valid poetic
models for social identity, our problems do not stop. Why should the
same gestures be available to contemporary poets? As we see most clearly
in Grecophiles like Hannah Arendt, values taken from the past tend to
be excuses for nostalgically evading the present. However bitter the pill,
it may be the case that we must let the poets express what values are
possible in a given time and try to adjust ourselves to them.[4]

Their track record is certainly better than that of critics. If social structures leave us only private lives to cultivate, and if intellectual shifts make
the speculative imagination appear a vestigial function, poets of the scenic mode may have a good deal to tell us. One can even make Ashbery,
if not Rich, our major poet on these determinist grounds. For if we have
the leisure, wealth, and education to be self-indulgent solipsists, we had
better make the most of that condition and heed the poet who in fact
makes the most of it by recapturing within such parameters the place of
lyric intelligence and a sense of the "big, / vaguer stuff" basic to the best
lyrical poetry in our canons.

It is not much of a consolation to say that this speculation is too general: If we cannot change what is fated, neither can we change our hope to produce change. But we still have to worry about the criteria we invoke in our claims that change is necessary. Where do I get my specific "ought," and what more capacious "oughts" sustain it? It is problematic enough to assume as I do that craft does not suffice, that major art projects qualities that we can imagine making a difference in how we live our lives. To this assumption I add a single, governing criterion for those qualities: that they make attempts at lucid self-consciousness about the poet's rhetoric and stance a basic vehicle for their lyric effects. This criterion can be somewhat flexible, can lead to praising both Ashbery and Rich, yet it clearly will not allow fully sympathetic treatments of all the poets discussed here or even a full development of the possible relationships among them that indicate dramas of pressure and counterpressure.[5]

Ultimately, we must ask, is it not possible to reverse my whole argument? Clearly, poetry need not be taken so philosophically, or perhaps so seriously. The elevation of poetry to the religion of culture codified by Matthew Arnold has probably not been beneficial to poetry, religion, or culture. Poetry should be a part of ordinary life in the same way as our playing and listening to music often is. A more conceptual version of this charge would insist that it is plausible to treat the true heroism or even true lucidity for contemporary poetry as the recognition that the most severe pressure of reality in our time is a compulsion to irony that undermines ideals of sincerity and makes our only interpretive orientation one that suspects the moral theater rather than applauding the moral performer. Being on stage and not acknowledging it is hardly the worst of sins, especially if what one stages seems to engage deep emotional and moral concerns. Counterpressure to this pressure of irony consists precisely in making stages where we can engage in experiences that focus and extend our qualities of perception and responsiveness to dramatic emotions. As Carl Dennis once said, poets provide an imaginative justice for lives and aspects of life that cannot represent themselves adequately. Moreover, there is no pressing intellectual need to announce the provisional quality of one's rhetorical stances. With a Johnsonian aloofness, one might ask who ever thought it otherwise. Literature is serious pretending – easily confused with serious pretensions – so that it is most fully self-reflexive when least self-divided, that is, when it is willing to explore the full intensity of a given stance or belief, even though it knows we know life is more complicated and less interesting. Self-consciousness about rhetoric need not be part of the message because it is built into the careful use of the medium. Writers can simply assume that they and their readers recognize that the greater need is not to free self-consciousness to its own resources but to create something sufficiently resonant and intense to have presence as an event focusing the reader's full emotional powers, as for example in the best work of John Logan.

III

My imagined critics present me with a difficult task. There is no point here in repeating my specific claims. But it should clarify their possible uses if I address the question of the status of those claims. What reasons can there be for practical, quite limited, perspectives that attempt to escape the subjective two-term relationship of sympathy for a three-term generalized assessment of an overall poetic climate? There is rapidly emerging a common theoretical response to this problem. It insists that a given partial stance is valuable to the extent that it seeks to express fully its own specific version of the material. Instead of seeking to subordinate differences to some impersonal discovery procedures, critics best address their society by so dramatizing their interests that they intensify disagreements. By disagreement we challenge one another to a keener statement of our differences and hence a deeper grasp of what our interests can and cannot produce. If we cannot have organic communities, we can at least be forced to take responsibility for our specific imaginative projections. In responsibility there might begin sharp definitions no longer tormented and blocked by the strategies we employ to gain a semblance of universality.

I accept this general position as the basic foundation for contemporary discourses about values. But I think its use for practical criticism requires substantial modification in how we understand what disagreements reveal and in how we decide what constitutes a strong version of a given stance. In the canonical statements of this view, the emphasis is on our recognizing the limitations of the critics' arguments. It is critical differences, not literary ones, that command our attention, with the role of literature reduced to the production of critical self-consciousness.

We need instead to see how the model of critical conflict leads us back to ways of describing the interrelationship of texts and extratextual realities. Why do we consider differences significant, and how might we use the differences themselves as indexes of a text's power? Simply asking these questions poses another possible level of inquiry where we might use our critical differences to locate shared concerns, if not answers. So I want to isolate that ground of potential agreement by distinguishing sharply between the level of argument, where we pose a variety of specific claims, and a possible level of deep questioning that reflects common desires which may in fact be rewarded by the play of differences. The power of a text, then, may be measured by its capacity to engage those questions or even to modify their terms. Our self-consciousness about the relationship between these differences and a possibly shared level of questioning can then lead us to recognize the cultural role criticism can play. If we only sharpen differences, we only focus ideological conflict. But if we locate shared concerns that the differences address, we can imagine our conflicts potentially changing our discourse about poetry by forcing us to reflect on the forms of questioning we can impose. This process in turn frees the critic to treat (or fantasize) antagonistic responses as heuristic. I am ultimately less interested in being right about Ashbery and Rich than in seeing critical discourse producing strong reasons for or against my judgments. It will be the reasons, not the judgments, that may leave a mark on literary culture.

In standard treatments of critical differences the emphasis lies on vulnerability. Conflict reveals contradictions and equivocations. But conflict also reveals strength, or, as I hope to show, the principles of what we mean when we speak of strong poetry. Through that revelation we can achieve a fuller grasp of the responsibilities of the critic. One obvious measure of strength is simply its capacity to endure criticism. But we get a more dramatic, qualitative sense of it if we look at the action from the inside, from the point of view of the way in which a person disposes him- or herself in relation to critical controversy. How we engage differences is ultimately the measure of our claims to power. In other words, for art it does not suffice to have influence or control. A reflective medium fulfills itself by its capacity to make self-interpretation part of the commanding stance. Art gains power in its efforts to understand how power is possible. But then power is strangely dependent on those it would influence. Unless we produce and preserve capacities to raise significant questions, we leave ourselves subject to models not worth appreciating, and we lack the terms to recognize what might most fully engage the deepest levels of our concerns.

These theoretical issues are at once sufficiently vague and sufficiently important to warrant a brief detour into a philosophical essay by Charles Taylor, "The Self in Question."[6] Taylor's goal is not assessing criteria for discourses but showing how some specific forms of ethical thinking are means to create terms for personal identity. In our context the model becomes a way of seeing how self-consciousness about our questions can be projected as an active principle for establishing values. Taylor's case develops from a simple, basic distinction between asserting preferences and making strong evaluations. Preferences are judgments of something as good simply by virtue of the direct satisfactions it produces. All preferences are in a sense equal, since there are no criteria beyond the specific desire of the chooser and no constraints except for practical considerations of possibility and consequences. I cannot satisfy preferences to visit

Paris and London at the same time, but the reasons involve only empirical contingencies. Similar contingencies would be the only constraints on sympathetic readings of poets. Strong evaluations, on the other hand, are second-order choices. One chooses something not because of what it is but because the choice involves the ways in which persons can represent themselves as being agents of a certain kind, that is as deserving certain predicates. Strong evaluations place a choice within a network of reasons, where the reasons in effect give one the right to the self-representation if they fit the situation. The clear sign of second-order status is the nature of the constraints one encounters in such choices. If I want to consider myself courageous, there are some cowardly things I cannot do – not because it is impossible or because I will be overtly punished but because the deeds are incompatible with a set of defining terms I have chosen for my actions. Critics incur the same obligations if they proffer general loyalties.

Second-order choices are contrastive because they are of meanings, not of objects, and thus are constrained by the network of public associations that establishes the relevant meaning. Selves have public identity when they consistently maintain the contrastive schemes projected in their reasons for actions. There is much room for casuistry here, but perhaps no more so than in utilitarian models and perhaps no less so than we need if we are to honor those who resist the temptation. No single contrast is definitive. This is a crucial fact about identity and about the culture that allows us to establish identities. The opposition of courage and cowardice can be interpreted in many ways. The traditional meanings can even be reversed. People constitute themselves precisely in continually testing their schemata, in establishing specific meanings for the contrast, and in acting in accord with the implications of that meaning. If we cannot see a connection between words and deeds or place deeds in a contrastive context, we simply cannot speak of moral identity at all. A person who calls him- or herself courageous but acts in what would normally be called cowardly terms while offering (explicitly or implicitly) no alternative interpretation of the terms has no public identity except perhaps as expressing symptoms. This person, I must add, could still have quite strong and determinate interests. What would be lacking would be any process of self-subsumption, any sense that the interests were determined by the person with a stake in being this kind of person.

Taylor is so clear and, I think, deep that the connections to criticism are not hard to draw. We must be careful to acknowledge that there are receptive, contemplative aspects of reading in relation to which it is crucial that we suspend all questions of personal identity. But when we act as critics and thus take public roles, I think it makes sense to speak of strong evaluations, to the extent that critics treat the contrastive schemes implicit in their questions as giving themselves and those who share their readings sets of personal qualities that can be assessed in relation to some plausible idealizations in the literary and cultural heritage. By this light, questions are more than remarks. They are forms of establishing identity, conditions of responsibility to a tradition, and projected extensions of critical into ethical attitudes. This is ultimately why aestheticism fails: It does not create a contrastive language with a substantial claim on non-literary forms of value. Conversely, when we understand how Taylor makes it possible to celebrate critical differences so long as the critics fully elaborate the consequences of their positions, we can use criticism itself as a powerful analogy for the basic ways poetry becomes valuable within practical experience.

What critics do only in a limited discursive sphere poets who understand the implications of their rhetoric can do in direct relationship to a variety of existential conditions. Critical strong evaluations show us how to define strong poets and, especially, how self-consciousness is crucial to the manifestations of strength. Strong poets provide, at least implicitly, structures of valuations defining and taking responsibility for an elaborate set of contrasts. They offer their readers distinctive qualities of vision and define ways those qualities might make a difference for those who try to live by them. Harold Bloom is right to insist that strong poets create and elicit interpretive conflicts. But the cause is less their psychological relation to their predecessors than their creative relations to the cultural theater where values are dramatized and discussed. Strong poets create sets of attitudes toward the contemporary scene in such a way that the attitudes expose the limitations of other writers and exemplify modes of feeling and thinking that allow deep engagements in the cultural and poetic problems dramatized. Strong poets convince us that theirs are the questions we must ask, because through them we see the pressure of reality in terms that allow significant counterpressures, even if we disagree on specific solutions. Stevens used the model of pressure in order to claim that the measure of poets is a capacity to involve the lives of other people in their work. They do that, we can add, by convincing us we need their creative acts to provide or elicit possible stances we can take in and toward our historical situation. Critical differences matter in relation to literary values to the extent that they help us formulate what these stances afford and how poets overcome the problems inherent in their projects.

When we turn from theory to practice, we immediately see that we have paid an enormous price for our poets' commitments to the expressive norm of sincerity and the thematic ideal of articulating a silence beyond cultural frameworks. In seeking absolutes, they cease to address one another or to take responsibility for making and testing contrastive languages. I think this is why we find almost all the instruments agreeing that ours is an age without much strong poetry. There are voices we sympathize with, but few presences we take into account when we elaborate our own contrastive frameworks for judging experience. As my evidence for this general malaise I need not rely on academic critics like Berthoff, Graff, and Perloff. As Berthoff shows, the poets themselves keep sprinkling statements of general dissatisfaction in with their politic praise. And increasing demands for discursiveness make clear poets' fears that variants of romantic, dramatic states of mind no longer generate levels of questioning about experience that allow poems to make some kind of difference in a public world. I am not sure that discursiveness will prove an adequate solution. But it seems quite clear that we need a more demanding level of discursiveness from critics if there is to be a climate in which significant new models of nondiscursiveness are to flourish. It may be the case that my opening call for a hero was a precise index of the basic challenge criticism must now face. Criticism must imagine plausible models of strong poetry and through the imagining produce a situation in which writers will bring these models into being. My own efforts to insist on this climate may be all too narrow. Rhetoricity may not be the fundamental area where lucidity can once again produce compelling lyrical states. But I hope engaging the questions I raise will make critics sufficiently self-reflexive about their commitments to demand the same self-awareness in the poetry they praise.

This is not to say that poetry should be versified extensions of criticism. But it does imply that unless one aspect of a poet's consciousness is devoted to how he or she can be read and judged in relation to the times, the poet is not likely to produce the deep and complex self-definition needed to be a strong poet. In poetry, at least, the humanist nostrum "know thyself" has a clear point: Until one establishes poetic identity one does not have a strong claim to occupy a site in the consciousness of readers. Poets' works fade into the sweet melancholy they share with the advertisements that surround them in the *New Yorker.*

IV

Were it not so self-congratulatory an ideal, I would insist that strong criticism and strong poetry must go together – as sharing a dynamic play of ideas and as forming an emblem of the creative spirit resisting the pressure of reality. But such normative pronouncements only dispel at the level of theoretical generalization energies we need for concrete analyses and arguments. So instead of *pronunciamenti,* I will close with a depressing contrastive example of why we need critical ideals of strong poetry and critical images of how our activity may contribute to producing that work. About three years ago I conceived the overall shape of this book. During the writing I half-hoped that poetry would stay as weak as it is so that I would have a valid case. As my illustration that the favor has for the most part been granted, I want to describe a recent essay that made me despair of poetry (and take considerable pleasure in myself). I offer it as an example of the forms of critical questioning the scenic mode elicits even from critics who have done much more profound work. Then I shall use my example as the vehicle for speculating on the reasons why poetry has today lost authority to speculative criticism and the ways in which poetry's institutional life seems to me unlikely to allow significant changes in the current situation.

Here is Helen Vendler in a recent *New York Review of Books:*

> Leithauser's other venture is far more his own – a series of poems on animals or natural scenes, poems formed in stanzas with a pattern of delicate and unemphatic rhymes. Their chief form of stylization is the framing of the scene stripped to essential detail and seen in a moment of insight . . . the mystery Leithauser sees in appearance is of course a reflection of his suggestible mind, which turns things over in attraction and fear . . . On many pages the reader is struck by the writer's interest in playing with scale, a resource frequently ignored by poets. Here is Leithauser on a patch of ground and an anthill:
>
> > two
> > long-necked dandelions sway
> > over a toiling community;
> > grain by grain
> >
> > coppery skin
> > blazing as if sweat-painted
> > the ants amass a sort of pyramid
> > on Mayan lines: broad
> > base and truncated cone.
>
> The anthill as Mayan pyramid is amassed with commensurate effort in these agglutinative lines; and the *mot juste* "sweat-painted" could be found for ants only by that leap we call imagination.[7]

Notice the price one pays for scenic lucidity. On the one hand, Leithauser and Vendler have located terms for preserving the lyric imagination. Nature need not be symbolic in order to be evocative of fine writing, and poetry need not be emotionally theatrical in order to make us feel the small intensifications that come with careful attention. The poem even offers an intriguing metaphoric suggestion that ants become in effect religious monuments to their own life of toil, and hence pure figures of bourgeois life. Yet imagine Milton alive at this hour to assess this poem. If this is the fate of lyric imagination, its successes become such mockery in relation to the past that the poet's efforts may bring more pain than pleasure. Vendler praises Leithauser's art because there is very little positive to say about his content. What significant questions get focused in this poem? What demands are there that one must change one's life, or even take self-reflexive responsibility for some features of it? Leithauser doubtless imagines his as a necessary response to experience: By reducing the scope of our questions we find a realm of playful, half-serious reflective perceptions important precisely because there is virtually no content until the poet creates *les mots justes*. However, within this framework there is ultimately very little way for the *mots* to be *justes*. Leithauser's is a poetry of epithets or adjectival play rather than a poetry of reflection that exemplifies a mental stance through which we can discover or reinforce significant values. If we remember Emily Dickinson on bees, the differences are all too evident. Leithauser's patch of ground and anthill become a depressing expression of just what kind of hero and what sites of being we are allowed under the new dispensation.

Ultimately, I am more troubled by Vendler than by Leithauser. We have much better poets; we do not have better critics, and we have no one else with her access to journals with a large, intellectual readership that might be led to care about poetry or be invoked as a means of making demands on poets. For that readership Vendler chooses to write about poems on patches of ground and anthills. And she makes her example of imagination a rather precious phrase like "sweat-painted," which simply extends the theme of toil and carries very little news even on a perceptual level. Worse, Vendler does not seem at all struck by the anomaly of presenting an elegant evocation of anthills in a journal issue that contains essays on the economy, the history of classical scholarship, and the concept of social risk. Vendler feels no need to justify her stance or show why what she praises in fact connects to the concerns addressed by the other essays. Sympathy has its limits, even sympathy with sympathy for ants, because as we get too close to phenomena we leave ourselves very little room for thought.

It is precisely Vendler's capacity for sympathy that makes criticism like this so disturbing a symptom. She reflects the intellectual stance the age's poetry demands, and she becomes an index of the quality of the questions or discourses the scenic mode can generate. From such examples it is all too evident why poetry now fails to play any formative role in our culture. By formative role I mean nothing exalted. Modernist poetry provides strong examples of two formative roles: a power to shape our models for reading and valuing literature and a power to establish images or models of mental activity that many agents in the literate culture treat as basic features in their self-representations. *The Waste Land* was instrumental in shaping the ways two generations imagined their relationship to history, and Yeats's poems actually seemed models showing the free man how to praise. Even in the heyday of New Criticism and later, during the revolutionary hopes of the sixties, poetry was the literary form most pronouncedly carrying the intellectual and emotional power to shape identities (and not merely to reflect their constituents, as popular novels do).

My aim is not merely to lament change. Lamentation is cheap, but knowledge about change may give us some control over our situation. We certainly need that control. This book has been written under one primary pressure: the fact that speculative criticism and literary theory now engage the interests and wield the authority that poetry did within modernism. Foucault or Derrida, or even their interpreters, draw larger, more attentive audiences than virtually any poet who came to prominence during the seventies. Moreover, if we look at what engages the passions of at least those in the academic community who once debated the values in and implications of poetry, we find criticism, not writing, the primary subject of concern. Vendler's essay helps make clear how our poetry and our descriptive criticism contribute to this state of affairs. Our poets assert what seems to them a heroic refusal of all illusions: Appearances must suffice; language and sympathy will make it so. They see the failure of poets' dreams in previous epochs, so they turn elsewhere in order to cultivate their isolated patches of ground.

Speculative criticism, on the other hand, seems intent on making Hegel a prophet for his claim that poetry would give way to a purer form of self-reflexive spirit. The spirit these critics pursue is a deliberate reversal of Hegel's, but it still performs in its perverse ways the curatorial role of preserving the energies and efforts of the past.[8] These critics repeat with a difference modernism's relation to a cultural heritage largely ignored by contemporary poets, and they may have developed critical terms intricate and self-qualifying enough to be sufficient for the life and variety of that past. Poets see the failures of the past and look elsewhere; our speculative critics also see the failures, but they make of those a way of returning to tradition where they locate a more capacious ground for the play of a lucid spirit than most dramas of the "self" can provide.

These reactions to the past then produce a strange irony. Left to its own resources, contemporary poetry must mark out a sphere where it has a cultural role not subordinate to the authority of some other discourse. Its basic means is retreat into an integrity and naturalness of voice that offers experience without opinions or overt arguments. But to suc-

ceed in this enterprise may be to lose, because once all claims to lucidity
are dropped, lyricism is too isolated to have much cultural force. Speculative criticism, by contrast, feeds on forms of discourse that apply to
several disciplines, so it brings emotional pressure and imaginative life
to topics by dramatizing how much depends on a given stance or how
much is buried within our traditional allegiances. However suspicious
we may be of speculative criticism, it is difficult to deny that it addresses
both of what may be the basic, incompatible demands on the contemporary imagination: that it invent ways of preserving in fresh terms a
sense of humane qualities and spiritual needs constructed by Western high-
cultural traditions and that it invent ways of deconstructing traditional
views of spirit so that new visions may emerge from beneath the tattered
rags of humanist ideals.

These speculative critics can make us recognize problems and cultural
possibilities, but the form of discourse will not carry a sufficient emotional burden or allow fine enough models for self-consciously defining
our own possible stances toward experience. Pater prepares the way for
Yeats, but his is decidedly not the greater achievement. However, before
we can once again use examples like those of Yeats, or even of Ashbery
and Rich, we will have to produce substantial changes in the intellectual
climate. Poets will have to reflect on what their work is a reflection of,
and they will probably have to combine the intensity of self-presentation
with the lucidity of dramatic self-criticism. And younger poets will have
to assume these tasks while facing serious problems from the heritage
bequeathed by the scenic mode. I refer now not to the ideological factors
we have been considering but to one basic institutional structure shaped
by those factors – the poetry workshop. These workshops and the mentality they encourage put poets in a situation closely parallel to that of
French painting in the 1850s. There, too, extraordinarily skillful artists
created a climate skeptical of any intellectual role for the medium, hence
trapping it within a narrow equation of lucidity with elegantly controlled
surfaces. Instead of a stress on ideas, there emerged an emphasis on craft
that in turn produced a highly inbred professionalism governing both
the training of artists and the judgment of their work. Rather than directly seeking sources of patronage among a consuming public, artists
received their commissions and praise largely by appealing to other
professionals. Their salon juries are our fellowship boards.[9]

This comparison is not entirely negative. It promises a rich vein of
minor poetry, and it suggests at least a possibility that in writers' attempts to transform or reject the dominant mode we will find our Mo-
nets, Gauguins, and Cézannes. Artists, like children, may profit from
developing under fairly strict and confining regimens. But for these positive things to happen we need a clearer view than we now have of where

and why this academicism gains its force. In the context I have attempted to provide, we can see the workshop as a material expression of the conditions of production and consumption basic to our poetic culture. The workshop is to the seventies (and, probably, the eighties) what the class on explication was to the fifties and the oral reading to the sixties.

This comparison, however, is somewhat too benign, because the workshops reinforce and reproduce the guidebook mentality prevalent in our culture[10] and, more important, because the specific features of writing they select for emphasis encourage those modes of lucidity to which poets most easily adapt. Instead of seeking defensible capacious modes of thinking, it is easier, perhaps even from many perspectives more useful, to rein in one's ambitions about content and bring to the fore the lucidity of a controlling craftsmanlike intelligence.[11] Plumly's essays are perfect cases in point, the *Summa* of the contemporary creative writing teacher, in that they emphasize scrupulous attention to craft and its effects while showing very little interest in the beliefs realized or the structure of affiliations that might provide nonliterary reasons for literary choices.

Notice that such concern for craft can be taught directly, like New Critical or neostructuralist reading skills, whereas developing in writers a sense of the quality and possible significance of content is a much more difficult task. The imperative in a workshop is to create an atmosphere where poets are encouraged to write, not to wait for the urgency of having something to say (the point is to be ready when that moment comes). Then, through discussion, poets can internalize the critical principles constituting a community of peers. Yet the emphasis on writing as simple invention risks creating too rhetorical an attitude toward poetry, and the requirements of correlating criticism and group dynamics tend to encourage concentration on craft and the importance of personal voices. Everyone is entitled to a voice, and differences over craft are more manageable and far less threatening to both the group and the individual than serious debates over the actual value of one's ideas or sense of experience.

Such structural arrangements cannot but produce a sense of professionalism, with its attendant virtues and vices. Professionals tend to view their work as a discipline, to stress successful adherence to loosely conceived rules of the game, and to minimize internal tensions so that the group can gain authority in relation to other groups. Professionalism also tends to make people stress sanity and decorum: In some respects the worst evil a peer can commit in professional groups is to be embarrassing, however useful the lessons learned from the risks taken. These reasons may explain why there are remarkably few negative reviews of poetry today and almost no public debate about the relative value of competing contemporary styles. There are shared objects of mockery but almost no conflicts among roughly equal talents. Even a critical essay like Plumly's bends over backward to insist on relative standards – indeed, tone becomes for Plumly essentially a critical device for emphasizing the expression of subjectivity and for ignoring questions about the value of poems as serious public discourse.

Finally, workshops tend to encourage what William Matthews calls a "middle range of rhetoric"[12] stressing muted, controlled feelings or ironic stances toward larger claims. Group situations produce an ethos in which one takes on poetic personas that are defensible in terms of ordinary models of civility. It is simply gauche to present to a group a bardic stance, to express the theatricalized questing of a Yeats or a Hart Crane, or to muster the cruel satiric energies of Irving Feldman's "My Olson Elegy." The most intense poetry, I suspect, can be written only out of a quarrel with the self or a quarrel with the world: When one's internalized audience consists of a discrete group, there is too much pressure toward subtle forms of self-defense, conformity, or reliance on shared values not common in the larger public world.

V

I hope I exaggerate the negative case. There is a rhetorical tendency in a conclusion to concentrate on one's general arguments and thus to forget the rich pleasures and qualities of sensibility that move one in particular poems. Ours is not an age demanding a Dunciad but one of talented, dedicated poets working under very inauspicious circumstances. There is even some evidence that fine younger poets, notably Charles Hartman, Tom Disch, Douglas Crase, Marjorie Welish, and David Lehman, are responding to these pressures by inventing promising new styles and voices. Poetry will survive both its critics and its practitioners. The nature of that survival, however, may depend to a considerable extent on criticism's playing a role that I consider nobler than the production of rather loose, derivative speculations. We must challenge our poets – not so that criticism will become an art form but so that poetry may fulfill its potential and our needs.

Strong poets are those who can challenge other voices and show how their stances produce images and breed languages that afford significant new perspectives on experience. Valuable criticism provides frameworks that prepare us for those poets and that may help them prepare themselves for us. The critic's power is to provoke strength by making anything less seem intolerable. No one critic can do that. But if we indulge our imaginations we can imagine another kind of critical discourse entering the poetry workshop. We can imagine sharp debates not about craft but about what craft is responsible to, both as cultural pressure and as an imperative imposed on us by the history of poetry. We can imagine our once again imagining, with Longinus, Plato, and Rousseau, that we offer to the judgment of a jury of heroes or gods those acts by which we most seek to be valued.

Above all, we can imagine cogent claims that we not yield too quickly to social definitions of maturity or narrow ideals of lucidity. All these imaginings may be delusions, but they are plausible enough to warrant the effort to make them real. Then we at least acknowledge and employ our capacities for anger and disappointment. Ultimately these capacities may lead beyond themselves, to moments when anger and disappointment prove misguided, and a resonant voice makes us understand what poets are for in a destitute time.

Afterword

I have been bothered by my inability in this book to be very forceful on why self-consciousness is so important a criterion for me. I fear that I overstress the defensive pole – self-consciousness as a lucidity that keeps one from narcissistic illusions and/or cheap emotional indulgences. But why are those states so bad, especially in a world that clearly does not indulge enough in the life of the emotions? Now that the book is written I think I have a better understanding of my own evaluative principles. So please allow me this last word.

Lyric poems, perhaps more than any other genre, seem to involve a tacit contract with the reader. No information is presented that is not more easily attained elsewhere. So the author must implicitly promise readers some other recompense for his careful, provisionally sympathetic attention. The best recompense, I think, is a display of the capacity of a given set of linguistic operations to give emotional and intellectual access to some dimension of experience that seems silly or banal when treated in prose. This access takes three basic forms: the text can provide accurate or memorable words for a common but evanescent or subtle experience; it can produce a stance that allows us to see particulars, feel emotions, or maintain tones toward experience to which we would otherwise be blind; or it can elaborate an image so that readers make the image into an ideal state, or a segment of such a state, which then becomes a principle of value readers employ in their self-representations and projects. In each case critical judgment must deal with the interaction between the capacity of the language to produce a sense of relevant mental powers and the possibility of those powers making a difference in the particular sphere of experience the poem implicates.

This connection between the linguistic, or writerly, and the existential provides the necessary foundation for my promised positive account of self-consciousness. Texts produce imaginary worlds that can be representative for existential contexts because we can use them for the purposes I have just mentioned. At the same time, the texts can refer to these extratextual concerns by virtue of what they exemplify as poetic powers for making these worlds. One could speak of powers to make us aware through language of our ability to specify complex or elusive qualities of the natural and social worlds, powers to express the emotional contours of the implied author's response to those qualities, powers to create and assess ideal projections, powers to embody within the work processes of judgment and identification that the work desires of its audience, and finally, powers to hold in synthesis the various relations between style and theme on which the work's force depends. All these powers can be representative in exactly the same way that the dramatic content is representative – as conditions we imagine to be applicable to our own lives. The route of identification, however, is not now by our interpreting characters in an imagined version of a real world but by our tentatively aligning ourselves with the capacities of the creative activity expressed in the work. What the work presents in its authorial act as the powers of consciousness becomes an emblem for what any mind can make of the pressures of reality that confront it.

When we evaluate poetry, then, we need two basic sets of criteria, each corresponding to a different general route of implication between the text and the world. The first set, that of how a work captures our realities, involves two basic norms: How complexly does the poet respond to the tension between lyricism and lucidity bequeathed by an immediate poetic heritage of failed prophetic ambitions, and how thoroughly does the poet engage the basic emotional problems inescapable within a narcissistic society. The second criterion – the one I have been calling the qualities of self-consciousness a poet exhibits – shifts our focus from the scenes presented to the author's wielding the poetic instrument itself as a form for expressing powers that extend beyond the text. Both criteria are obviously necessary. (The "negative" test of lucidity concerns the author's ability to master certain aspects of the world the poems allude to.) It is the second, however, that I think demands greater critical attention than it usually receives. On methodological principles alone we are likely to get better critical dialogues on this subject because it admits a greater degree of shared grounds than criteria of content. We probably find it easier to abstract from our differences and grant the plurality of vital poetic worlds when we shift from the specific assertions about a world that a work offers to the means it brings to bear on that enterprise. Moreover all poets face the problem of making their means a significant emblem of human powers, whatever the particular beliefs or values they choose to express. Finally, as Stevens made stunningly clear in "Of Modern Poetry," an age without god, or without any shared and fixed script, probably cannot maintain faith in any content unless the faith is anchored in dramatic evidence that we possess, and desire, the particular powers used in asserting that content.

When I have invoked this second criterion, I hope I have isolated recurrent tendencies in contemporary poetry that block much of it from projecting a very rich, complex, or engaging sense of what the linguistic instrument can accomplish. The poets are quite self-conscious about the craft of poetry – but not about the powers one can offer an audience by treating craft metaphorically. The dominant style vacillates between minute attention to a subdued elegance of technique and the most general leaps into the metaphoric infinite, without allowing the style itself to invoke powers of mind capable of making the infinite seem, in fact, within our grasp. Where there is not sufficient emphasis on how constructive acts enable the tonal flexibility or states of vision a poem celebrates, the celebration collapses into a passive, self-satisfied indulgence in the lyrical. The poem itself mediates only by setting scenes and creating "slips inward," never by dramatizing its lyric visions as hard-earned rewards for what its own linguistic intensity manifests. Rilke's Angel rarely looks out from these texts.

Contrasts with modernist poetry should make all this clear. There is no poet more self-conscious than James Merrill. Yet all his technical skill does not produce the power to carry out an argument on the important questions he raises or even to use the issues to justify his imaginative stance. We are led to participate in an elegant display of complex personal bonds. But language can only sweeten this pathos, not transform it or even do much to deepen the sense of what it is in consciousness that enables such relations or makes them the grounds for forms of action that do more than celebrate small supportive communities. Yet Merrill at least raises important public issues. Poets such as Wright and Plumly never get there at all. In another register, we find Kinnell locked into an essentially narrative approach to nightmare, and nature poets like Stafford and the later Merwin relying almost entirely on scenic effects and melodramatic metaphors. Compare Stevens, Eliot, and Williams. For Stevens it was style that produced the "precious portents of our own powers" by which one could face and measure the claims of science without retreating into escapist mysticism. Eliot had his nightmares, but rendering them became in *The Wasteland* a process of testing the capacity of an entire culture to come to terms with the realities implicit in its traditional sources of symbolic meaning. Finally, Williams treats the desire for a vital sense of nature as a continual pressure on our powers to construct responsive attitudes and clean, hard-edged interrelationships: So much depends on the composition of a responding sensibility.

At stake in the contrasts I have been attempting to draw is a great deal more than the question of how we judge individual poets. For that question depends on a prior one, best put by Heidegger's "What Are Poets For." An "Afterword" is not the place to begin a lengthy answer, of course. But our historical situation allows considerable brevity. We face essentially the same cultural pressures as did the modernist poets: The interpretive languages that hold authority over our social life are devoted to mapping human motives and powers of agency into the discreet, manageable structures proposed by the social sciences. These languages serve the laudable goal of finding principles that might allow them to propose interventions in a social order clearly in need of some intervening. Yet one effect of such desires is a dangerously reductive image of human agency. Our needs and desires become equivalent to whatever social science can hope to manage or to predict. And we tend to define our basic values in accord with these descriptions: What we value depends on what we take to be our basic needs and capacities.

Poetry, at least poetry in the twentieth century, has as one of its primary social functions the production of images that resist such pressure from the social sciences. As our most concise and demanding form of linguistic expression, poetry can demonstrate the range of powers and needs we have by virtue of our existence in the culture language provides. A fully self-conscious poetry can display both a variety of mental actions and an intensity of mental energies that warrant very different models of human agency. Instead of the rational decision maker of economics or what we might call sociobiology's egoistic disseminator, poetry presents persons confronted with the pains and pleasures of a complex, endlessly dissatisfied structure of demands and adjustments.

The specific content of the contrasts poetry dramatizes will change. Modernism's frontal assaults on empiricist values must yield to the more indirect forms of assertion we find in Ashbery and Hass or to the equally direct but politically different model of powers Rich tries to manifest. Nonetheless poetry's obligations remain constant, requiring us to hold contemporary poets to the highest standards developed by our cultural heritage. Without such critical pressure we may hasten a day when that heritage is in fact as irrelevant as it is often claimed to be. For we will no longer recognize ourselves as capable of sharing the desires it cultivates and the powers it provides. The only good news in this situation may be the fact that we will be spared most of the pain because we will lack what is necessary to counter the lies we tell ourselves in order to evade seeing what we have become.

Notes

1. Self and sensibility in contemporary poetry

1   For my citations from Young see *A Field Guide to Contemporary Poetry and Poetics,* ed. David Young and Stuart Friebert (New York: Longman, 1980), pp. 155, 162–6, 168, 128–33. Stafford's poem is from William Stafford, *West of Your City* (Los Gatos, Calif.: Talisman Press, 1960), p. 12.

2   I somewhat overstate the problem in critics like Gerald Graff (*Literature against Itself* [Chicago: Univ. of Chicago Press, 1979]) and Werner Berthoff (*A Literature without Qualities* [Berkeley: Univ. of California Press, 1980]). Both in fact make several telling points, and both (see especially Berthoff, pp. 7–11) are quite good on what society needs from literature. Nonetheless, I think my remarks are justified by the fact that both are so caught up in general symptoms of malaise that they pay remarkably little attention to the specific ways poets describe and try to engage what they too understand as problematic. The best contrast to them I know is Douglas Crase, "The Prophetic Ashbery," in *Beyond Amazement: New Essays on John Ashbery,* ed. David Lehman (Ithaca, N.Y.: Cornell Univ. Press, 1980). See also my debate with Graff in *Par Rapport* 2, no. 2 (1979), pp. 87–106, 123–38.

3   Helen Vendler, *Part of Nature, Part of Us* (Cambridge: Harvard Univ. Press, 1980). It is difficult to demonstrate briefly the cloying effect of reading Ven-

dler's essays together and thus seeing the prejudices so gorgeously cloaked by her elegant and deep responses to specific subjects. For a good overview of the limitations in such work see Marjorie Perloff's review of *Part of Nature* in *Contemporary Literature* 22 (1980–81), pp. 96–103. We might note here how frequently values of sincerity, personal voice, and especially domesticity reinforce exactly those assumptions about poetry which I try to show become problematic when viewed in terms of general cultural problems and pressures. See for pronounced examples pp. 107–10, 206–9, and 229–31, on Bishop and on Merrill, as well as her quite noble attempt to domesticate the speculative romantic Stevens into a poet of "hints and faint transfigurings," while still acknowledging (if not fully appreciating) his insistence on the difficulties and ultimately antidomestic ferocity of the imaginative effort to transfigure.

For another discriminating criticism devoted to specifying the qualities of individual sensibilities, see David Kalstone, *Five Temperaments* (New York: Oxford Univ. Press, 1976). If we turn to poet-critics, we find some efforts to create comparative terms, but with the emphasis primarily still on specific rhetorical effects. See especially Stanley Plumly, "Chapter and Verse," *American Poetry Review* 7 (Jan.–Feb. 1978), pp. 21–35, and (May–June 1978), pp. 21–32; and Jonathan Holden, *Rhetoric of the Contemporary Lyric* (Bloomington: Indiana Univ. Pres, 1980). Another poet-critic, Charles Molesworth, has some exemplary writing on poetry and culture with respect to the previous generation of poets in his *The Fierce Embrace* (Columbia: Univ. of Missouri Press, 1979). Finally, I see my criticisms of the contemporaries largely as an extension of Robert Pinsky's *The Situation of Poetry* (Princeton, N.J.: Princeton Univ. Press, 1976). I disagree, however, with his version of a cure, as I will elaborate in Chapter 4.

4   The ideology informing most creative writing classes is well represented in *Poets Teaching: The Creative Process,* ed. Alberta T. Turner (New York: Longman, 1980). One could say that my analysis is circular: She picks those poets she identifies with. But since there is no competitor for this book, I take its circle as matching a cultural one.

5   Holden, *Rhetoric of the Contemporary Lyric,* pp. 5, 6, 17, 9, 11, 36–7. Notice how many forms of immediacy his account of it leaves out – e.g., the immediacy of writing, of composing arguments, of associating thoughts, etc.

6   I want to echo Kuhn on paradigms here in order to bring into focus similarities and differences between dominant modes in poetry and "normal practice" in science. The prevalence of the workshop makes laboratory conditions basic to both disciplines, and as literary study gets increasingly ahistorical it approximates the scientific reliance on textbooks. Finally, even Kuhn's anomalies have as their parallel the gradual realization that a style has grown conventional. But here two interesting differences emerge. In science anomalies are what resist the common practice; in literature anomaly conditions that threaten a dominant mode prevail when it proves all too easy to adapt real contradictions to a single common rhetoric. Because of this distinction our awareness of anomalies derives less from contradictions within poetic

practice than from the pressure of events whose nature and force reside outside the technical practice and produce too much unity within it.

7 I develop this dichotomy at length by an analysis of Tennyson and Arnold in "The Plight of Victorian Lyricism as a Context of Modernism," *Criticism* 20 (1978), pp. 281–306. I must note affinities with Northrop Frye's distinction between myths of freedom and myths of concern, which itself links to a lengthy tradition going back at least to Pascal's *l'esprit geometrique* and *l'esprit de finesse*.

8 This, I think is the most compelling feature of Graff's attack on the romantic tradition. It is made explicit in Robert Pinsky's more sensitive but less theoretically elaborate *Situation of Poetry*.

9 In "Rhetoricity in the Sonnet," *Tennessee Studies in Language and Literature* 25 (1980), pp. 1–23, I try to distinguish between rhetoric, the study of how language is controlled for specific ends, and rhetoricity, a reflective attitude toward what persons reveal about their nature and their culture from changing and fairly permanent characteristics of how rhetoric is used. For other theoretical assumptions involving concepts of actions and the situating of them in history see my *Act and Quality: A Theory of Literary Meaning and Humanistic Understanding* (Amherst: Univ. of Massachusetts Press, 1981). I ought also to elaborate on my earlier comment on the major difference between this work and my book on American poetry in the 1960s, *Enlarging the Temple* (Lewisburg, Pa.: Bucknell Univ. Press, 1979). There I concentrated on individual poets as they engaged in personal dialectics intended to work out new models of values that lyric poetry can exemplify. Here I concentrate on a dialectic the critic constructs among poets. The different approach is required, I think, because a younger generation of poets is interested less in exploring values associated with general ideas than in testing what is emotionally possible within various choices among styles and rhetorics all the poets can use. Where *Enlarging the Temple* dealt with poets, I deal here with poetic positions the self can occupy. Individual poets explore usually several positions, but some remain typical for them, and it is these I hope to describe and evaluate.

10 John Ashbery, *The Double Dream of Spring* (New York: Dutton, 1970), p. 18. I should add that the criticism of Ashbery edited by David Lehman in *Beyond Amazement* is the best general example of the issues and themes that are the likely consequences of such a shift in sensibility.

11 The works of social criticism I find most useful in setting the stage on which poets perform are Philip Rieff, *The Triumph of the Therapeutic* (New York: Harper & Row, 1966); Christopher Lasch, *The Culture of Narcissism* (New York: Norton, 1978); and Richard Sennett, *The Fall of Public Man* (New York: Vintage, 1978); as well as the intense psychoanalytic concern for disorders of the self that one finds best articulated in Heinz Kohut's work. One reason I do not use these sources explicitly is that I think the social critics have as much to learn from poets as they have to teach readers of poetry. For example, the works I cite here suffer from taking their critical stances too seriously and not sympathizing with the actual interpretations and de-

sires of those experiencing the narcissistic anxieties. For two very different accounts of such narrowness see my "Ecce Homo: Narcissism, Power and the Status of Autobiographical Representations, *boundary 2* 9 and 10 (1982), pp. 389–413; and Alan Stone, "Stress and Coping among Young Adults in the Decade of the Eighties," in a forthcoming collection of essays on marriage edited by Kingsley Davis and Amyra Grossbard Shechtman.

12   The best text I know on the duplicities of inside and outside is Jacques Derrida, "Fors," *Georgia Review* 31 (1977), pp. 64–120. Other texts basic to my understanding of problems in the concept of self are P. F. Strawson's and John Perry's work on indexicals, especially the essays cited later in my discussion of Ashbery. On my next point, the problem of closure, contemporary criticism has all too many interesting accounts. Two that are most useful for seeing very different thematic and formal dilemmas within modernism, dilemmas which I claim that the dominant mode evades, are Leo Bersani, *A Future for Astyanax* (Boston: Little, Brown, 1976); and Marjorie Perloff, *The Poetics of Indeterminacy: Rimbaud to Cage* (Princeton, N.J.: Princeton Univ. Press, 1981). Finally, for problems of rhetoricity and tensions between sincerity and self-consciousness, I find Paul de Man's Sartrean lucubrations the best critical source. See especially *Blindness and Insight* (Oxford: Oxford Univ. Press, 1971) and the essays on Rousseau and Nietzsche in *Allegories of Reading* (Ithaca, N.Y.: Cornell Univ. Press, 1980).

13   Thus the new poets make an interesting contrast to my description in *Enlarging the Temple,* chap. 1, on the way romantic themes of nausea and narcissism were repeated in the sixties. The change requires a more psychological, less ontological, critical vocabulary.

14   This is one instance of Burke's paradox of substance, developed in his *Grammar of Motives* (1945; rpt. Berkeley: Univ. of California Press, 1969), and underlying most of the slippages or duplicities "explored" by recent criticism. Perhaps the richest poetic intellectual grasp of the consequences of such duplicities as they require us to live amid complex and multiple systems may be found in David Antin's work, especially "Radical Coherency," *O.ARS* 1 (1981), pp. 175–94; and "Tuning," in his forthcoming *Tuning* (New York: New Directions). See also my argument with Graff in *Par Rapport.*

15   For the best texts on the negative consequences of this shift and on Enlightenment reason's becoming a self-devouring serpent to be understood by myths of external recurrence, see the last chapter of Michel Foucault, *The Order of Things* (New York: Random House, 1970); James Ogilvy, *Multi-Dimensional Man* (New York: Oxford Univ. Press, 1978); and a problematic but powerful work I use later on, André Glucksman, *The Master Thinkers,* trans. Brian Pearce (New York: Harper & Row, 1980). The best account I know of the resulting sense of irony is Alan Wilde, *Horizons of Assent: Modernism, Post-Modernism and the Ironic Imagination* (Baltimore: Johns Hopkins Univ. Press, 1981). But the speculative project I am trying to describe at this third level is devoted to providing some larger framework than the ironic. Wallace Stevens is our best guide in his proposing to "live in the world, but outside of existing conceptions of it" (quoted by Crase "The Prophetic Ashberry," p. 34). And perhaps the best general case for the kind

of self involved in this vision, a sense basic to all of Wittgenstein, is John Koethe, "The Metaphysical Subject of John Ashbery's Poetry," in Lehman, *Beyond Amazement.*

16 Richard Rorty, *Philosophy in the Mirror of Nature* (Princeton, N.J.: Princeton Univ. Press, 1979).

17 Ihab Hassan, *The Right Promethean Fire* (Urbana: Univ. of Illinois Press, 1980), especially in the chapter "Indeterminacy, Immanence, and Cultural Change."

18 For the best instance I know of how such thinking changes our perspective on traditional hierarchies, consider Wittgenstein, *Culture and Value,* ed. G. H. Von Wright (Chicago: Univ. of Chicago Press, 1980), p. 31A: "Kierkegaard writes: 'If Christianity were so easy and cosy, why should God in his Scriptures have set Heaven and Earth in motion and threatened *eternal* punishments?' – Question: But in that case why is this Scripture so unclear? If we want to warn someone of a terrible danger, do we go about it by telling him a riddle whose solution will be the warning? – But who is to say that the Scripture really is unclear? Isn't it possible that it was essential in this case to 'tell a riddle'? And that, on the other hand, giving a more direct warning would necessarily have had the *wrong* effect? God has *four* people recount the life of his incarnate Son, in each case differently and with inconsistencies – but might we not say: It is important that this narrative should not be more than quite averagely historically plausible *just so that* this should not be taken as the essential, decisive thing? So that the *letter* should not be believed more strongly than is proper and the *spirit* may receive its due. I.e. what you are supposed to see cannot be communicated even by the best and most accurate historian; and *therefore* a mediocre account suffices, is even to be preferred. For that too can tell you what you are supposed to be told. (Roughly in the way a mediocre stage set can be better than a sophisticated one, painted trees better than real ones, – because these might distract attention from what matters.)"

2. The dominant poetic mode of the late seventies

1 The best descriptive accounts I know of the narrow poetic conventions for which I try to produce a context are Marjorie Perloff, "From Image to Action: The Return of Story in Post Modern Poetry," *Contemporary Literature* 23 (1982), pp. 411–27; and her "One of the Two Poetries," *PN Review* 19 (Dec. 1980), pp. 47–51. Many of the strictures raised by Robert Pinsky, Charles Molesworth, and Paul Breslin against the earlier dominant mode, the poetics of "the emotive imagination," still apply.

2 Roland Barthes, *Critical Essays* (Evanston, Ill.: Northwestern Univ. Press, 1971), pp. xvii–xviii.

3 Stanley Plumly, "Chapter and Verse," *American Poetry Review* 7 (Jan.–Feb. 1978), p. 24.

4 Ibid., p. 21.

5 Ibid., p. 24.

6   For Stevens's basic statements on the pressure of reality and the counter-pressure of imagination, see *The Necessary Angel* (1951; rpt. New York: Random House [Vintage Books], 1965), pp. 20, 36. Also important for the concept of pressure is Kenneth Burke's work on how changes in conceptual grammars occur, requiring the critic to find ways of revealing "the strategic spots at which ambiguities necessarily arise." See his *Grammar of Motives* (1945; rpt. Berkeley: University of California Press, 1969). I quote from p. xviii.

7   Robert Creeley, ed., *The Selected Writings of Charles Olson* (New York: New Directions, 1951).

8   Robert Lowell, "Night Sweat," in *For the Union Dead* (New York: Farrar, Straus & Giroux, 1964), p. 68.

9   Ibid.

10   I quote Bly from "The Dead World and the Live World," *The Sixties,* 8 (1966), p. 4. These paragraphs summarize chap. 2 of my *Enlarging the Temple* (Lewisburg, Pa.: Bucknell Univ. Press, 1979).

11   The term "emotive imagination" was coined by Donald Hall and then used as the basis for critical descriptions in Ronald Moran and George Lensing, *Four Poets and the Emotive Imagination* (Baton Rouge: Louisiana State Univ. Press, 1976). For Breslin, see "American Poetry and/or Surrealism: How to Read the New Contemporary Poem," *American Scholar* 47 (1978), pp. 357–76.

12   Robert Pinsky, *The Situation of Poetry* (Princeton, N.J.: Princeton Univ. Press, 1976), p. 77.

13   Robert Bly, *Silence in the Snowy Fields* (Middletown, Conn.: Wesleyan Univ. Press, 1962), p. 15.

14   The best cases for the tension between irony and analogy in romantic poetry may be found in Paul de Man, "Intentionality of the Romantic Image," in *Romanticism and Consciousness,* ed. Harold Bloom (New York: Norton, 1970); and Octavio Paz, *Children of the Mire* (Cambridge: Harvard University Press, 1974). I defend my claims that attention to the stance of mind or act projecting the analogies can be a successful evasion of irony in "Wordsworth's 'Preface' as Literary Theory," *Criticism* 18 (1976), pp. 122–46.

15   Galway Kinnell, *The Book of Nightmares* (Boston: Houghton Mifflin, 1971), p. 59.

16   Charles Molesworth, *The Fierce Embrace* (Columbia: Univ. of Missouri Press, 1979), pp. 269–74. On the problematic nature of the view of emotions in the poetry of the sixties, Joyce Carol Oates, "On Sylvia Plath," in *Contemporary Poetry in America,* ed. Robert Boyers (New York: Schocken Books, 1974), pp. 139–56, is very suggestive, although probably too optimistic in its view of alternatives.

17   James Wright, *Collected Poems* (Middletown: Wesleyan Univ. Press, 1971), pp. 157, 113, 114.

18   Ibid., p. 151.

19   The formula is evident in "A Blessing . . ." and "Lying in a Hammock . . . ," as well as in the following poems from *Shall We Gather at the River:* "Gambling in Stateline, Nevada," "Living by the Red River," "Late No-

vember in a Field," "Listening to the Mourners," "Rip," "The Lights in the Hallway," and "Two Postures beside a Fire."

20 Wright, *Collected Poems,* p. 152; Robert Bly, *The Light around the Body* (New York: Harper & Row, 1967), p. 62.
21 Stanley Plumly, *Out-of-the-Body Travel* (New York: Ecco Press, 1979), p. 8.
22 Plumly, "Chapter and Verse," p. 30.
23 Plumly, "Chapter and Verse," May–June 1978, p. 25.
24 Charles Wright, *Bloodlines* (Middletown, Conn.: Wesleyan Univ. Press, 1975), p. 56. Helen Vendler, in a fine essay celebrating Wright (*Part of Nature, Part of Us* [Cambridge: Harvard Univ. Press, 1980], pp. 280–1) reads this poem as praising transcendence. Plumly's reading of Wright in "Chapter and Verse" is closer to mine; he stresses "the body corporeal made 'the breath of the dream,'" but he sees the dreams' dependence on temporality. Finally, Pinsky's criticisms of Wright's style in general (*Situation of Poetry,* pp. 111–18) help show how his weaknesses can be seen as representative of those of a substantial body of contemporary poetry.

3. The pressure to transform

1 As support for my criticisms consult Werner Berthoff's summary of poets' negative comments on the poetry of the age (*A Literature without Qualities* [Berkeley: Univ. of California Press, 1980], pp. 89–97), or check the vague cautionary generalization in the columns of the *American Poetry Review.* Yet, as in life, all this criticism seems ultimately to free the critic to indulge in what he clearly sees as problematic in others.
2 Charles Simic, *Dismantling the Silence* (New York: Braziller, 1971), p. 55.
3 I take the idea of poems as transforming other styles from Herbert Schneidau, "Style and Sacrament in Modernist Writing," *Georgia Review* 31 (1977), pp. 427–53, but I modify it considerably.
4 Stephen Dunn, *Looking for Holes in the Ceiling* (Amherst: Univ. of Massachusetts Press, 1974), pp. 47–8. Jonathan Holden, in *Rhetoric of the Contemporary Lyric* (Bloomington: Indiana Univ. Press, 1980), has an excellent chapter on Dunn that concentrates on his uses of voice and his making poetry of pure middle-class life, a final triumph of lyricizing what I call in *Enlarging the Temple* (Lewisburg, Pa.: Bucknell Univ. Press, 1979), with respect to Lowell, the world of pure prose.
5 *Salmagundi,* no. 50–1 (1980–1), p. 23.
6 *Poetry* 157 (1981), p. 23.
7 *New Republic* (May 30, 1981), p. 30.
8 Robert Hass, *Praise* (New York: Ecco Press, 1979), pp. 4–5.
9 Ibid., p. 1.
10 Ibid., pp. 67–8.
11 John Ashbery, *The Double Dream of Spring* (New York: Dutton, 1970), p. 18. As a general description of works that play against the logic of causal narrative, see David Lodge on metonymy and metaphor in *The Modes of Modern Writing* (London: Edward Arnold, 1977). Charles Hartman, *Free Verse: An Essay on Prosody* (Princeton, N.J.: Princeton Univ. Press, 1981), pp. 168–

71, is quite good on a related distinction between poems stressing sense and poems stressing reference. See also the works cited in note 12 to chapter 1 on the subject of resisting closure, but a sense of irony or pure freedom from conventions will not suffice to explain why poets are fascinated by more conjectural modes. I will develop this theme when I discuss Ashbery.

12 Albert Goldbarth, *Comings Back* (Garden City, N.Y.: Doubleday, 1976), p. 36.

13 The best contemporary statement I know on middles is Ursula K. Leguin, "It was a Dark and Stormy Night; or Why We Are Huddling about the Campfire," *Critical Inquiry* 7 (1980), pp. 191–9. The first critical use of the term I know of is Geoffrey Hartman's discussion of extended middles in "The Voice of the Shuttle," in *Beyond Formalism* (New Haven: Yale Univ. Press, 1970). I elaborate that idea in part 1 of "The Qualities of Action: A Theory of Middles in Literature," *boundary 2* 5 (1977), pp. 323–50; and others use versions of it to establish a middle ground between piety and irony – for example, Gerald Bruns, "Allegory and Satire: A Rhetorical Meditation," *New Literary History* 11 (1979), pp. 121–32.

4. The paradoxes of contemporary antiromanticism

1 I confess to a somewhat melodramatic affinity with images of contamination, even when I cannot define a condition of health that justifies a term like "disease." Let "dis-ease," then, be understood as the prevalence of the problems I shall try to make explicit in this chapter.

2 Jonathan Holden, *Rhetoric of the Contemporary Lyric* (Bloomington: Indiana Univ. Press, 1980), p. 136. Another index of Holden's limitations is that he must treat Ashbery in terms of epistemological despair because he lacks sufficient critical terms to capture the ways poems exemplify new possibilities of making sense.

3 Ibid., p. 119.

4 E.g., ibid., p. 49.

5 Ibid., p. 135.

6 Ibid., p. 58.

7 Ibid.

8 Compare Brooks: "In the unified poem, the poet has 'come to terms' with his experience . . . The unity is achieved by a dramatic process, not a logical one; it represents an equilibrium of forces, not a formula. It is 'proved' as a dramatic conclusion is proved; by its ability to resolve the conflicts which have been accepted as the donnés of the drama." I quote from the last chapter of the *Well Wrought Urn,* as cited in *Critical Theory since Plato,* ed. Hazard Adams (New York: Harcourt Brace Jovanovich, 1971), p. 1038. See also, from Brooks's "Irony as Principle of Structure," the following passage (again cited from Adams, p. 1048): "What we do ask is that the poem dramatize the situation so accurately, so honestly, with such fidelity to the total situation that it is no longer a question of our beliefs, but of our participation in the poetic experience." It is also worth noting that Plumly performs a reduction similar to Holden's when he equates symbolism simply with a rhet-

oric of correspondence, without an account of the ontological warrant for treating art objects as making real the mental energies that produce and thus in a way sanction the correspondence. See Plumly's "Chapter and Verse," *American Poetry Review* 7 (May–June 1978).

9 Mark Strand, *The Story of Our Lives* (New York: Atheneum, 1977), p. 3.

10 Ibid., p. 10.

11 Robert Pinsky, *The Situation of Poetry* (Princeton, N.J.: Princeton Univ. Press, 1976), p. 8. It is on this point that Pinsky comes closest to Graff, and both come closest to Yvor Winters. I think, therefore, that some of my closing remarks on Graff in the *Par Rapport* symposium (vol. 2, no. 2 [1979], pp. 87–106, 123–38) apply also to Pinsky. Both writers, I should admit, are thoroughly aware of the dangers I cite but feel morally compelled to risk them. Such risks, however, seem to me to miss the crucial point that great modernists like Yeats, Stevens, and even Eliot do not deny the generalizing value of semantic utterances. It is not words they want to escape, but reductions to a simple communicative sense of the overall utterance. They do not want to avoid language's powers but to cast poems in ways that let us most fully reflect on those powers as powers.

12 Pinsky, *Situation of Poetry*, pp. 4, 12, 11, 163.

13 Ibid., pp. 133, 162, 144.

14 Ibid., p. 134.

15 Robert Pinsky, *An Explanation of America* (Princeton, N.J.: Princeton Univ. Press, 1979), p. 7.

16 Ibid., p. 23.

17 Pinsky is too good a scholar not to play off here two ideas of "idea" – a simple prose sense that every father has a version of his daughter whom he fantasizes as someone he can fashion and a Coleridgean sense of idea as the genetic model or ideal type whom one approaches by the imagination. One meaning is self-defensive, the other romantically assertive; Pinsky stands uncomfortably in the middle.

18 Pinsky, *Explanation of America*, p. 30.

19 Pinsky, *Situation of Poetry*, p. 164.

20 Louis Zukofsky, "An Objective," in *Prepositions: The Collected Critical Essays of Louis Zukofsky* (London: Rapp & Carroll, 1967), pp. 210–21. This essay is a revision of "Sincerity and Objectivity," *Poetry* 37 (1931), pp. 269–78. See also interviews with Zukofsky, Oppen, Rakosi, and Reznikoff in "The Objectivist Poet: Four Interviews," ed. L. C. Dembo, *Contemporary Literature* 10 (1969), pp. 155–219. For critical accounts of objectivist principles, and for objectivism's continuing vitality as a critical model, see two works by Hugh Kenner: *The Pound Era* (Berkeley: Univ. of California Press, 1971); and *A Homemade World* (New York: Morrow, 1975).

21 Charles Olson, "Projective Verse," in *Selected Writings of Charles Olson*, ed. Robert Creeley (New York: New Directions, 1966), p. 18.

22 Zukofsky, *Prepositions*, p. 12.

23 Percy Bysshe Shelley, "Ode to the West Wind," in *Selected Poetry and Prose*, ed. Kenneth N. Cameron (New York: Holt, Rinehart and Winston, 1961), pp. 387, 390; S. T. Coleridge, "Dejection: An Ode," in *Selected Poetry and*

Prose of Coleridge, ed. Donald Stauffer (New York: Modern Library, 1951), pp. 80–1.

24   Robert Bly, "Poem in Three Parts," in *Silence in the Snowy Fields* (Middletown, Conn.: Wesleyan Univ. Press, 1962), p. 21.

25   *Chicago Review* 30, no. 3 (1979), p. 127. This issue is devoted to objectivism as a tradition that retains its vitality.

26   Robert Creeley, *For Love: Poems 1950–60* (New York: Scribner 1962), p. 109. The best critical commentaries on Creeley are Warren Tallman, "Three Essays on Creeley," reprinted in *Godawful Streets of Man* (Toronto: Coach House Press, 1976); and "Creeley Issue," ed. William M. Spanos, *boundary 2* 6–7 (1977). I realize that Creeley's poem was written before the dominant mode I say it opposes indeed became dominant. But the vices of the dominant mode as a structural model have a long history. For more recent objectivist uses of the personal, see Joel Oppenheimer's "Houses" (pp. 89–99) and my commentary on it (pp. 21–2) in the objectivist issue of the *Chicago Review.*

27   Zukofsky, "Sincerity and Objectivity," p. 271.

28   Zukofsky, *Prepositions,* p. 24.

29   George Oppen, "Interview," *Contemporary Literature* 10 (1969), p. 161.

30   Ron Loewinsohn, "To the Most Gorgeous Among the Dancers," in John Freeman, ed., *Poetry in English Now* (Cardiff, Wales: Blackweir Press, 1978), p. 15.

31   Zukofsky, "Three Poems by André Salmon," *Poetry* 37 (1931), p. 293.

32   Carl Rakosi, "Shore Line," in *Amulet* (New York: New Directions, 1967), p. 32.

33   Ron Loewinsohn, *Goat Dances* (Santa Barbara, Calif.: Black Sparrow Press, 1976), pp. 11–13.

34   For an excellent discussion (with a view similar to mine) of the strengths and weaknesses of objectivism with respect to Oppen, see Norman Finkelstein, "Political Commitment and Poetic Subjectification: George Oppen's Test of Truth," *Contemporary Literature* 22 (1981), pp. 22–41.

5. Robert Creeley's poetics of conjecture

1   John Koethe, in *Beyond Amazement: New Essays on John Ashbery,* ed. David Lehman (Ithaca, N.Y.: Cornell Univ. Press, 1980), distinguishes a Cartesian, a Humean, and a Wittgensteinian (of the *Tractatus*) self that one can find respectively in Lowell (or, I add, in those working within the poetics of sincerity), in Frank O'Hara, and in Ashbery. Creeley does not have Ashbery's Stevensian background, so we shall see his versions of multiplicity serve primarily as vehicles for complicating what remains a Cartesian self. It is also worth noting that when Plumly, in "Chapter and Verse," *American Poetry Review* 7 (May–June 1978), pp. 19–28, speaks about poets in a symbolist tradition, he attributes the pursuit of transpersonal meaning to the emblem or book, that is, to a rhetorician's view of control that ignores questions of philosophical grounds for the abstracting power of poetry.

2 The first quotation, in a context discussing collage, is from Phil Gerber, "Interview with Robert Creeley," *Athanor* 4 (1973), p. 13, and the second from Terry Bacon, "How to Know When to Stop: Creeley on Closure," *American Poetry Review* 5 (Oct. 1976), p. 6. The best critical text providing a general foundation for concerns in poetry for collage structure is David Antin, "Modernism and Post-modernism: Approaching the Present in American Poetry," *boundary 2* 1 (1972), pp. 98–133.

3 Warren Tallman, "Three Essays on Creeley," reprinted in *Godawful Streets of Man* (Toronto: Coach House Press, 1976), pp. 109–10, is very good on Creeley's poems as pieces in an unfolding sense of personal condition. Linda Wagner makes a similar observation about Creeley's recent work in "The Latest Creeley," *American Poetry Review* 4 (Sept.–Oct. 1975), p. 42. She also makes a useful comparison of Creeley's stress on process to Williams's objective mode. Finally, I want to acknowledge excellent work on Creeley's prose poems, which I saw after finishing this chapter, in Stephen Fredman, *Poet's Prose: The Crisis in American Verse* (Cambridge: Cambridge Univ. Press, 1983).

4 Robert Creeley, *A Day Book* (New York: Scribner, 1972), pp. 22–4. (I have determined page numbers for *A Day Book* by counting only the pages of poetry.)

5 Both "closure" and "mimesis" are much-abused critical terms that I use loosely here to capture what I take to be Creeley's sense of them. A more technical analysis of "closure" would have to begin with the recognition that the term is a relative one. Any unit of meaningful discourse must possess a kind of closure if it presents a coherent meaning. Aesthetic closure is a more complex state that usually is achieved by making the achievement of coherence a function of and comment upon the major patterns in the discourse, so that the ending seems a fulfillment of established expectations – either formal or narrative, argumentative, or dramatic. Jacobsen on the axis of combination replacing the axis of selection as a model for the poetic function is the clearest abstract model for this patterning. See his "Linguistics and Poetics," in *Style in Language,* ed. T. Sebeok (Cambridge: MIT Press, 1960), pp. 350–77. Creeley resists this sense of aesthetic closure by refusing to allow the conclusion to seem in retrospect required by the beginning and by, in this poem, denying the endings our sense of lyric form leads us to expect. Plotting, in effect, appears to be preferable to the constraints of plot, however plodding the results sometimes are. For two good essays on the sense of historical condition leading post-modern poets to resist closure, see Cary Nelson, "The Resources of Failure: W. S. Merwin's Deconstructive Career," *boundary 2* 5 (1977), pp. 573–98; and Cary Nelson, "Whitman in Vietnam: Poetry and History in Contemporary America," *Massachusetts Review* 16 (Winter 1975), pp. 55–71.

Such problems have special relevance when one is dealing with a poetics of thinking because it is so difficult to distinguish process and product in the art object. That is, many poems that give the appearance of relying on the processes of the writing mind are actually carefully wrought products in which the illusion of free play depends ultimately on considered aesthetic choices not foregrounded by the poem's surface. Other poems actually try to record acts of thinking in the process of writing and do not submit these to a preconceived plan. These poems, like Cowper's *Task,* are pure process. A considerable part of Ashbery's power to fascinate lies in his ability to dance between these two alternatives so that neither suffices by itself.

6   Bacon, "How to Know When to Stop," p. 5.

7   Gerber, "Interview," pp. 14, 13.

8   Robert Creeley, *Mabel: A Story and Other Prose* (London: Marion Boyars, 1976), p. 41. (The prose from *A Day Book* and "Presences," as well as "Mabel: A Story," is cited from this edition.)

9   Robert Creeley, *Hello: A Journal, February 29–May 3, 1976* (New York: New Directions, 1977), p. 22.

10   Ibid., p. 20.

11   Gerber, "Interview," p. 78; see also "Transcript of Creeley at the 1965 Berkeley Poetry Conference," *Athanor* 4 (1973), pp. 37–45.

12   "Transcript of Creeley," p. 39. (The ellipsis after "duration" is Creeley's.)

13   Creeley, *Mabel,* p. 15.

14   Creeley, *Hello,* p. 38.

15   I elaborate from Wittgenstein a related concept of judging understanding by whether or not one can go on, and how fully one can continue a project, in "Going On and Going Nowhere: Wittgenstein and Criteria for Literary Understanding," in *Literature and Philosophy,* ed. William Cain (Lewisburg, Pa.: Bucknell Univ. Press, 1984).

16   Creeley, *Hello,* p. 39.

17   There is some justification for claiming a historical shift in emphasis if one takes as historically "modernist" the writers seen by other influential writers and critics at the time as representative of basic new modes of writing not aimed primarily at popular consumption. But it is also important to recognize that the main retrospective value of distinctions like modern and postmodern is to identify from clear examples forces that have in fact been in tension in most significant writers in the past 180 years. I should add that in the following remarks I try to give a more abstract and more flexible version of distinctions between "modernist" symbolist modes and post-modernist experiments with immanence than I offered in *Enlarging the Temple* (Lewisburg, Pa.: Bucknell Univ. Press, 1979), where I have an extensive discussion of Creeley's poetry up through *Pieces.*

18   In connecting Creeley to Wittgenstein's methods of projection, I rely on my *Act and Quality: A Theory of Literary Meaning and Humanistic Understanding* (Amherst: Univ. of Massachusetts Press, 1981).

19   I describe this metonymic mode in "Objective Image and Act of Mind in Modern Poetry," *PMLA* 91 (Jan. 1976), pp. 101–14.

20   Creeley, *Mabel,* p. 171. For Creeley on relaxation, see Gerber, "Interview," p. 11. In his essay on Creeley in the same issue of *Athanor* (vol. 4, 1973), "Robert Creeley, the Domestic Muse and Post-modernism," Jerome Mazzaro makes some comments useful for thinking about relaxation. If we take Creeley's comments on later Williams as an index of his thinking about a

relaxed mode, we see him stressing as its major value the sense of personal condition conveyed; see Mazzaro, "Robert Creeley," p. 33.

21 William Carlas Williams, *Pictures from Brueghel* (New York: New Directions, 1962), pp. 177–8, 179. Williams's poem "Shadows," in ibid., pp. 150–2, reveals the similarities between his later style and Creeley's in an even clearer way, with several close parallels to the poem "Thinking."

22 Robert Creeley, *Away* (Santa Barbara, Calif.: Black Sparrow Press, 1976), p. 39.

23 See Wittgenstein's *Tractatus Logico-Philosophicus,* trans. D. F. Pears and B. F. McGuiness (London: Routledge & Kegan Paul, 1961), entries 6.62, 6.64. I make the parallel explicit because I think that someone better versed in Wittgenstein than I am could give a fuller description of how Creeley treats solipsism in his recent work. Koethe's essay is one example of this possibility.

24 Creeley, *Mabel,* pp. 59, 49.

25 Bacon, "How to know When to Stop," p. 7.

26 Gerber, "Interview," p. 46. Alain Robbe-Grillet, "Order and Disorder in Film and Fiction," and Robert P. Morgan, "On the Analysis of Recent Music," both in *Critical Inquiry* 4 (1977), pp. 1–20 and 33–53, give useful descriptions of arbitrary substitution sets that evade a sense of loss.

27 Creeley, *Mabel,* p. 28.

28 Creeley, *Day Book,* p. 28.

29 "Craft Interview with Robert Creeley," *New York Quarterly,* no. 13 (Winter 1973), p. 37.

30 I remember Michel Foucault making a distinction between commentary on the Bible, the main mode before the controversies of the Reformation, since there was little controversy on the sense of the whole, and interpretation that requires positing interpretations for the whole (and hence making God in one's own image). More needs to be made of this distinction.

31 Creeley, *Mabel,* pp. 36, 40.

32 Ibid., pp. 22–7.

33 Ibid., p. 23.

34 Ibid., p. 25.

35 Ibid., pp. 9–11, 17–18, 130–2. I see the fear of tautology both as a danger in pure prose consciousness, where the lack of lyric intensity makes all facts of equal importance, and as a consequence of the nausea at pure objectivity I describe in *Enlarging the Temple.* "Fucking is fucking" (*Mabel,* p. 7) is a good example: Here honesty admits no mystification but leaves one linguistically and perceptually with indifferent objects of attention. In tautology the predicate is swallowed up in the subject, so no meaningful extension of the subject is possible. Grammar is a warning to the solipsist. For Creeley's fullest statement on a fear of pure objectivity, see *Mabel,* p. 49.

36 See Creeley, *Mabel,* pp. 37–9.

37 Creeley, *Mabel,* p. 27.

38 The dating that stresses the diary form of *A Day Book* is not in the original edition. It may have been added in *Mabel* in order to stress the contrast with the more abstract organizing principles of the latter two entries, which break

from even temporal linearity. I also find interesting the fact that Creeley manages in *Mabel* to find sustaining contexts for *A Day Book* after stating that the poetry joined to the prose in the original volume did not work because "the prose was so contained as one unit of writing that the poems never get a chance to work in and out of it" (Bacon, "How to know When to Stop," p. 6).

39   Robert Creeley, *Later* (New York: New Directions, 1979), pp. 13, 121.
40   Creeley, *Mabel,* pp. 113–15.

6. John Ashbery: discursive rhetoric within a poetics of thinking

1   The poem whose conclusion this is opens Ashbery's *Houseboat Days* (New York: Penquin, 1977, p. 3) and thus sets the project for the volume. Charles Berger, in *Beyond Amazement: New Essays on John Ashbery,* ed. David Lehman (Ithaca, N.Y.: Cornell Univ. Press, 1980), pp. 163–81, shows how Ashbery structures *The Double Dream of Spring* in a similar fashion. (New York: Dutton, 1970).

2   Since I wrote the essay on which this chapter is based, a surprising amount of fine criticism, especially that in Lehman, *Beyond Amazement,* and David Kalstone, *Five Temperaments* (New York: Oxford Univ. Press, 1976), has covered many of the facets of his work I cover here. I think, nonetheless, that my synthesis is original, as is the way I try to place Ashbery in context. Both the context and the synthesis seem to me necessary to right the balance set astray by essays like Helen Vendler's "Understanding Ashbery," *New Yorker* (March 16, 1981), pp. 119–35, which try to explain Ashbery's thematic content and attitude and thus make equations to writers like Keats. This is not wrong, and Vendler does her usual superb job, but it does domesticate the poetry and eliminate the philosophical and affective dimensions that matter precisely because they (and we) are so different from Keats.

3   Ashbery, *Houseboat Days,* p. 34.
4   John Ashbery, *As We Know* (New York: Penguin, 1979), p. 110.
5   Ashbery, *Houseboat Days,* p. 15.
6   John Ashbery, *Three Poems* (New York: Viking, 1972), p. 112.
7   *The Craft of Poetry: Interviews from the New York Quarterly,* ed. William Packard (Garden City, N.Y.: Doubleday, 1974), p. 128.
8   Ashbery, *Three Poems,* pp. 103–4.
9   Packard, *Craft of Poetry,* pp. 123–4.
10   See ibid., p. 127; and "Recital," in Ashbery, *Three Poems.*
11   Ashbery, *Houseboat Days,* p. 50.
12   Wallace Stevens, *The Necessary Angel* (1951; rpt. New York: Random House [Vintage Books], 1965), pp. 123–4.
13   The best negative article on Ashbery is Charles Molesworth, "This Leaving Out Business: The Poetry of John Ashbery," *Salmagundi,* no. 38–9 (1975), pp. 20–41. See also Paul Breslin, "Warpless and Woofless Subtleties," *Poetry* 137 (1980), pp. 42–50.
14   John Ashbery, *Self-Portrait in a Convex Mirror* (New York: Viking, 1975), pp. 55–7. I want to distinguish decreation from deconstruction, even though

deconstruction is increasingly shifting from a tool for dismantling arguments to a tool for creating new spaces for lyric vision within the interstices of old texts. Decreation I take to be a deliberate poetic act intending to disclose possible forms of relatedness, and consequently other possible grounds for identity and value, sharply different from the host forms or conventional expectations that the decreation parasitically restructures. Decreation, in essence, is a means for working within the seams and expectations of dominant modes of discourse by disclosing fresh ways of making sense. It blends the parodic and the transcendental because it continues to seek qualities of perception and forms of poetic knowledge by cleansing and transforming outmoded expressive or descriptive vehicles. Decreation alters the economy of consciousness by exploring new modes of exchange among its used and usurious coins. Deconstruction, on the other hand, invokes the spirit of skeptical lucidity without a lyric counterpressure. Deconstruction, in its original formulations, was primarily a way of gaining freedom from the past (rather than a sense of presence) by dramatizing the interstices in arguments where incompatible claims were necessary as underpinning or to create transitions among points. For the best overview of the concept of deconstruction as it appears now, see Rudolf Gasché, "Reconstruction as Criticism," *Glyph* 6 (1979), pp. 177–215.

15 Packard, *Craft of Poetry*, p. 111.
16 My claims here are partially an argument with Marjorie Perloff, *The Poetics of Indeterminacy: Rimbaud to Cage* (Princeton, N.J.: Princeton Univ. Press, 1981), and partially an attempt to find a theoretical way to account for her superb examples of the kinds of reading required by poets like Stein and Ashbery. I would like to say, but cannot yet demonstrate, that her indeterminate poets represent a form of what I called in *Enlarging the Temple* (Lewisburg, Pa.: Bucknell Univ. Press, 1979) a poetics of immanence. They seek an immanence in thinking or in writing, as opposed to the forms of illusionistic immanence figured in scenes of disclosure that one finds in Bly, Snyder, and some Williams and Pound. But indeterminacy is only one means toward breaking down expectations to allow new forms of direct presence. In trying to make it the only means or, often, the end, Perloff is compelled to treat Pound's and Ashbery's forms of defamiliarization as essentially the same. And she has no way to speak about poetic precision or significance. She is right in seeing a modernist strand that resists conceptualization, but I think that emphasis ought to be placed on the ends sought by such resistance. This process leads to making a distinction among a poetics of thinking, a constructivist aesthetic, and a variety of expressivist forms of immediacy.
17 Packard, *Craft of Poetry*, pp. 118–19.
18 Ibid., p. 121.
19 The *locus classicus* for demonstrating the psychological appeal of dialectical thinking is Derrida's "Hegel without Reserve," in *Writing and Difference* (Chicago: Univ. of Chicago Press, 1980). For the complications of internal and external that deconstruct classical ideals of expression, see Derrida's "Fors," *Georgia Review* 31 (1977), pp. 64–120.
20 Ashbery, *Three Poems*, pp. 27, 93.

21   Ashbery, *Double Dream,* p. 24. See also "And Other, Vaguer Presences," in Ashbery, *Houseboat Days,* p. 48.

22   For a summary of themes associated with the materiality of motives, see Rosalind Coward and John Ellis, *Language and Materialism* (London: Routledge & Kegan Paul, 1977). In relating this view of motive to metaphor, I must also acknowledge the ideas provided to me by Alan Singer in conversation.

23   W. B. Yeats, *Collected Poems,* (New York: Macmillan, 1956), p. 284.

24   Ashbery, *Self-Portrait,* pp. 68–83.

25   Ashbery, *Three Poems,* p. 118. The conclusion of *Three Poems* is relevant here on many levels. Not only does it state a similar thematic resolution to the need for reconciling oneself to dreams from the past, but it also presents a similar insistence on resolution as essentially a "fusion" or gathering or "conjugating" of dispersed details into a state of consciousness "both intimate and noble" (ibid.).

26   Ashbery, *As We Know,* p. 3.

27   I use indexicals to speak about the self because of the work of John Perry. See especially "The Importance of Being Identical," in *The Identities of Persons,* ed. Amelie Rorty (Berkeley: Univ. of California Press, 1976), and "Perception, Action, and the Structure of Believing," which I saw in typescript and which is to be published in a festschrift for Paul Grice. Also very useful for clarifying the problem that artists like Ashbery face – how there can be something transpersonal that does not fit any of our tests for objectivity – are the concluding chapters of Thomas Nagel, *Moral Questions* (Cambridge: Cambridge Univ. Press, 1978).

28   Ashbery, *Houseboat Days,* pp. 45–6.

29   I cannot find the documentation. The metaphor, however, is worth including on its own merits.

30   Ashbery, *As We Know,* p. 79.

7. Self-reflection as action: the recent work of Adrienne Rich

1   John Ashbery, *The Double Dream of Spring* (New York: Dutton, 1970), p. 18.

2   I quote from "I Dream I'm the Death of Orpheus," in Rich's *The Will to Change* (New York: Norton, 1971), p. 19.

3   Adrienne Rich, "Poetry, Personality, and Wholeness: A Response to Galway Kinnell," in *A Field Guide to Contemporary Poetry and Poetics,* ed. David Young and Stuart Friebert (New York: Longman, 1980).

4   Several of the best woman critics of contemporary poetry seem embarrassed by the ideological narrowness of Rich's recent work and attack the poetry for what I shall try to show are themselves narrowly aesthetic standards. See Helen Vendler, "All Too Real," *New York Review of Books* (Dec. 16, 1981), pp. 32–5; and, for different, radically modernist aesthetic values, Marjorie Perloff, "Private Lives/Public Images," *Michigan Quarterly Review* 22 (Winter 1983), pp. 130–42. They are in part justified by the largely uncritical adulation that Rich gets from feminist critics. See, for example, the essays

by Wendy Martin, Erica Jong, and Nancy Milford in *Adrienne Rich's Poetry,* ed. Barbara Charlesworth Gelpi and Albert Gelpi (New York: Norton, 1975). Even the best reading of Rich, David Kalstone's *Five Temperaments* (New York: Oxford Univ. Press, 1976), cannot satisfactorily bridge the competing frameworks for viewing her work. By concentrating on temperament he gets beyond aesthetic criteria, but he does not provide the contrastive framework that I think necessary for judging her significance to contemporary poetry. I elaborate the model of reading abstractly that I mention here in my "The Idea and Ideal of a Canon," *Critical Inquiry* 10 (1983), pp. 37–60.

5 Gelpi and Gelpi, *Adrienne Rich's Poetry,* p. 98.
6 Adrienne Rich, *A Wild Patience Has Taken Me This Far: Poems, 1978–81* (New York: Norton, 1981), p. 4.
7 Gelpi and Gelpi, *Adrienne Rich's Poetry,* p. 96.
8 Adrienne Rich, *The Dream of a Common Language: Poems, 1974–77* (New York: Norton, 1978), p. 20.
9 Ibid., p. 28.
10 Ibid., pp. 72–7.
11 Adrienne Rich, *Diving into the Wreck: Poems, 1971–72* (New York: Norton, 1973), p. 6.
12 Ibid., p. 12.
13 Perloff attacks Rich for claiming a radical politics within a thoroughly establishment style that co-opts the assertion. The irony is that when Rich becomes relatively experimental in style, she cannot carry off her vision. Since the core of her politics is a quite traditional notion of self and will, she must use a straightforward style. That becomes radical in itself when, as Gerald Graff argues in *Literature against Itself* (Chicago: Univ. of Chicago Press, 1979, pp. 98–101), experiment has become standard. Rich, in other words, is sustenance for the claims of Lukács and Marcuse against Brecht.
14 Rich, *Will to Change,* p. 18.
15 Gelpi and Gelpi, *Adrienne Rich's Poetry,* p. 94.
16 Rich, *Diving into the Wreck,* p. 19.
17 Gelpi and Gelpi, *Adrienne Rich's Poetry,* p. 93.
18 Ibid., pp. 114–17.
19 Ibid., pp. 114, 119.
20 Rich, *Dream of a Common Language,* p. 3.
21 Rich, *A Wild Patience,* pp. 3–5.
22 Ibid., pp. 8–9.
23 Ibid., p. 20.
24 Ibid., p. 22.
25 Ibid., p. 23.
26 Ibid., p. 30.
27 Ibid., pp. 50–1.
28 Ibid., pp. 46–8.
29 Ibid., pp. 40–5.
30 Perhaps the best index to the political attitude of this volume is Rich's footnote to the Colter poem: "Colter's life work – a remarkable achievement for

a woman architect – was thus inextricable from the violation and expropriation of native culture by white entrepreneurs. Yet her love for that culture was life long" (ibid., p. 61).
31   Ibid., p. 59.

8. Epilogue

1   *Beyond Amazement: New Essays on John Ashbery,* ed. David Lehman (Ithaca, N.Y.: Cornell Univ. Press, 1980). It is their inability or unwillingness to grapple with such attitudinal qualities, which can give a work significant content and power of implication without inviting a concern for thematic assertions, that makes criticisms of contemporary writing like Graff's or Berthoff's seem inappropriate to what they purport to account for.

2   In all fairness, I must admit that this conflict lies at the heart of *Three Poems* (New York: Viking, 1972), but Ashbery concludes by insisting that our imaginative dreams have their place only in a spectral theater.

3   Although I find little of use in Harold Bloom's effusions on Ashbery in "John Ashbery: The Charity of the Hard Moments," *Salmagundi,* no. 22–23 (1973), pp. 103–23, his brilliant remarks on poets' having to forge relations between ethos and pathos and the different ways they do so seem to me perhaps the most suggestive materials we have for a close study of the history of poetry from modernism to the present. See the last chapter of his *Wallace Stevens: The Poems of Our Climate* (Ithaca, N.Y.: Cornell Univ. Pres, 1977).

4   Cary Nelson's fine *Our Last First Poets* (Urbana: Univ. of Illinois Press, 1982) uses the clever strategy of praising poets because their problems reveal clearly the poverty of our cultural situation. I regret coming on this book too late to take up its arguments in my text.

5   I am of course aware that my map leaves out whole territories. Yet I suspect that my outline could locate those territories without too much trouble by treating poets' basic concerns in terms of the ways in which they address the problems I have concentrated on. This is why emphasizing a few exemplary tensions seems to me far more productive than the kind of survey one finds in Daniel Hoffman's section of the *Harvard Guide to Contemporary American Writing* (Cambridge: Harvard Univ. Press, 1980) or in Roberta Berke's *Bounds out of Bounds: A Compass for Recent British and American Poetry* (New York: Oxford Univ. Press, 1981). I must confess, however, that my model breaks down or needs several epicycles to cover poetry written for highly specific political purposes. But such poetry is usually not a part of dialogue with the style and structure of other poetic modes. Indeed, part of Rich's greatness is that she insists on this dialogue.

6   Charles Taylor, "The Self in Question," in *The Identities of Persons,* ed. Amelie Rorty (Berkeley: Univ. of California Press, 1976), pp. 281–300. I discuss Taylor at length in chap. 6 of *Act and Quality: A Theory of Literary Meaning and Humanistic Understanding* (Amherst: Univ. of Massachusetts Press, 1981).

7   Helen Vendler, "The Creeping Griffon," *New York Review of Books* (Sept. 23, 1982), pp. 42–43.

8 My argument about the curatorial role of poststructuralist theory is elaborated in Geoffrey Hartman, *Saving the Text* (Baltimore: Johns Hopkins Univ. Press, 1980). Marjorie Perloff is responsible in my mind for insisting on the importance of the issue as a measure of the way contemporary poetry is so limited.

9 I owe this idea to Michael Maratsos, who was speaking of modern music. The controversies surrounding the NEA creative writing fellowships for 1980–1 indicate amusingly but disturbingly just how true and bothersome this peer-judgment model is. For a summary see Hilary Masters, "Go Down Dignified: The NEA Writing Fellowships," and David Wilk, "A Restrained Response to 'Go Down Dignified,'" both in *Georgia Review* 35 (1981), pp. 233–58. Wilk bases the NEA procedures "on the assumption that art professionals are the best judges of contemporary art" (p. 247). They are certainly among the best judges, at least of the craft of writing. But because the panel includes no critics or educated nonprofessionals, it then finds itself in a situation where it is all too easy to claim that political toleration plays a larger role than critical judgment.

10 I use "guidebook mentality" as shorthand for the reliance on the discourse of professionals that Michel Foucault has made a pressing object of concern.

11 I must repeat that there are valid perspectives from which all my complaints appear virtues. Certainly creative writing classes cannot aim to produce Whitmans, and mastery of craft in itself is a pleasurable experience that makes greater things possible. I complain, nonetheless, because we must recognize how our loves diminish along with our enmities, so that the more we internalize workshop values, the more likely it will be that we will not get past the virtues of literary civility so fostered.

12 William Matthews, in conversation.

Index